LIFE

BUTCH CASSIDY AND THE SUNDANCE KID

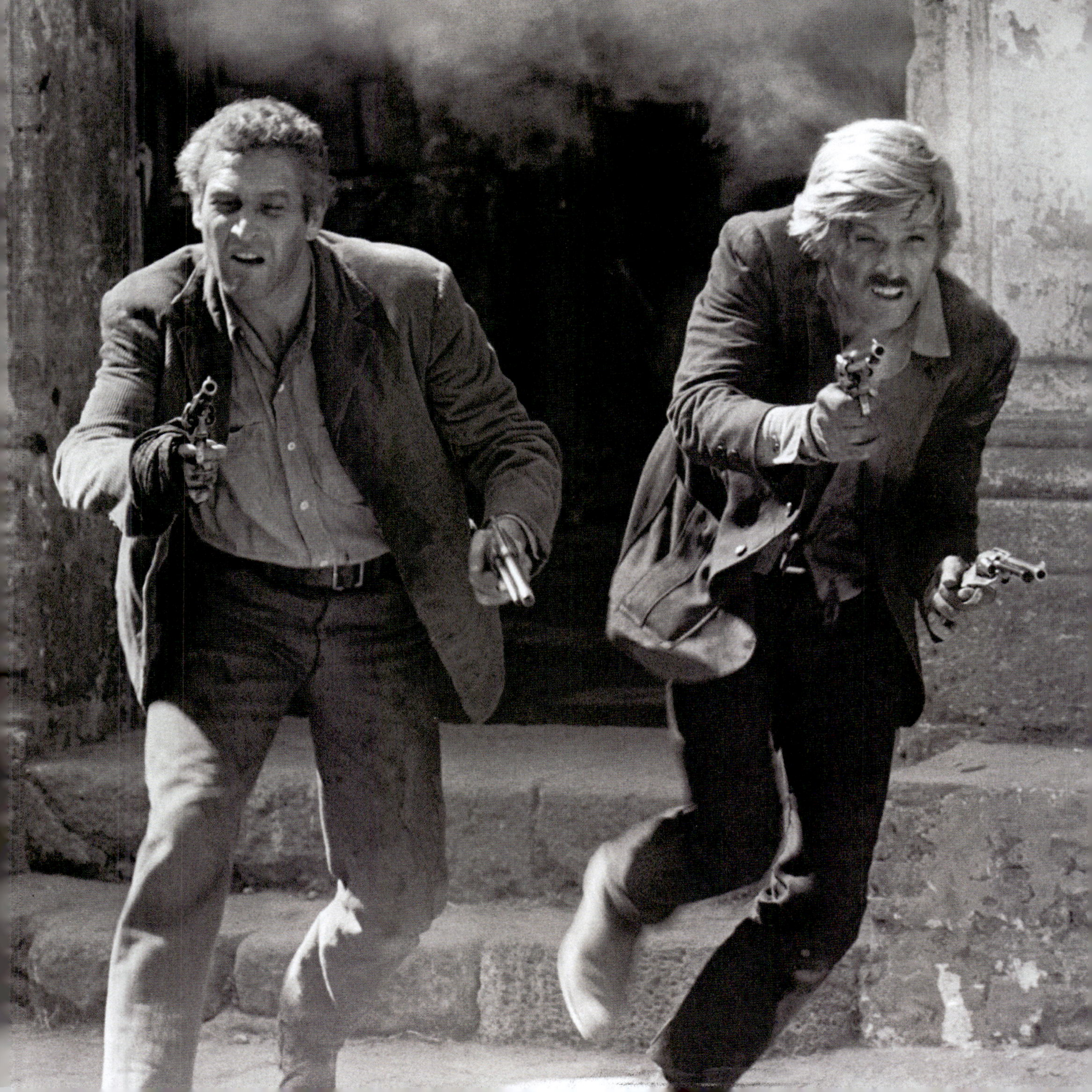

LIFE

Butch Cassidy and the Sundance Kid

meredith

For information on bulk purchases, please contact Christi Crowley in the Special Sales Department at Christi.Crowley@meredith.com.

For syndication requests or international licensing requests, e-mail syndication@meredith.com.

PRINTED IN THE USA

Vol. 19, No. 24 • August 30, 2019

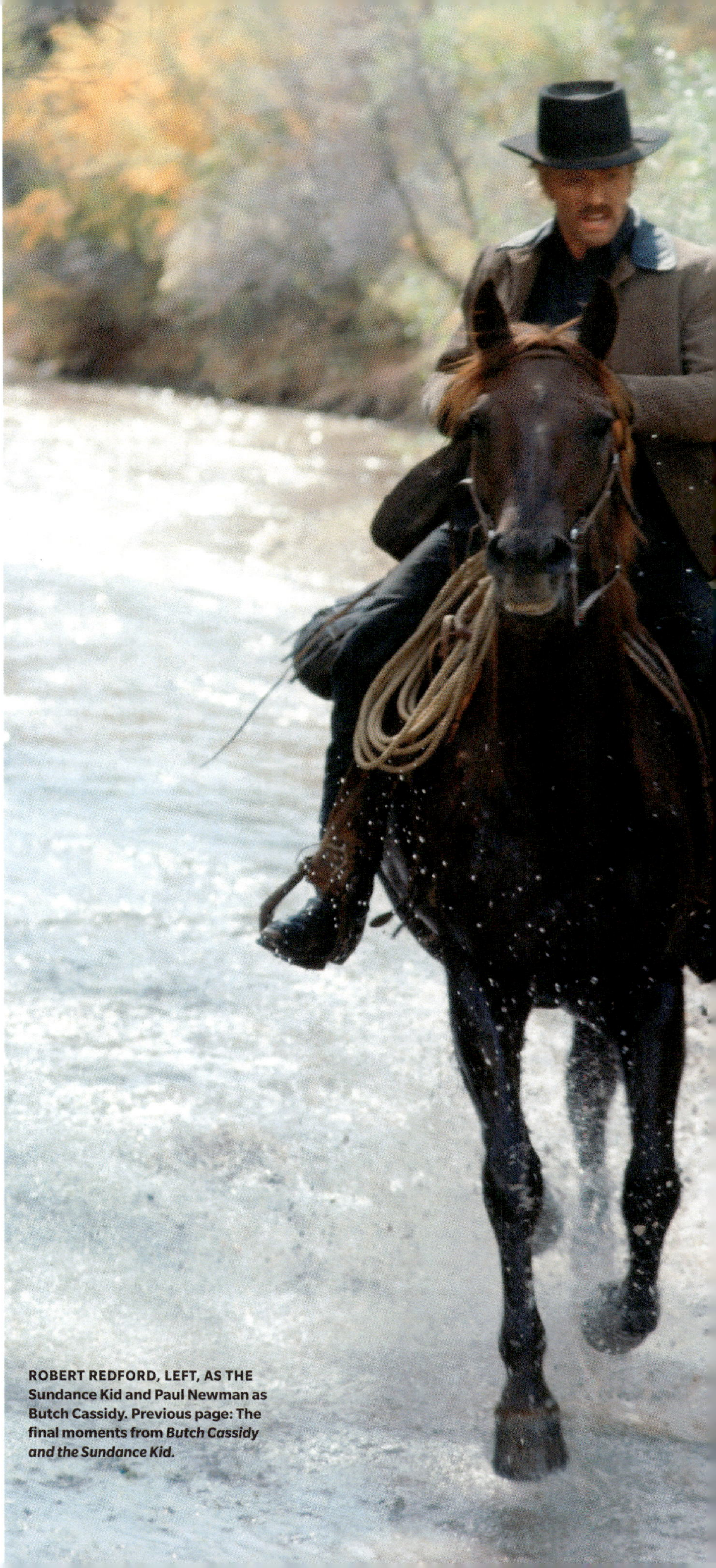

ROBERT REDFORD, LEFT, AS THE Sundance Kid and Paul Newman as Butch Cassidy. Previous page: The final moments from *Butch Cassidy and the Sundance Kid.*

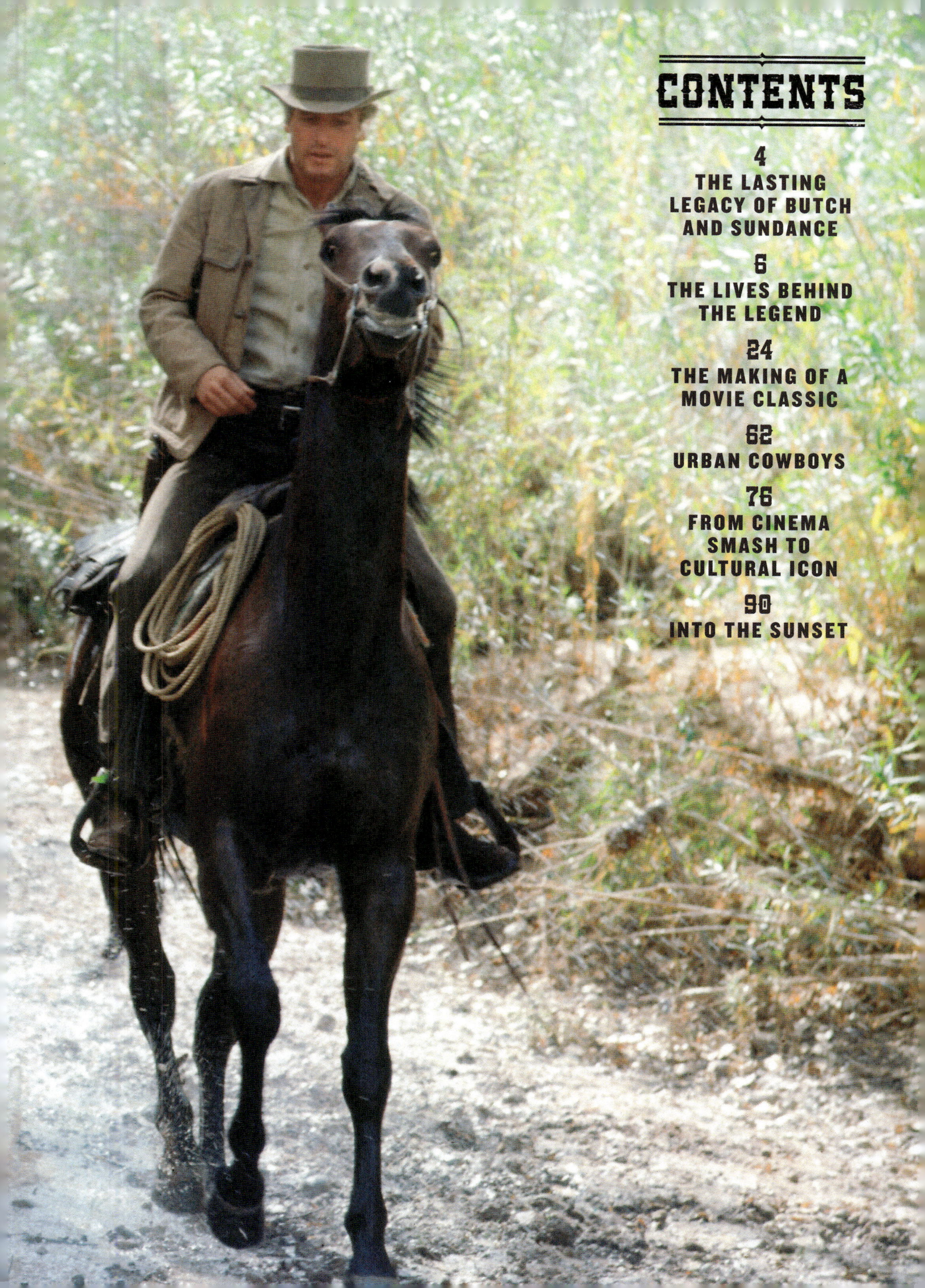

CONTENTS

INTRODUCTION

The Lasting Legacy of Butch and Sundance

BUTCH CASSIDY AND THE SUNDANCE KID'S CRIMINAL EXPLOITS MADE THEM FOLK HEROES IN THE WANING DAYS OF THE OLD WEST. THEN A SMASH 1969 MOVIE ENSHRINED THE PAIR AS AMERICAN LEGENDS

BY DANIEL S. LEVY

BUTCH CASSIDY AND THE SUNDANCE KID was an unexpected hit, a film about a duo of wisecracking Western outlaws who ran their mouths more than they pulled their triggers. Paul Newman and Robert Redford played those 19th-century villains as likeable antiheroes who inhabit a Western fantasy set to a 1960s pop-music tune. And 50 years ago, the movie seemed just the magical, side-show elixir Americans hankered for. When *Butch Cassidy* opened in September 1969, audiences ignored naysaying critics, massed in lines, grabbed some popcorn and soda pop, and enjoyed nearly two hours of sweet escapism. Perhaps they yearned for a respite from the barrage of wrenching news, as U.S. troops fought in Vietnam, antiwar protests overran college campuses, fires scorched inner cities, and a murderous cult called the Family gripped America's attention with what became known as the Manson killings.

With Newman, Redford, and Katharine Ross, as Redford's lady friend, Etta Place, *Butch Cassidy and the Sundance Kid* stole the hearts of millions, made off with the equivalent of more than $700 million in current dollars, won four Academy Awards, and launched the 33-year-old Redford into superstardom. While Redford and Newman never made a sequel, they did team up again with *Butch Cassidy* director George Roy Hill for another film about a bunch of relatable, albeit shady, grifters: 1973's *The Sting*, which won seven Academy Awards. And *Butch Cassidy* created a cottage industry of films and TV shows that explored various iterations of the pair while also spawning the modern bromance.

Of course, the spectacular success of *Butch Cassidy*—and its long, profitable afterlife—would have been impossible without the intriguing real-life figures who inspired William Goldman's Oscar-winning screenplay. The film follows the strange but true tale of Robert Leroy Parker and Harry Alonzo Longabaugh, sons of devout and impoverished families who in the long tradition of American pioneers set out in search of a different life. But instead of homesteading a spread of land, Parker and Longabaugh reinvented themselves as two feared and trail-worn outlaws called Butch Cassidy and the Sundance Kid.

They enjoyed a pretty good run in their few years of fin de siècle lawlessness. But all bad things come to an end—and so their days riding the range, robbing banks, trains, and mines with the Hole-in-the-Wall Gang were soon curtailed by swift Western justice. While marshals, troops, and rangers hunted, jailed, and killed their mates, Butch and Sundance, along with Etta,

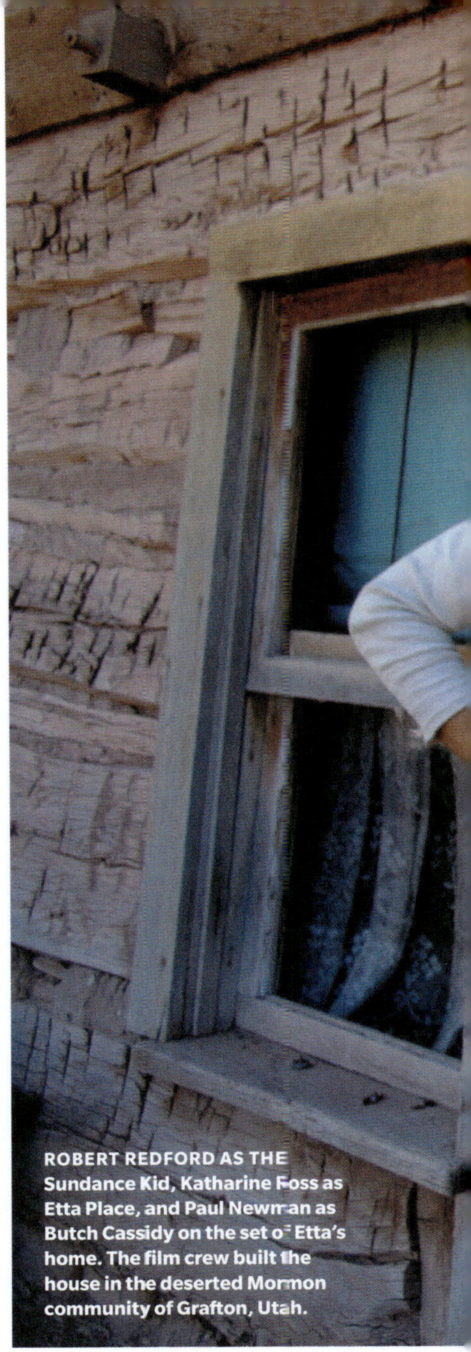

ROBERT REDFORD AS THE Sundance Kid, Katharine Ross as Etta Place, and Paul Newman as Butch Cassidy on the set of Etta's home. The film crew built the house in the deserted Mormon community of Grafton, Utah.

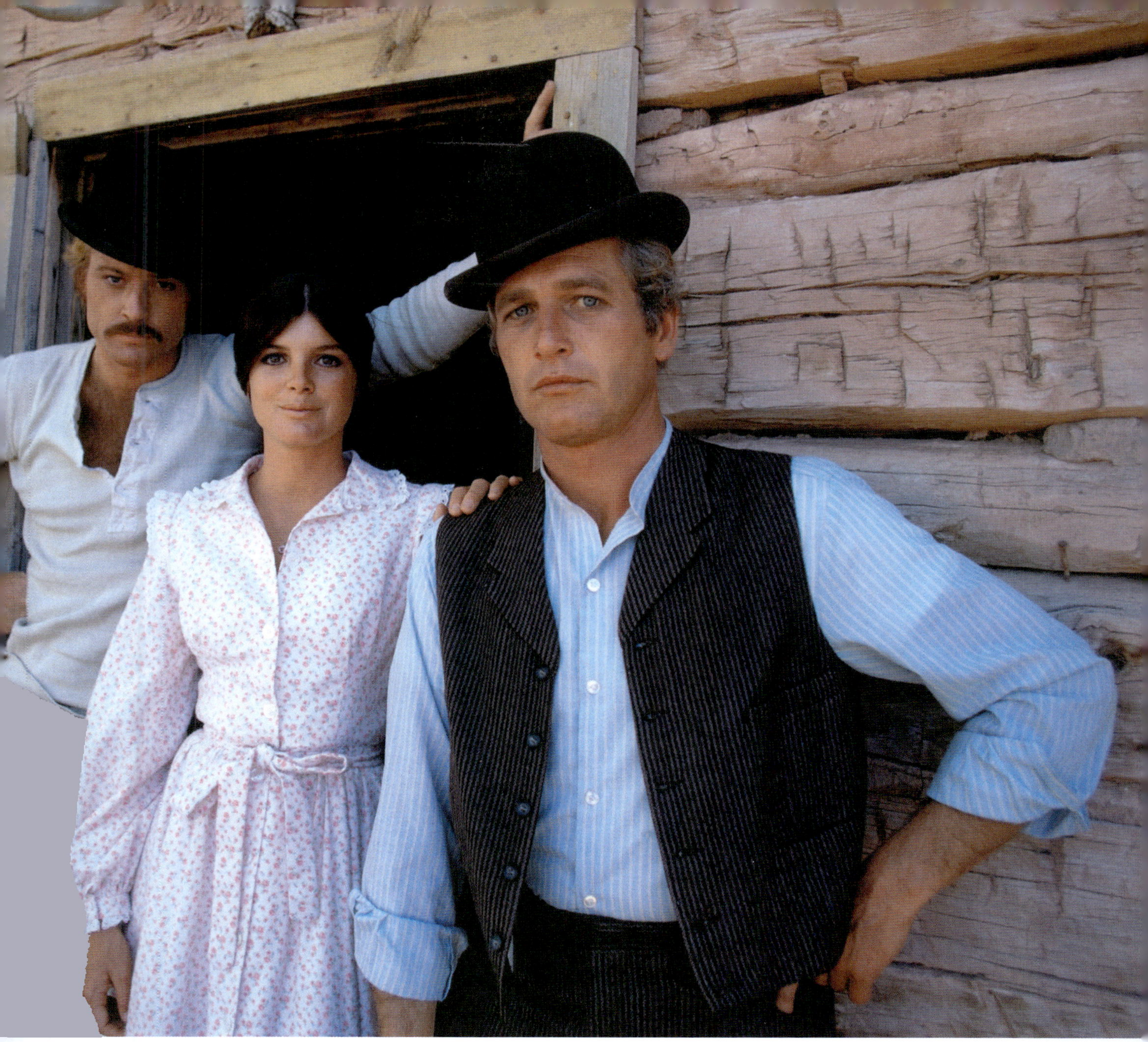

eluded the law. Just like that once wide-open territory Americans had spent a century corralling and mythologizing, Butch and Sundance seemed to vanish. Their disappearance aptly symbolized the swan song of the Wild West, as that rugged, untamed land yielded to the march of civilization.

Yet amazingly, even as the American frontier closed, it would not signal Butch and Sundance's final act. In classic American fashion they transformed their lives again, and unexpectedly reappeared in a less celebrated Wild South. Down in Argentina and Bolivia Butch and Sundance tried their hands at ranching. But they did not take to a settled life. Something about riding trails and drinking campfire coffee must have made the outlaws feel like strapping on their six-shooters and returning to their old ways. And that's just what Butch and Sundance did—until they robbed the Aramayo silver mine in November 1908. The law cornered them in the sleepy town of San Vicente, Bolivia. Military surrounded *los bandidos yanquis*; a gunfight broke out, and soldiers killed the two pals.

Or maybe they didn't. Maybe, just maybe, Butch and Sundance escaped.

Indeed, there are still questions about what really happened to them. And that only makes the legend of Butch Cassidy and the Sundance Kid more fascinating and enduring. Just like those 19th-century dime novels that brimmed with larger-than-life characters embracing the freedom of the land—and the 1969 film, with Newman and Redford's irresistibly engaging portrayals of the pair—these two outlaws maintain their hold on the popular imagination. More than 100 years after their Bolivian gunfight, we beckon them to return to America and continue to inhabit our fantasies about that place we call the Wild West. ✦

CHAPTER ONE

THE LIVES BEHIND THE LEGEND

HOW TWO BOYS FROM GOOD, GOD-FEARING FAMILIES WENT IN SEARCH OF FORTUNE AND ADVENTURE, THEN BLAZED A CRIMINAL—AND COLORFUL—TRAIL ACROSS THE WESTERN FRONTIER

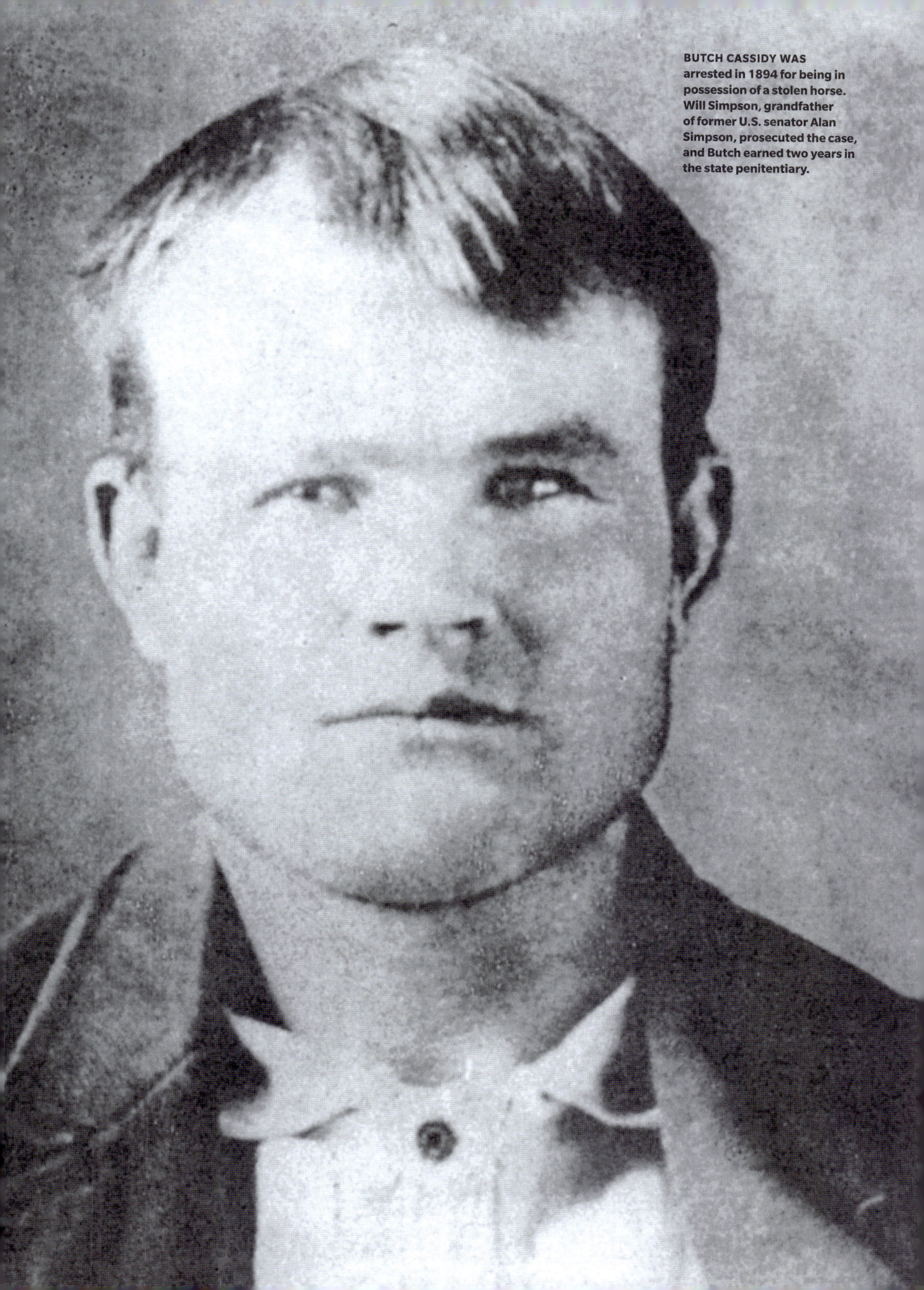

BUTCH CASSIDY WAS arrested in 1894 for being in possession of a stolen horse. Will Simpson, grandfather of former U.S. senator Alan Simpson, prosecuted the case, and Butch earned two years in the state penitentiary.

JUST AFTER TWO IN THE MORNING ON June 2, 1899, two men carrying lanterns flagged down the Union Pacific Railroad's No. 1 train. Engineer William Jones, assuming the pair had come to warn him that the bridge near Wilcox, Wyoming, had been washed out, braked the engine. Two men wearing masks then hopped on board and ordered Jones to cross the bridge. When the engineer didn't move fast enough, he was coldcocked with the butt of a Colt revolver.

After the train passed to the other side of the wooden trestle, the bandits blew up the structure. Then they uncoupled the passenger cars. At that, four more villains climbed on and advised the passengers that no one would be harmed as long as they stayed calm. When the outlaws made it to the mail car, clerks Robert Lawson and Burt Bruce didn't open the door fast enough, so it was blown off. The gang found little of value, so they headed to the express car. Cowering inside was messenger Charles Woodcock, who, despite his fear, refused to unlock the door—so the robbers blew it wide open, demolishing the side of the car. Though dazed from the explosion, the resolute Woodcock wouldn't reveal the safe's combination, so the robbers set off another blast—and made off with $50,000 in cash along with jewelry, gold, and diamonds.

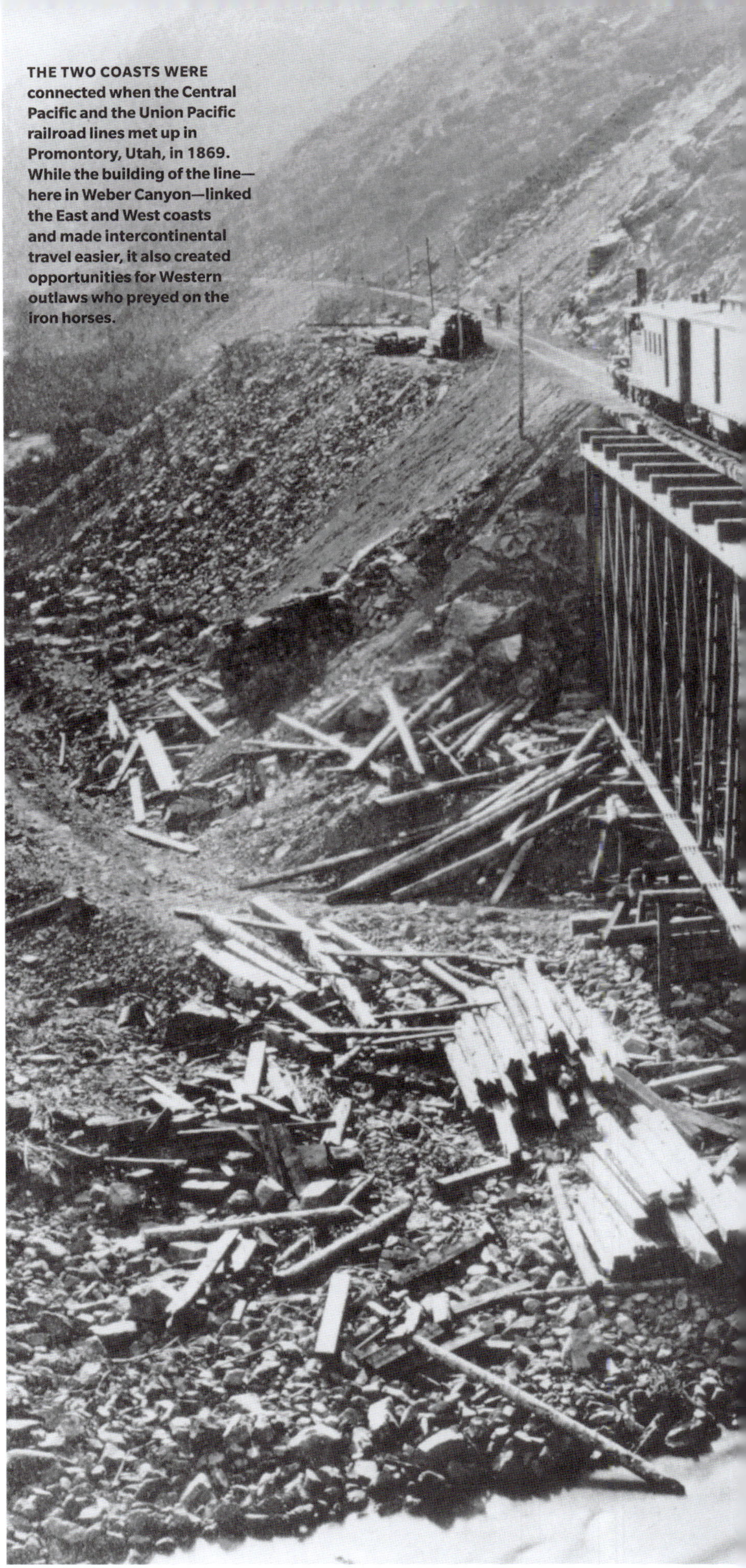

THE TWO COASTS WERE connected when the Central Pacific and the Union Pacific railroad lines met up in Promontory, Utah, in 1869. While the building of the line—here in Weber Canyon—linked the East and West coasts and made intercontinental travel easier, it also created opportunities for Western outlaws who preyed on the iron horses.

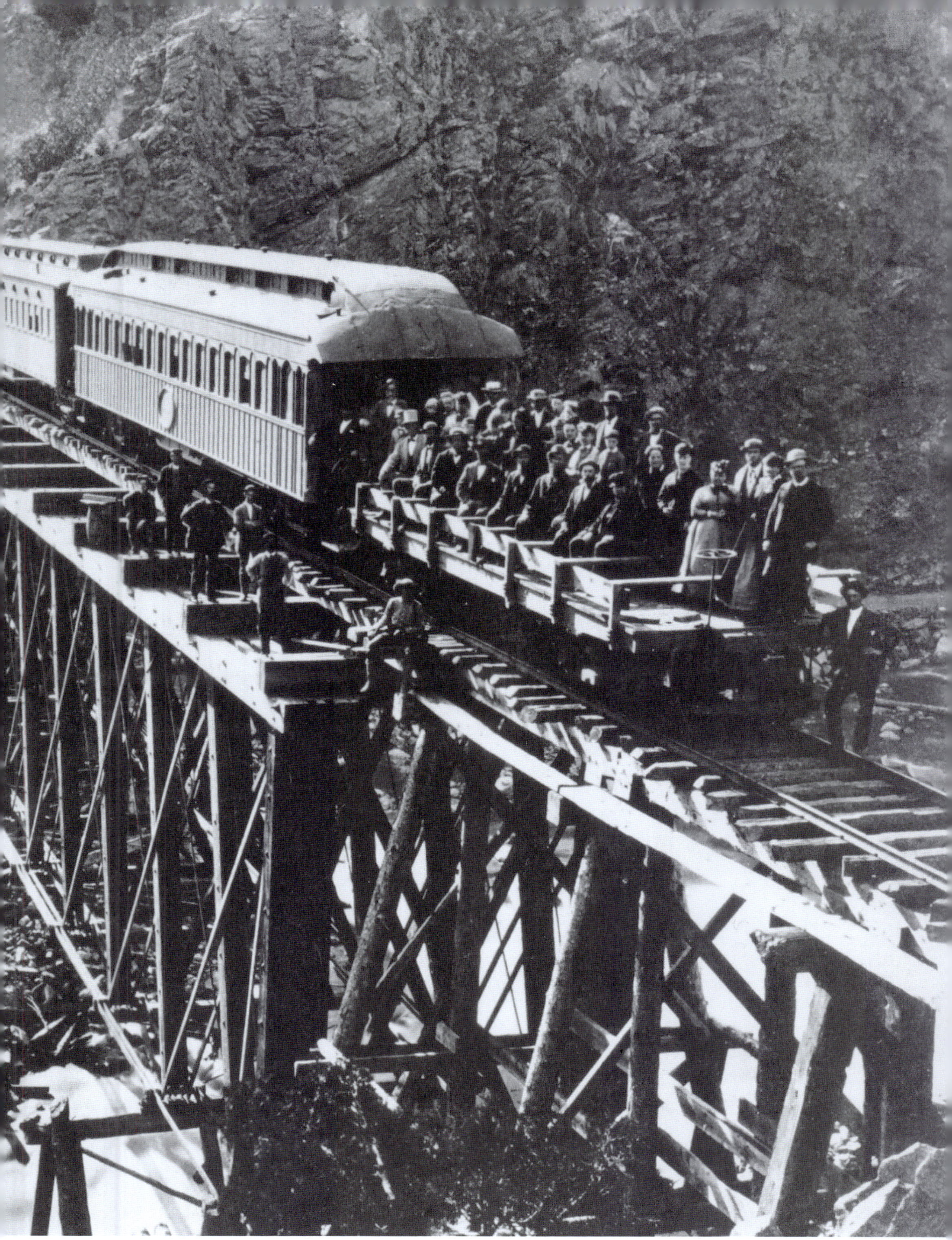

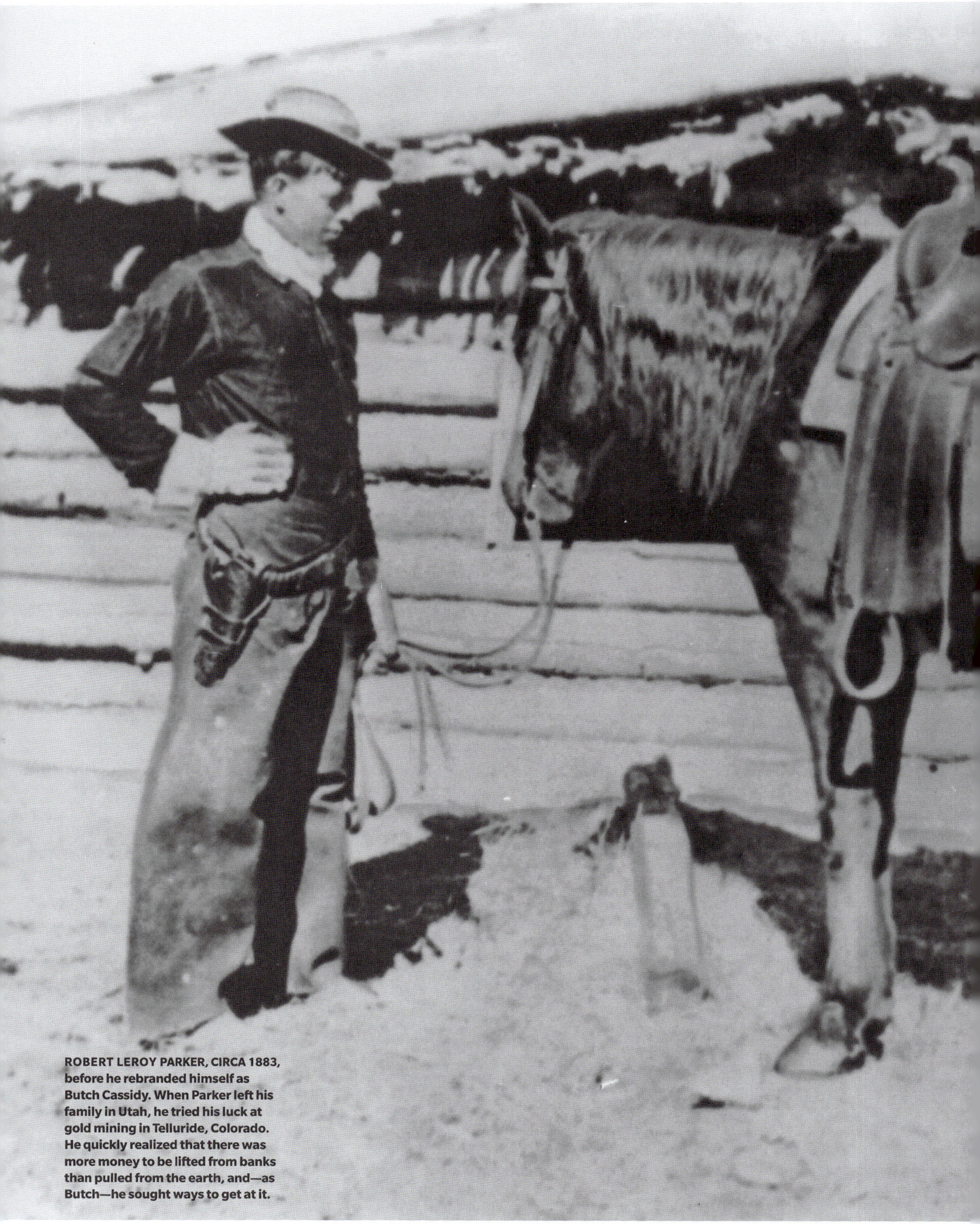

ROBERT LEROY PARKER, CIRCA 1883, before he rebranded himself as Butch Cassidy. When Parker left his family in Utah, he tried his luck at gold mining in Telluride, Colorado. He quickly realized that there was more money to be lifted from banks than pulled from the earth, and—as Butch—he sought ways to get at it.

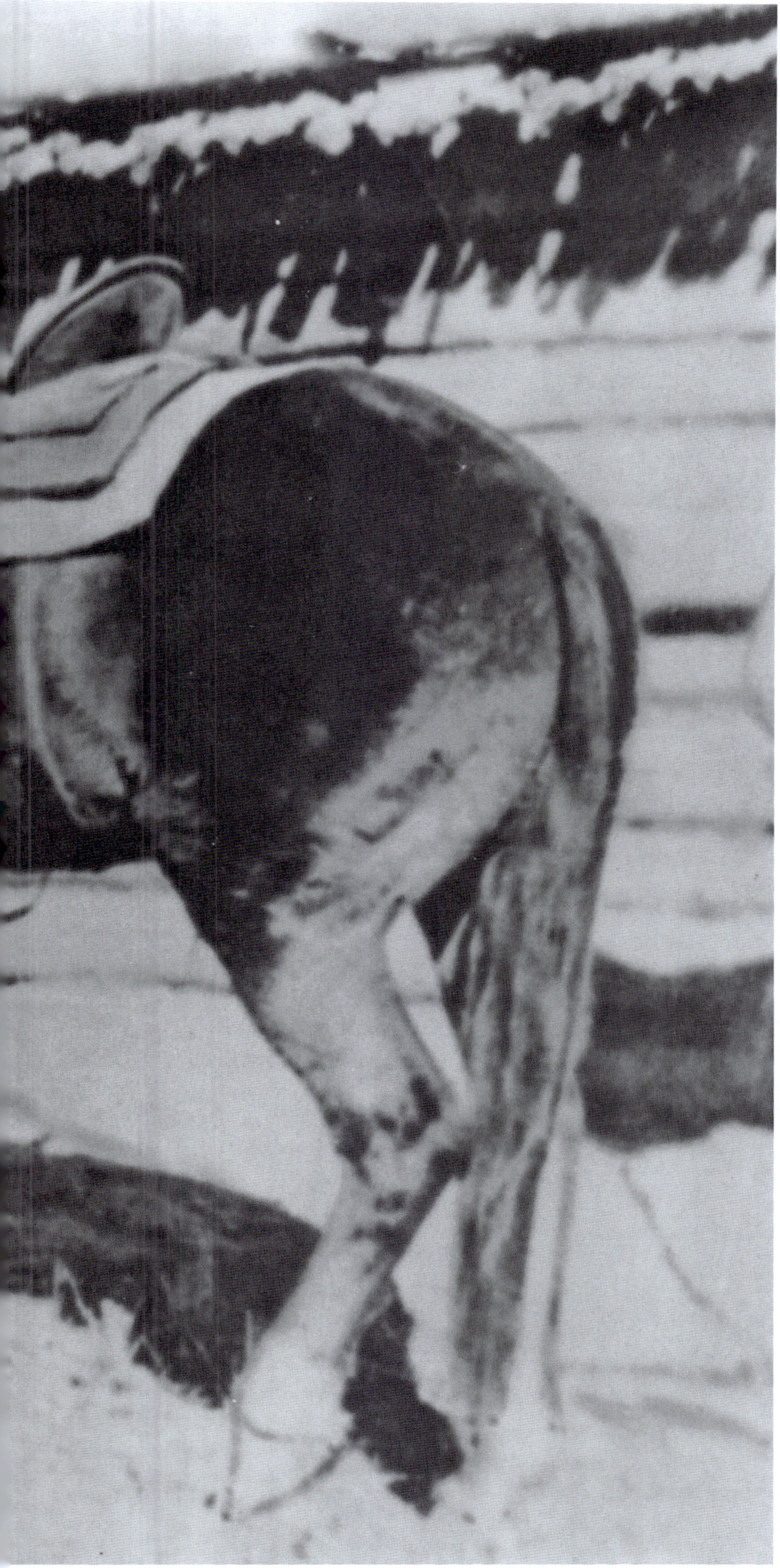

The Sundance Kid led the heist. While the head of the gang, Butch Cassidy, wasn't there, he had orchestrated the robbery and arranged horse relays to help his men get away. So by the time engineer Jones arrived in Medicine Bow, Wyoming, and shot off a telegram—"First Section No. 1 held up a mile west of Wilcox. Express car blown open, mail car damaged. Safe blown open; contents gone"—the Hole-in-the-Wall Gang had vanished.

As infamous outlaws, Butch and Sundance had come quite a way from their humble, God-fearing origins. Cassidy was born Robert Leroy Parker on April 13, 1866—the year outlaws Jesse and Frank James robbed their first bank—to a family of devout Mormons. His mother, Ann, and

SUNDANCE HEEDED THE WORDS OF EDITOR HORACE GREELEY, WHO WROTE, "GO WEST, YOUNG MAN."

father, Maximilian, were early settlers in Circleville, Utah. Maximilian toiled long hours as a farmer, while Ann homeschooled her brood of 13, teaching them fundamentalist values. As the oldest, much work fell to Robert; at 13 he headed to a nearby ranch to make money for the family. There he met a horseman, cattle rustler, and gambler named Mike Cassidy. Cassidy was not a churchgoing man, and he taught Parker many of the ungodly things he knew—including how to make a better, if distinctly dishonest, living.

At 18 Parker abandoned his family's impoverished land. In the summer of 1884 he landed in the mining boomtown of Telluride, Colorado, where gold fever filled the bars, gambling dens, and brothels. By then, though, the major gold claims had been staked, so Parker found a job hauling ore down

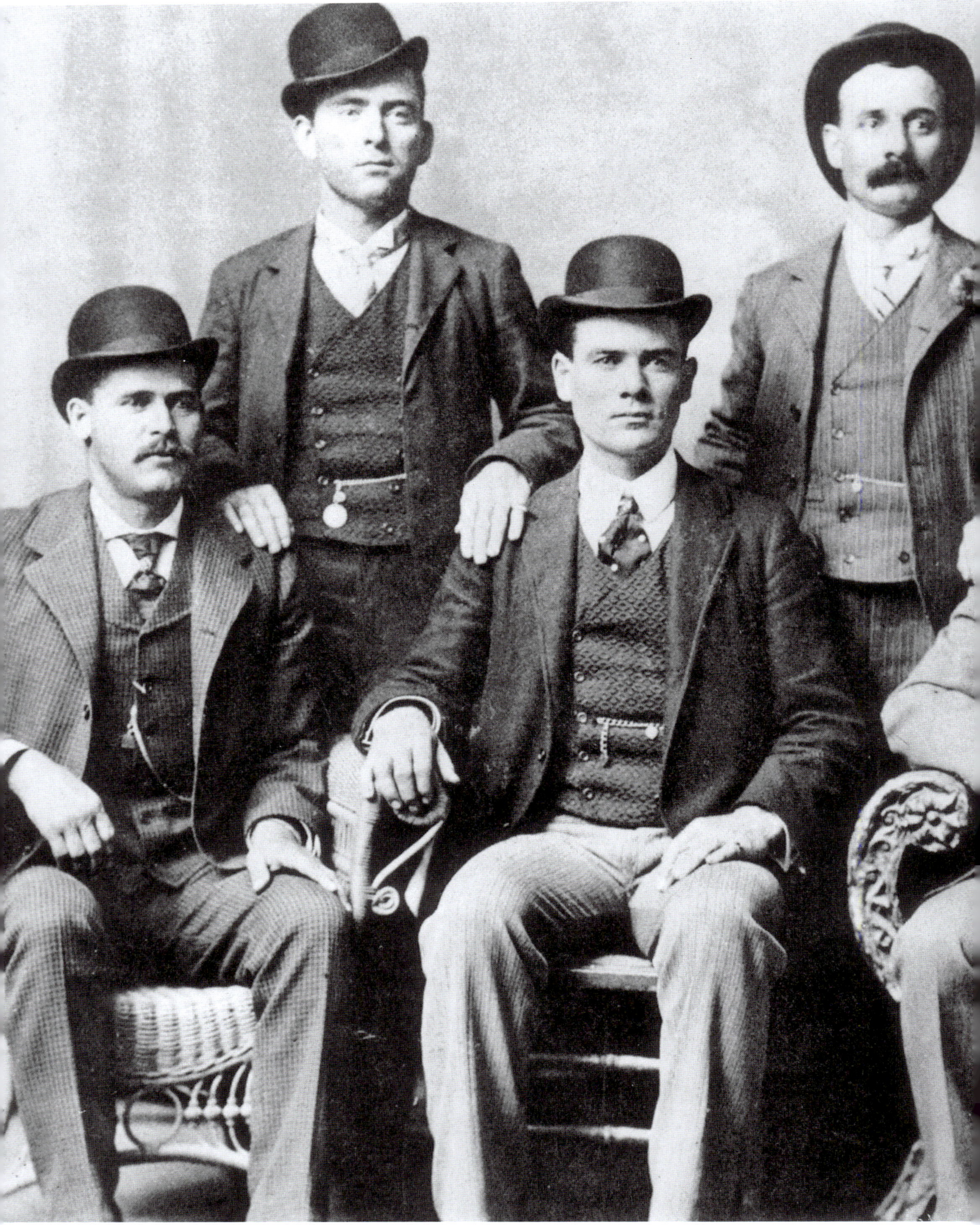

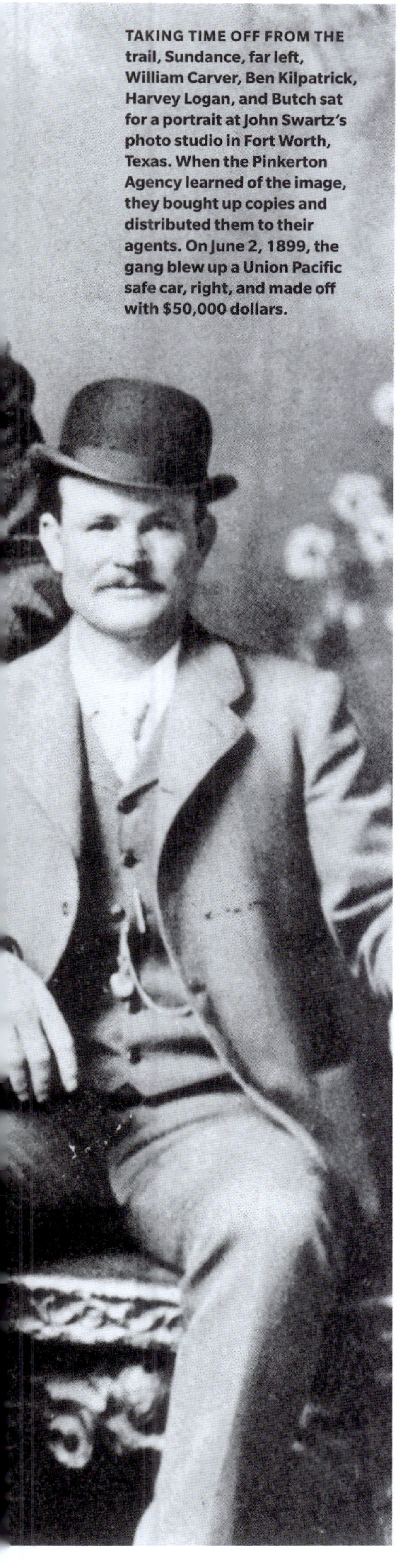

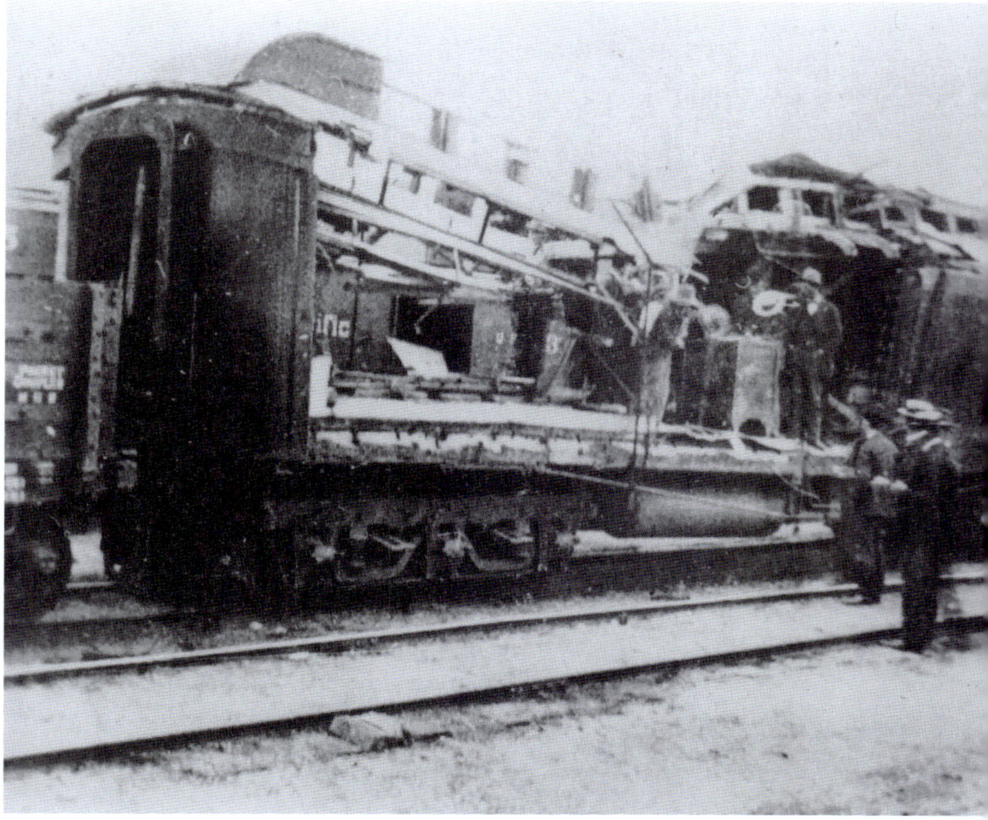

TAKING TIME OFF FROM THE trail, Sundance, far left, William Carver, Ben Kilpatrick, Harvey Logan, and Butch sat for a portrait at John Swartz's photo studio in Fort Worth, Texas. When the Pinkerton Agency learned of the image, they bought up copies and distributed them to their agents. On June 2, 1899, the gang blew up a Union Pacific safe car, right, and made off with $50,000 dollars.

the mountains. Looking for an easier way to make a greenback, he noticed the town's San Miguel Valley Bank. Parker cased the building and figured out when the money came in and left. Then, on June 24, 1889, with three others, he waited till most of the staff was gone, and made off with $20,000.

Parker not only planned the heist, but knowing they would be chased, set up fresh horses along the escape route so his team could race away and avoid capture. Now a wanted man, he feared embarrassing his mother, so he changed his name to George Cassidy in honor of his mentor. And because he had once worked as a butcher, he soon started to go by Butch Cassidy. In 1894 he landed a two-year stint in prison for possessing a stolen horse.

Cassidy wasn't the only one aching for a new life. Harry Alonzo Longabaugh came from a family of strict Baptists in Phoenixville, Pennsylvania. Born in 1867 to Josiah and Annie Longabaugh, he had worked on the canals, and at the local library he checked out pulp novels and probably read about the exploits of Buffalo Bill, Jesse James, and Calamity Jane. For a restless youth, the frontier offered adventure, and like many others he heeded the words of *New York Tribune* editor Horace Greeley, who wrote, "Go west, young man." In 1882, at the age of 14, Longabaugh found work on his cousin's Colorado ranch. There he learned to be a cowboy, and ended up laboring all over Wyoming and Montana. But when work dried up, he turned to petty crime, and at 20 spent a year in jail in Sundance, Wyoming, for stealing horses. When released, he called himself the Sundance Kid.

THE WEST HAS A HISTORY OF men who, like Butch and Sundance, reinvented themselves as they sought to make a dishonest living. Their opportunities increased in May 1869 when the Central Pacific Railroad linked up with the Union Pacific. With the ceremonial driving of a final golden spike at Promontory, Utah, the train lines joined the East and the West Coast, creating cross-continental travel, turning trains into easy targets, and giving birth to a golden age of Western banditry.

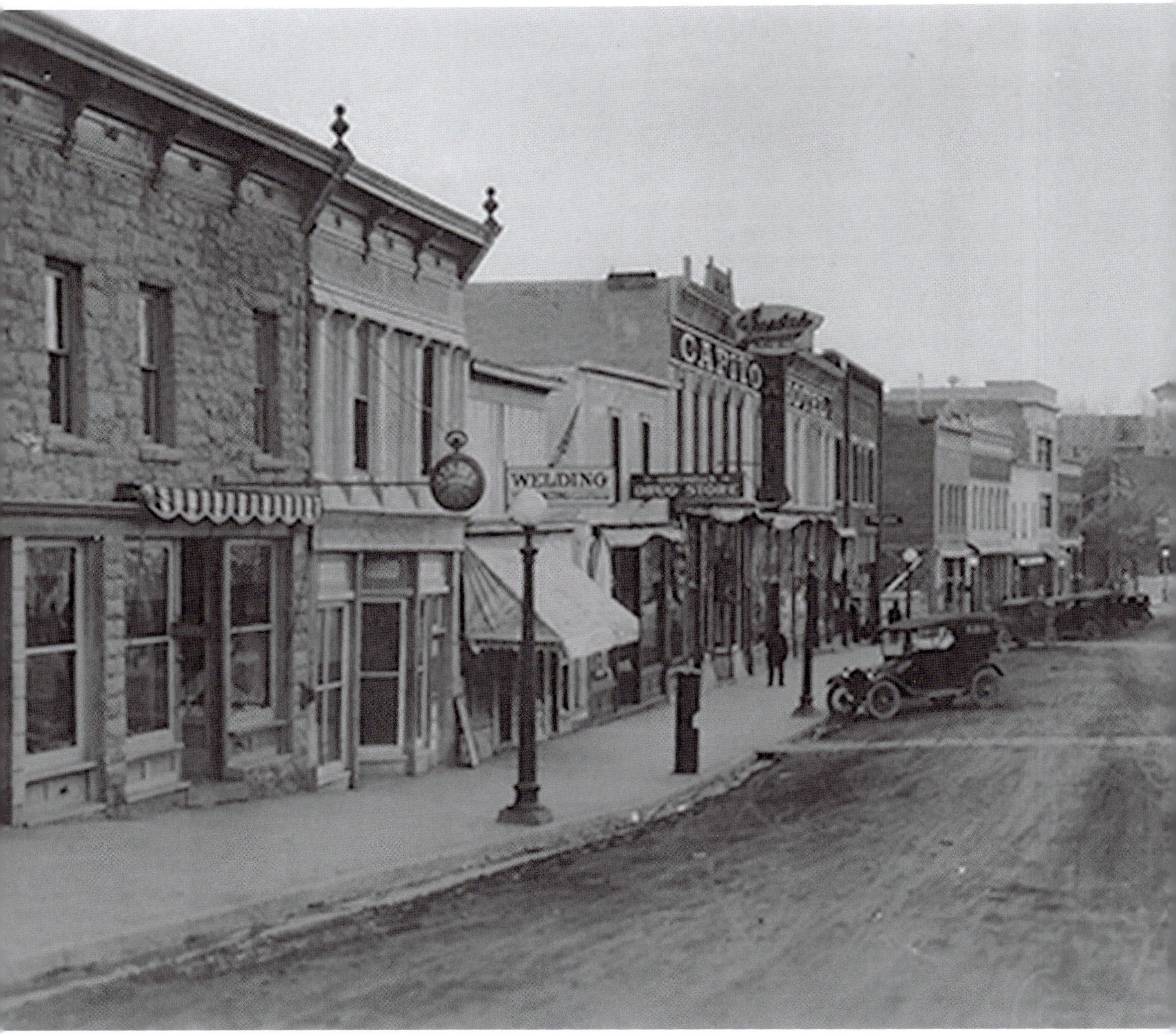

There were a lot of criminals out there eager to take advantage of the opportunities, some famous like Sam Bass, the James boys, and William "Billy the Kid" Bonney Jr., and others now lost to history. They and their gangs searched for easy pickings, and many found refuge in a vast series of hideouts along the Outlaw Trail, which stretched from Montana down through Wyoming, Colorado, Utah, New Mexico, Arizona, and into Texas and Mexico. The area offered cover and anonymity, with outlaws frequenting places like the steep-walled canyons of Utah's Robbers Roost, the wastelands of Colorado's Brown's Hole, and Wyoming's Hole-in-the-Wall Pass. There they received the support of some farmers and ranchers who felt that the banks and big mining companies were pushing them out; these locals supplied the men with lodging, horses, and food. One former Union Pacific conductor supposedly even offered information about when the trains contained gold shipments. In return, the settlers received much-needed cash.

In the mid 1890s, on the Outlaw Trail, Cassidy and Sundance first met. The two men developed a close friendship and learned to trust each other. Butch was the gregarious and charismatic one. The handsome Sundance proved to be quieter, and his quick draw earned him a reputation as the best shot around. On August 13, 1896, Cassidy led a bank robbery in Montpelier, Idaho, making off with between $5,000 and $15,000. According to local lore, five days later, he called together more than 200 like-minded outlaws at Brown's Hole and called on them to pool their talents and form a "Train Robbers' Syndicate."

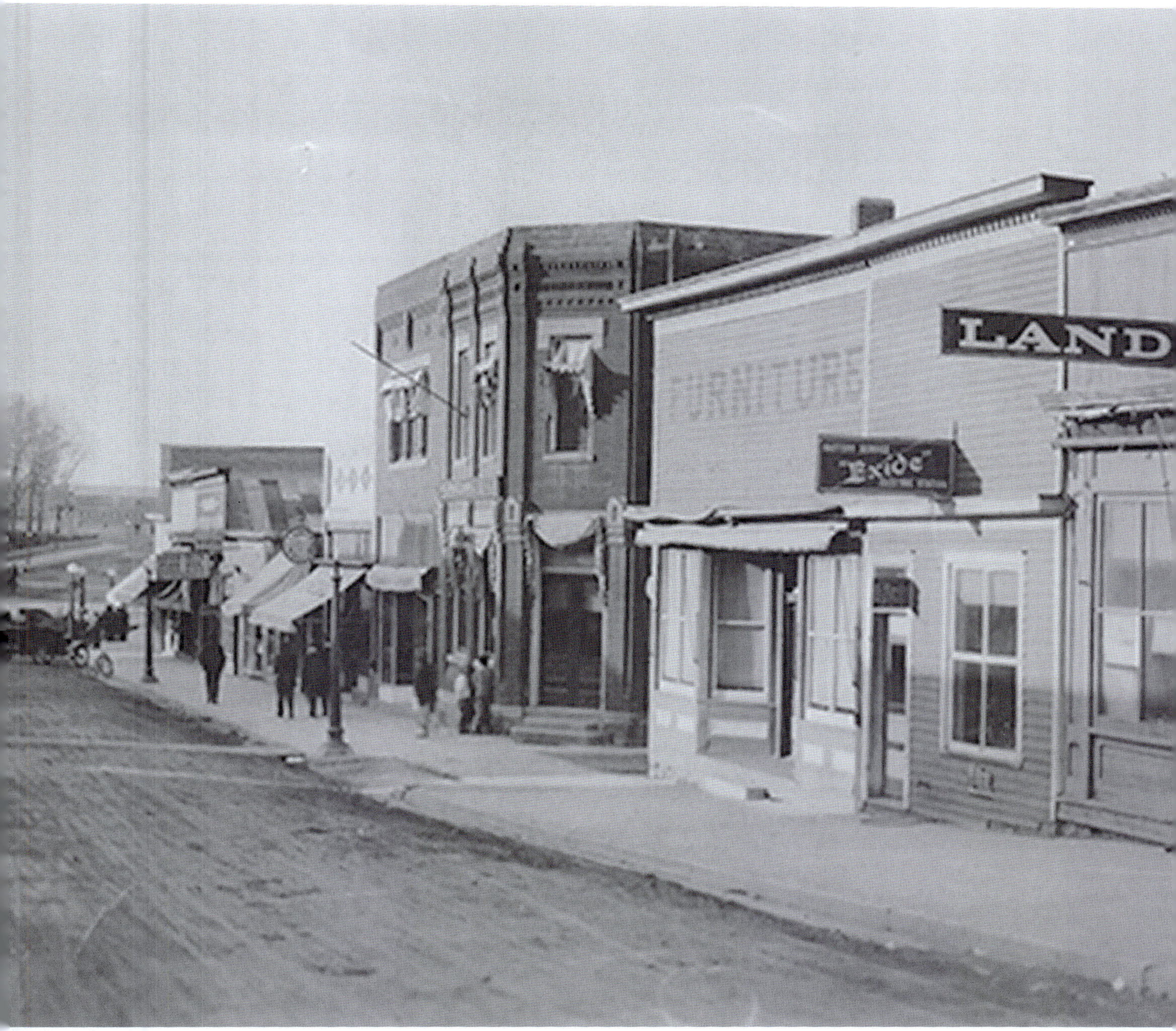

BUFFALO, WYOMING (SEEN here in 1919), lies in the foothills of the Bighorn Mountains, not far from Butch and Sundance's Hole-in-the-Wall hideout. Now and then, the outlaws were known to come to town—they even stayed at the Occidental Hotel.

The organization was really a loose confederation of groups with fluid memberships. Butch's shrewd leadership skills made him a natural chief of the Hole-in-the-Wall Gang, some 20 colorfully named bandits, desperados, and good-for-nothin' characters. The gang included Sundance, Harvey "Kid Curry" Logan, his brother Lonnie Logan, William "News" Carver, William Ellsworth "Elzy" Lay, George "Flat Nose" Currie, Ben "Tall Texan" Kilpatrick, "Laughing" Sam Carey, Tom O'Day, Laura Bullion, Orlando Camilla "Deaf Charley" Hanks, and the brothers Sam and Tom "Black Jack" Ketchum.

Butch and Sundance's group was different from the others. Despite Harvey Logan's violent tendencies, Butch stressed the use of kind persuasion with the hint of deadly repercussions. And while Butch took the lead in planning, he welcomed the others' thoughts and insights as they plotted out which banks, mining companies, and trains to rob.

The outlaws kept busy as they headed out in assorted teams. In an April 1897 daylight robbery at the Pleasant Valley Coal Company in

Castle Gate, Utah, they snatched $7,000, cut the telegraph wires, and raced away. Two months later, they robbed the Butte County Bank in Belle Fourche, South Dakota, but made off with only $87. On July 14, 1898, the gang hit Southern Pacific passenger train No 1. When a messenger refused to open the express car, the outlaws detonated dynamite outside as a show of force. The messenger quickly complied, and Cassidy's boys gathered up some $26,000 in cash and jewelry. And in June 1899 the gang held up Union Pacific No. 1—the train Woodcock worked on; *The Rawlins Semi-Weekly Republican* reported that after placing an excessive charge on the safe, the gang "wrecked the car, blowing the roof off and sides out, portions of the car being blown 150 yards."

Then, in July 1899, the Hole-in-the-Wallers descended on a train near Folsom, New Mexico, and made off with $70,000. But a posse was soon in hot pursuit, and in a gun battle Sam Ketchum and Elzy Lay were wounded and arrested. Ketchum died, and Lay earned a prison sentence. On August 29, 1900, the gang robbed Union Pacific train No. 3 out of Tipton, Wyoming. When the man inside the express car refused to open it, they set dynamite. Only then did the door slide open and reveal the unfortunate Woodcock from the Wilcox heist. The outlaws pilfered about $55,000, and as they left, Cassidy reportedly said, "Goodbye, boys." In September 1900 they slipped into Winnemucca, Nevada, and robbed the First National Bank of $32,640.

Butch & Co. hunkered down on the Outlaw Trail, squandering their

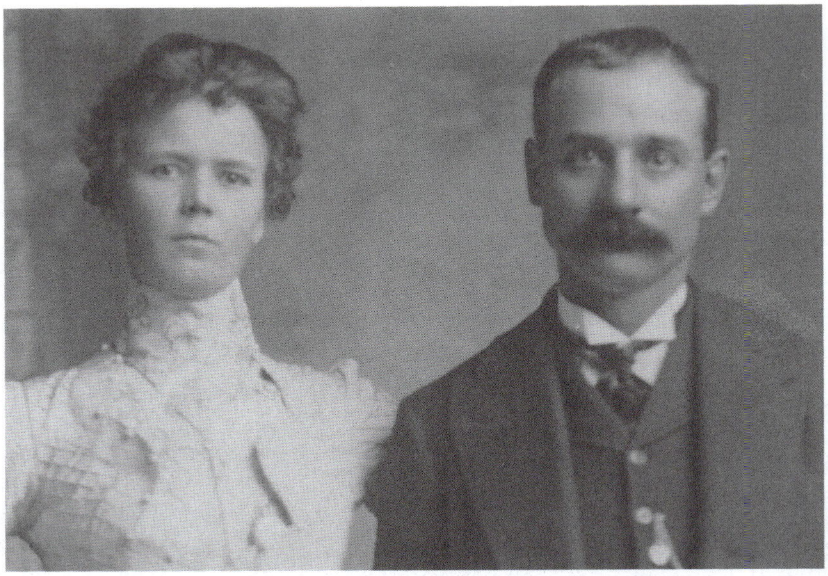

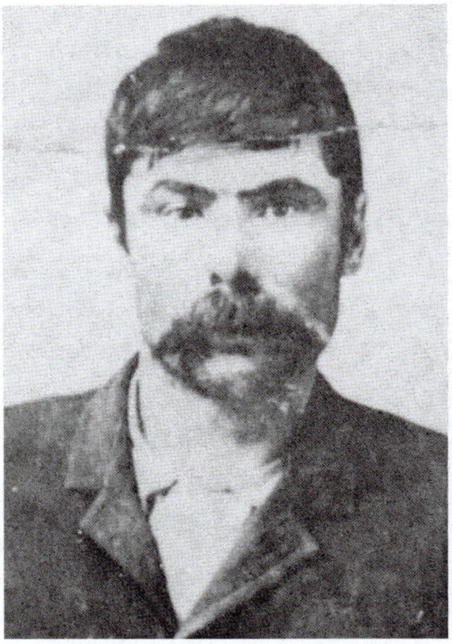

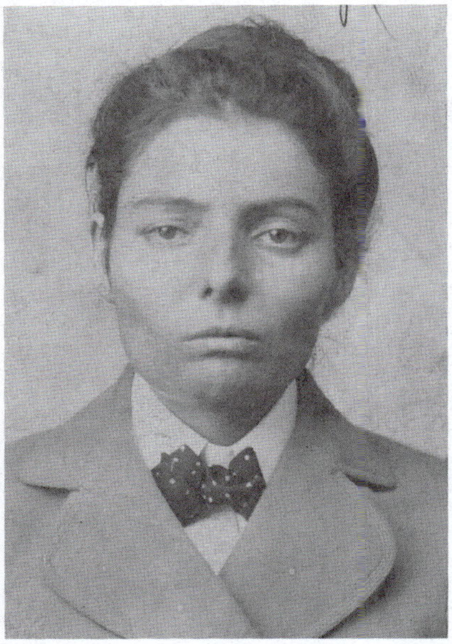

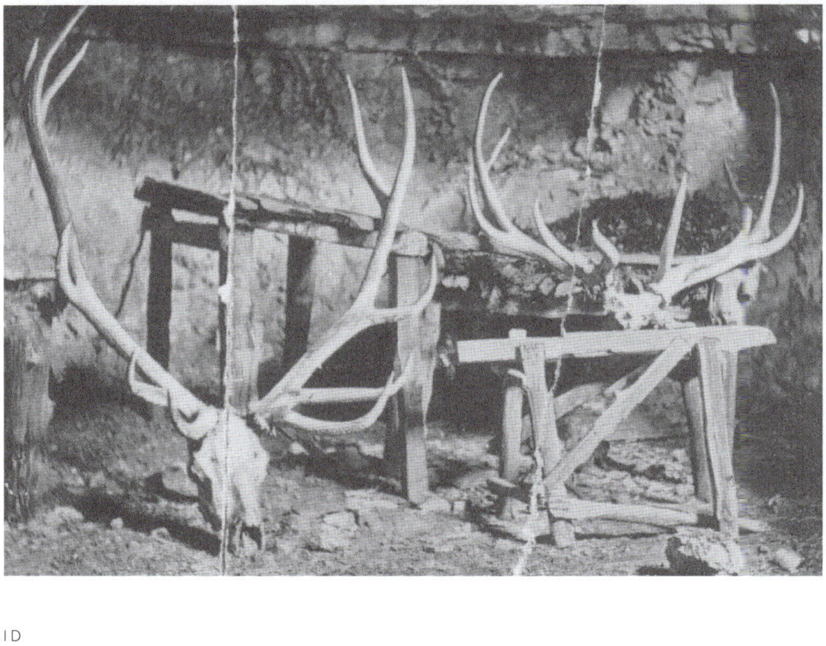

HOLE-IN-THE-WALL GANG member Harvey "Kid Curry" Logan with his girlfriend, Annie Rogers, top. Middle: Tom O'Day (left) and Laura Bullion, also in the gang. Bottom: One of the Hole-in-the-Wall caves the gang hid out in. Butch's activities drew the unwanted attention of the law, and earned a hefty price on his head, opposite.

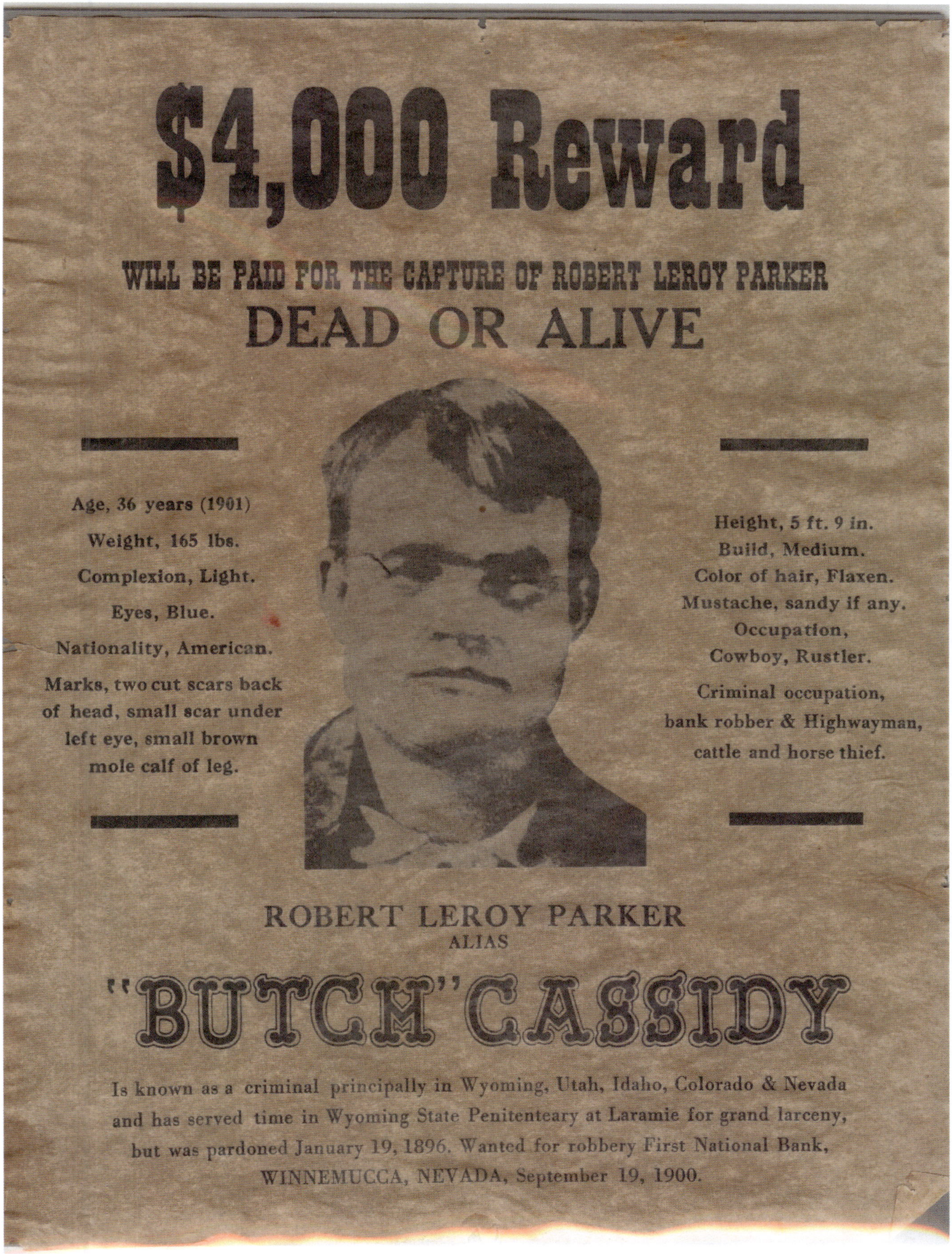

$4,000 Reward

WILL BE PAID FOR THE CAPTURE OF ROBERT LEROY PARKER

DEAD OR ALIVE

Age, 36 years (1901)
Weight, 165 lbs.
Complexion, Light.
Eyes, Blue.
Nationality, American.
Marks, two cut scars back of head, small scar under left eye, small brown mole calf of leg.

Height, 5 ft. 9 in.
Build, Medium.
Color of hair, Flaxen.
Mustache, sandy if any.
Occupation, Cowboy, Rustler.
Criminal occupation, bank robber & Highwayman, cattle and horse thief.

ROBERT LEROY PARKER
ALIAS

"BUTCH" CASSIDY

Is known as a criminal principally in Wyoming, Utah, Idaho, Colorado & Nevada and has served time in Wyoming State Penitenteary at Laramie for grand larceny, but was pardoned January 19, 1896. Wanted for robbery First National Bank, WINNEMUCCA, NEVADA, September 19, 1900.

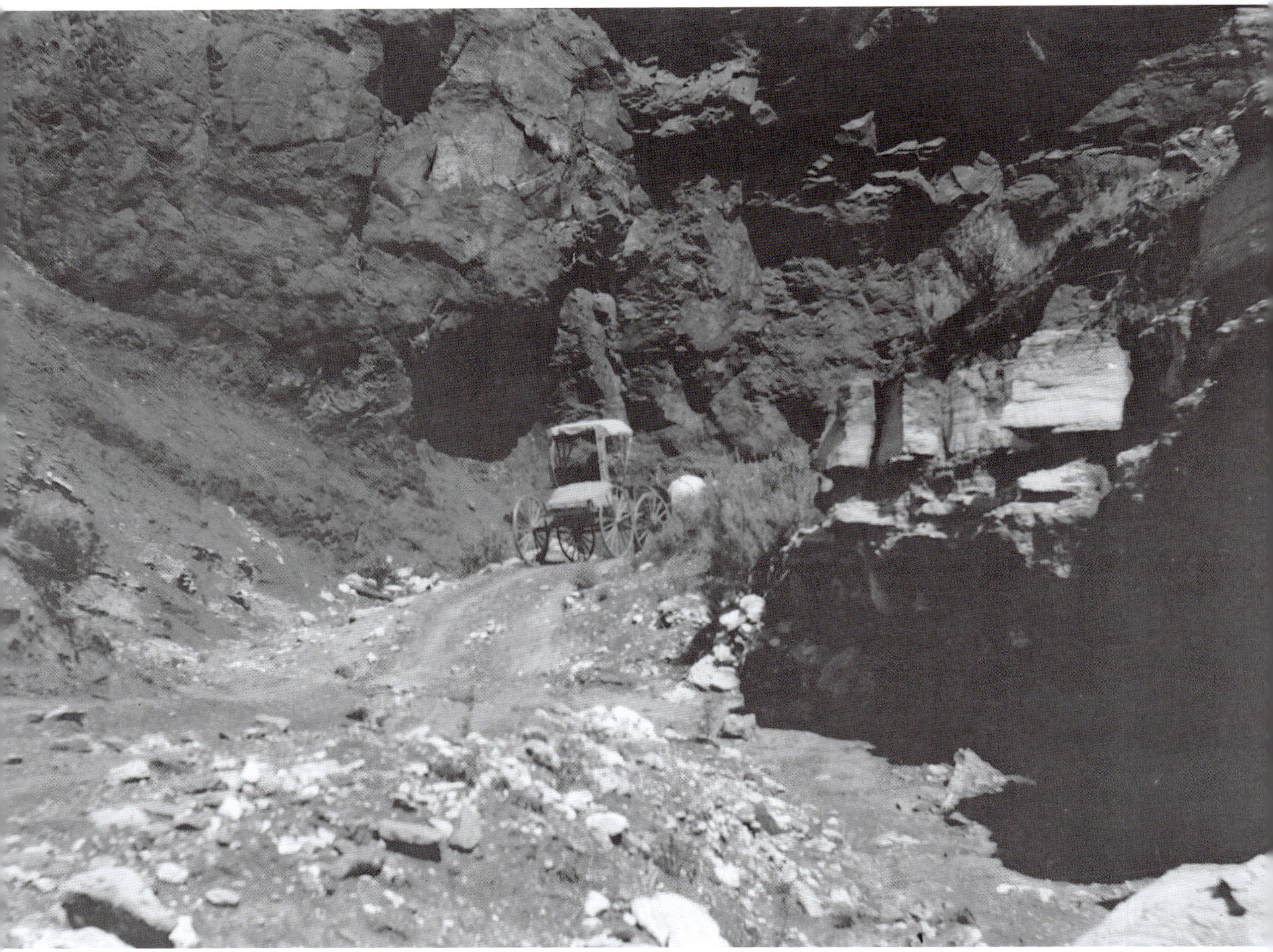

earnings on drink, cards, and women. A popular spot was Herb Bassett's ranch along northern Utah's Green River. Bassett had a large library, and let Cassidy look through his books. He also had a daughter, Ann, who became involved with Cassidy. Sundance, meanwhile, had been seeing Ethel "Etta" Place, whom he probably met at Fannie Porter's brothel in San Antonio. It is not certain that Place was really her last name, since it's also Sundance's mother's maiden name.

BUT EVEN THOUGH THE HOLE-in-the-Wall gang was laying low, their success drew unwanted attention. Butch's Wyoming mug shot was circulated, and by 1898 their robberies made headlines. The *Omaha Daily Bee* declared CASSIDY IS A BAD MAN: LEADER OF THE ROBBERS' ROOST GANG AND HIS ADVENTURES. TERROR TO MEN OF THREE STATES. His gang started to assume a mythic stature—all crimes were laid at their feet—and earned coverage in the Eastern press and inclusion in the pantheon of dime novels. "They were lawless men who have lived long in the crags and become like eagles, shunning mankind, except when they swooped down upon some country bank to rob it at the point of a pistol, or rode out on the range to gather in the cattle or horses of other men," reported the *New York Herald*. Many even saw them as heroes; a report that Butch returned money to a widow following a bank robbery earned him the nickname "Robin Hood of the West."

By then, the West was changing, and railroad executives, mining kings, and others wanted to halt the attacks. The June 1899 Wilcox robbery prodded the Union Pacific to track down the Hole-in-the-Wall Gang. The railroad put out a reward and hired the Pinkerton Detective Agency. Pinkerton's motto, "We never sleep," offered a clue to their approach, and in no time their detectives and police scoured the West for the group they dubbed the Wild Bunch. So while Butch might have been a meticulous planner, Pinkerton's 2,000 full-time agents and 30,000 informants and part-timers proved to be relentless investigators. They painstakingly catalogued the men's characters and physical traits, listed their scars and how they dressed, and distributed the information.

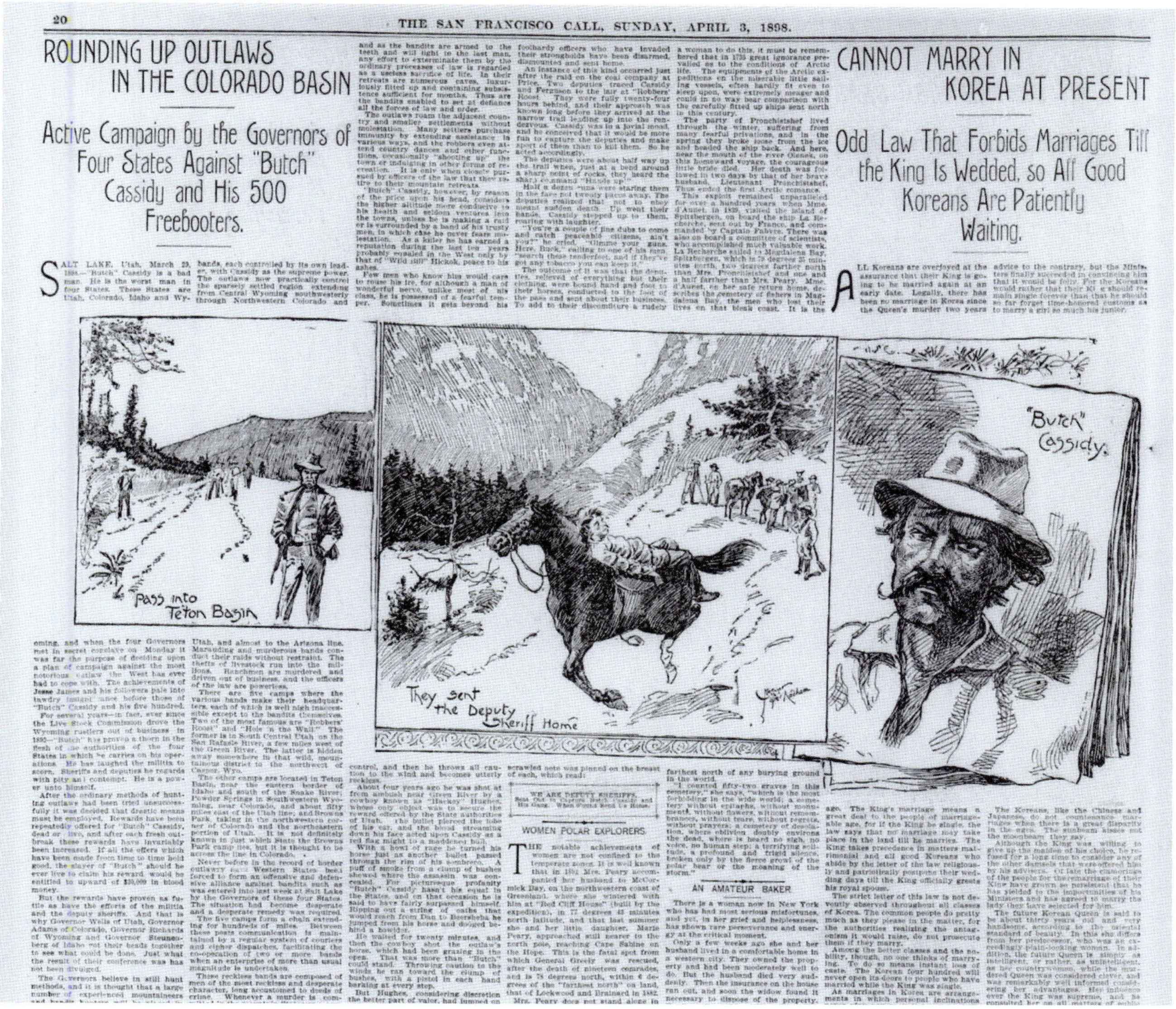

20 THE SAN FRANCISCO CALL, SUNDAY, APRIL 3, 1898.

ROUNDING UP OUTLAWS IN THE COLORADO BASIN

Active Campaign by the Governors of Four States Against "Butch" Cassidy and His 500 Freebooters.

CANNOT MARRY IN KOREA AT PRESENT

Odd Law That Forbids Marriages Till the King Is Wedded, so All Good Koreans Are Patiently Waiting.

WOMEN POLAR EXPLORERS

AN AMATEUR BAKER

THE HOLE-IN-THE-WALL PASS, in Wyoming's Bighorn Mountains was an inaccessible area (opposite) that offered outlaws easy refuge. While it might have been hard for lawmen to find them, the gang drew the attention of papers like the *San Francisco Call* in an article from 1898, above.

To help with the investigation, the Union Pacific stocked a special train with agents, food, horses, and equipment, and dispatched it in pursuit. Also on the case were Burlington Railroad detectives and state militia. They all searched for banknotes and coins from the Wilcox heist based on serial numbers as well as telltale signs of damage from the explosion. These efforts began to bear fruit. United States Marshal Frank A. Hadsell wrote of finding in Rawlins, Wyoming, "powder-burned currency," as well as "a lot of gold coin that seemed to be blackened or burned considerably."

Needing a break from their holdups, in November 1900, Butch, Sundance, Carver, Kilpatrick, and Harvey Logan went to the cattle town of Fort Worth to relax. They stayed at the Maddox Hotel and hung out in the local red light district called Hell's Half Acre. While there, the men cleaned up, donned their Sunday best, and posed at Swartz View Company. Knowing he'd photographed celebrities, John Swartz proudly displayed a copy of his work in his window. When the Pinkertons learned of the image they bought copies.

With such an invaluable clue, the Pinkertons further closed in on their prey. Realizing that they had sizable bounties on their heads and detectives on their heels, Butch and Sundance wisely considered a career change. Seeking a safer place, the two men, along with Etta, decided to head to South America. En route the trio stopped in New York City in February 1901, where they did the town, sightseeing, attending plays, and eating sumptuously. Sundance and Etta had a portrait made at DeYoung Photography Studio. At Tiffany's he bought her a gold lapel pendant watch and selected a diamond stickpin for himself, while Butch picked up a gold watch. Then on February 20 they sailed away and sought to reinvent themselves.

THE REST OF THE WILD BUNCH also should have hightailed it, for their wild days were nearing an end—a violent one, for most. Lonnie Logan, who had used some of the damaged Wilcox money in Montana, was tracked down to his hideout in Dodson and killed in February 1900. Two months later, Sheriff Jesse Tyler killed Flat Nose Currie in Moab County, Utah. On April 2, 1901 News Carver met his maker in Sonora, Texas. Officers captured Laura Bullion in 1901 with money from that year's Great Northern robbery. Following her release, she moved to Memphis and worked as a seamstress, dying there in 1961. Deaf Charley Hanks also took part in the Great Northern heist, and was gunned down in 1902. Captured in 1902, Kid Curry Logan earned a prison sentence, escaped the next year, and when surrounded by lawmen in 1904 in Rifle, Colorado, shot himself. Tall Texan Kilpatrick had been captured in 1901, and after his release from prison took up his old ways; he was killed during a 1912 train robbery. Elzy Lay, who was imprisoned in 1899, earned his freedom in 1906 and headed to Wyoming, where he opened a saloon; he eventually moved to California and died in 1934. And Laughing Sam Carey simply vanished from history. As the law rounded them up, the group earned a fitting epitaph from Chicago's *Inter Ocean* paper, which noted that the Wild Bunch "has disappeared with the march of civilization . . . wiped out by death and imprisonment."

Things were more peaceful in Argentina, a land with plenty of opportunities for cattlemen and settlers. Butch, Sundance, and Etta ranched a homestead in Patagonia and lived in a four-room timber ranch house decorated with framed pictures and brass lamps. Butch called himself James Ryan, Sundance went by Harry Place, and they had 300 head of cattle, 1,500 sheep, and 28 horses. They even had a pet dog. The threesome became part of the community and appear to have reformed, though the men always had their pistols strapped on.

But while they no longer led a life of crime, the outlaws weren't forgotten back home. Indeed, references to them were popping up all over. In November 1901 the *Salt Lake Herald* wrote of Cassidy: "This redoubtable gentleman of the ready revolver has aided in more fiction than any outlaw the boundless West has produced. Mr. Cassidy had been captured by sheriffs almost without number . . . Some bright morning we'll hear that M. Butch de Cassidy has been nabbed in sunny France, or that Butchovitch Cassidowsky is in the hands of the czar's policeoff. With Cassidy anything seems to be possible except really being caught."

ONE CHICAGO NEWSPAPER OBSERVED THAT BUTCH'S GANG "DISAPPEARED WITH THE MARCH OF CIVILIZATION."

And the Pinkertons persisted in their quest. In the winter of 1903 the agency intercepted a letter Sundance sent to his family in Pennsylvania. Agents headed to South America and distributed wanted posters. With the detectives closing in, Butch and Sundance pulled up stakes. Etta went back to the States and vanished.

The men made their way to Chile and then Bolivia and resumed robbing banks and mines. Carrying

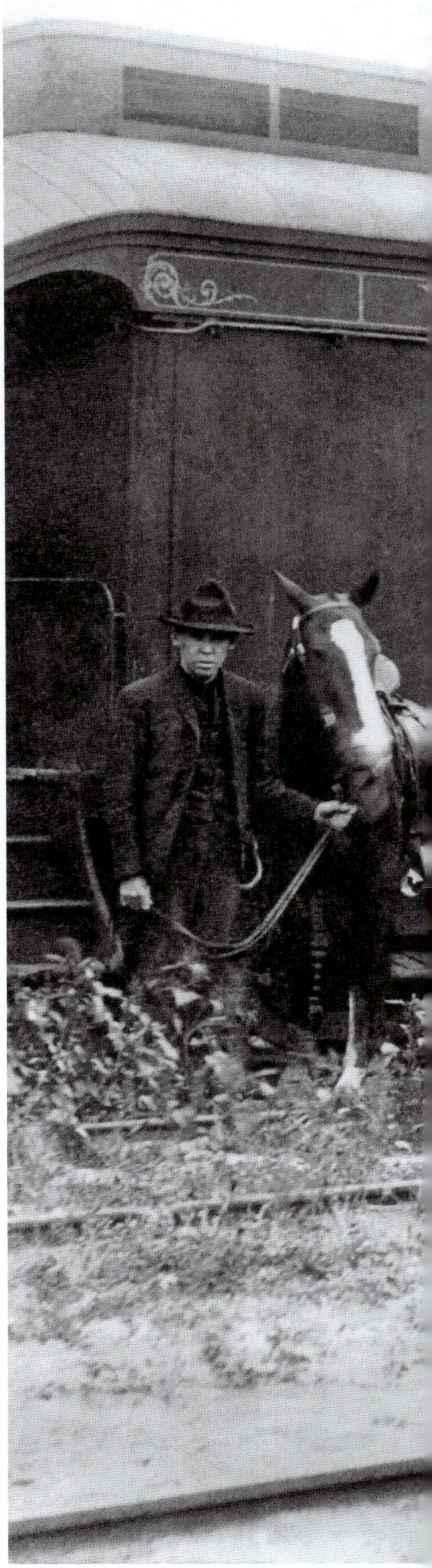

TO TRACK DOWN THE HOLE-IN-the-Wall Gang, the Pinkerton detective agency had the Union Pacific outfit a special train car, which transported rangers, horses, supplies, and plenty of guns.

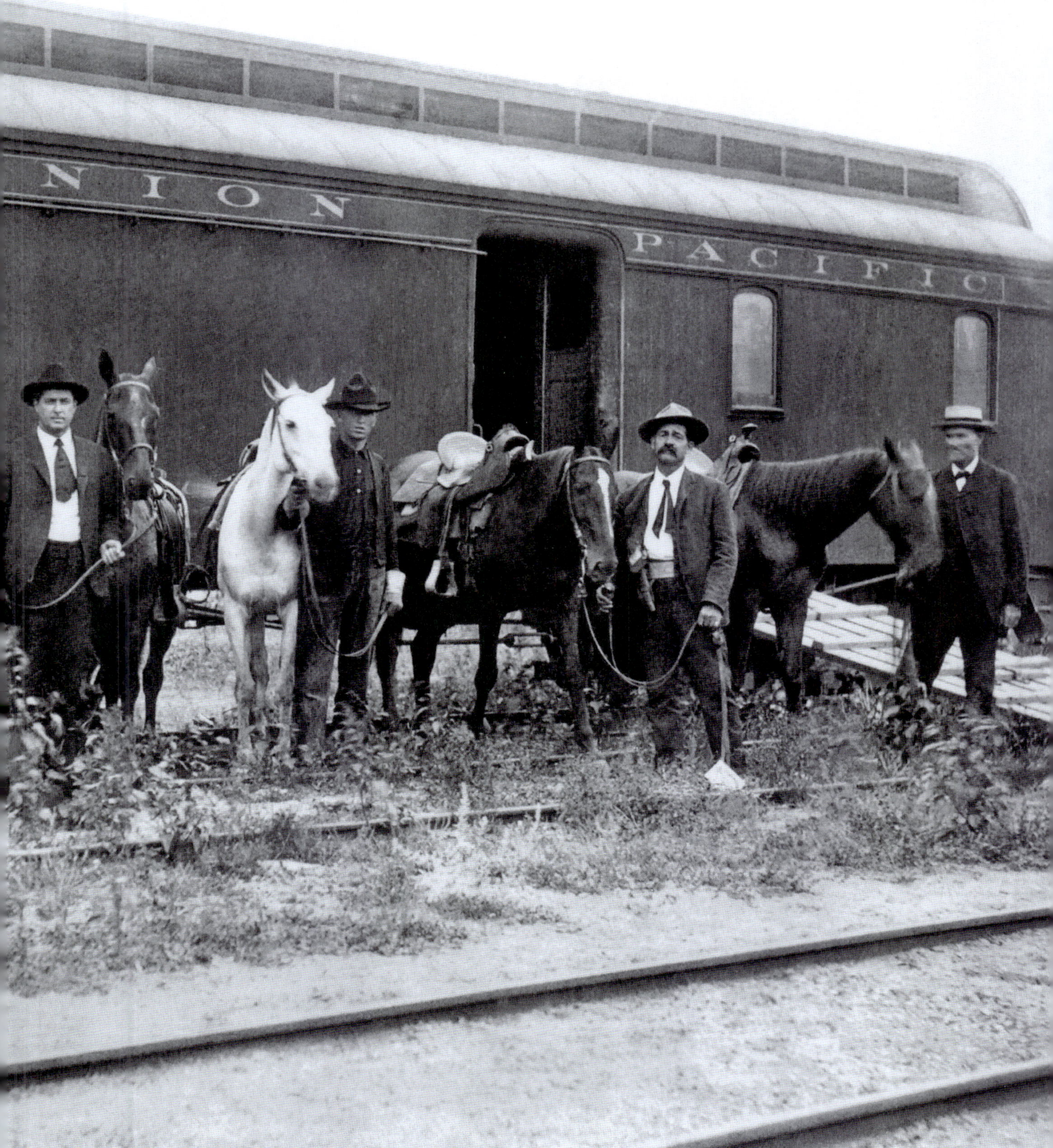

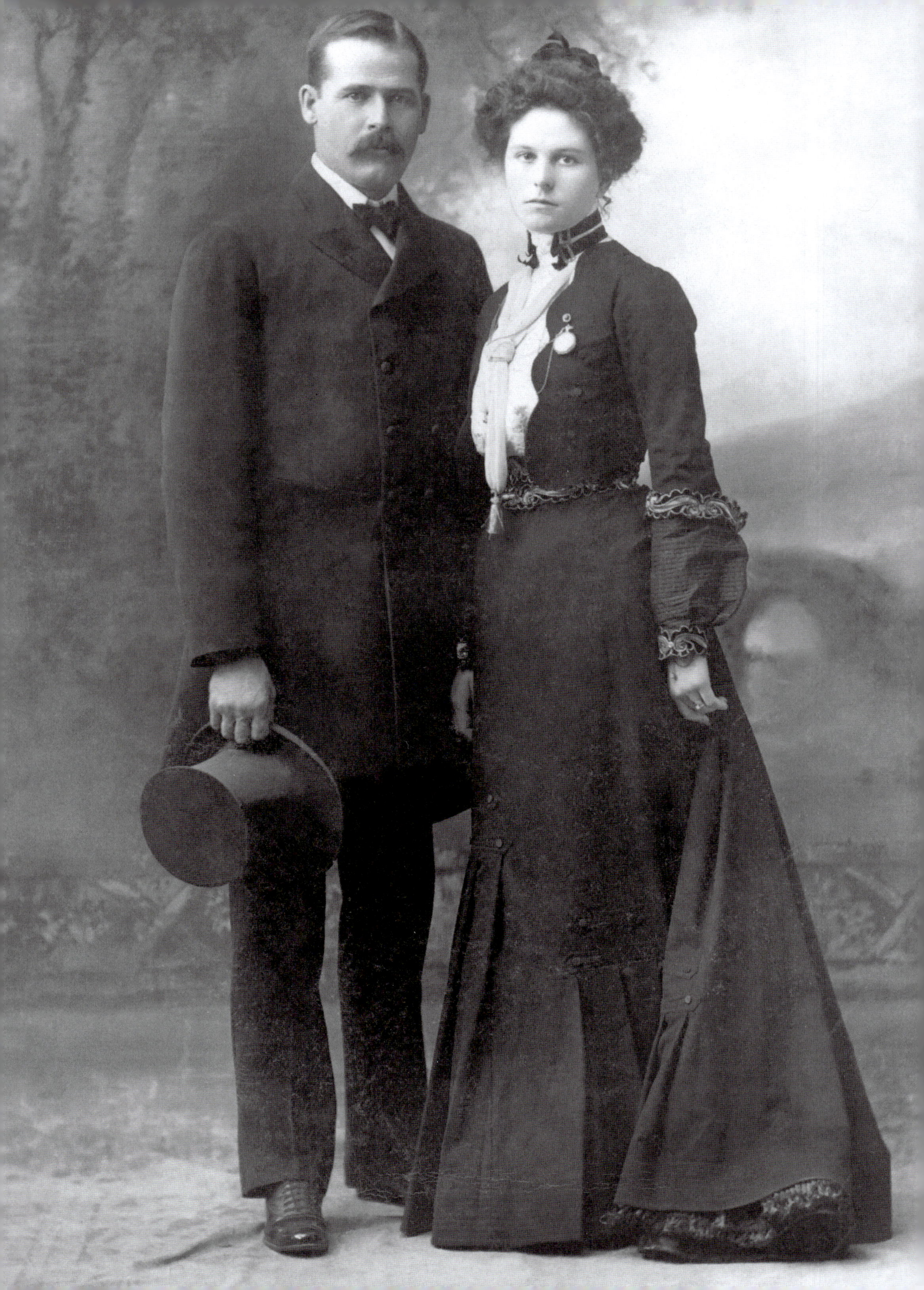

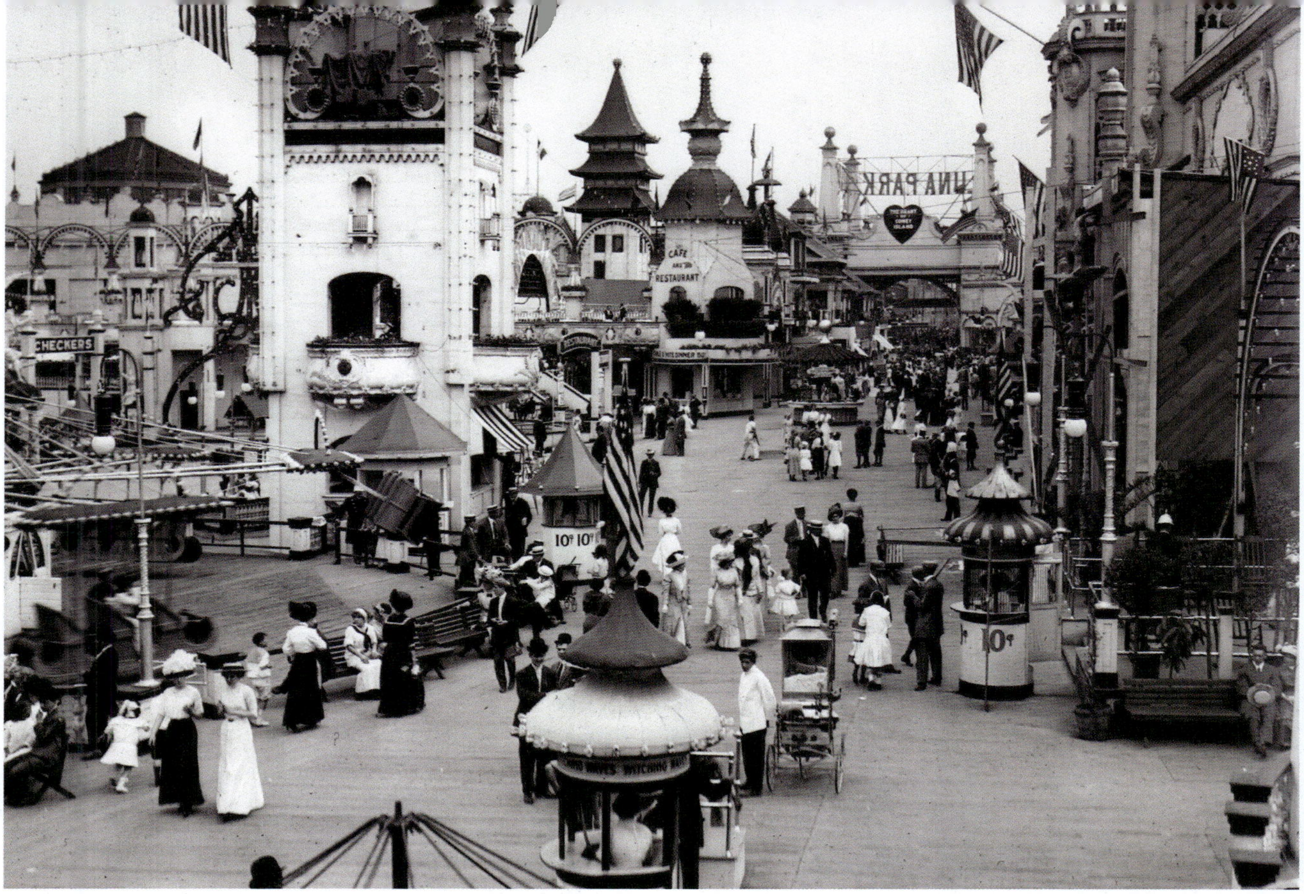

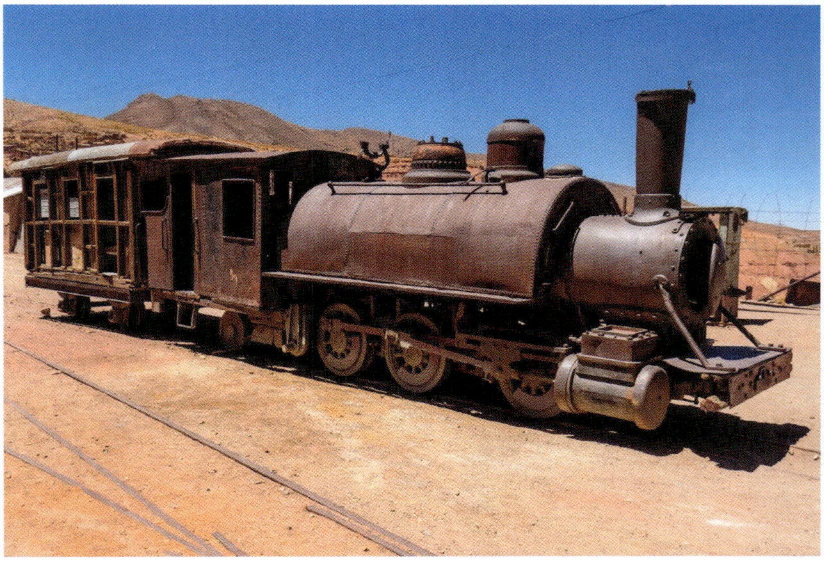

Mauser carbines, Browning and Colt revolvers, and plenty of ammo, on November 4, 1908, the boys held up payroll guards from the Aramayo, Franke and Co. Silver Mine. "At 9:30 in the morning we encountered two well-armed Yankees who waited for us with their faces covered by bandanas and their rifles ready," recalled mine official Carlos Peró. But instead of finding the half million they hoped for, Butch and Sundance made off with only a few thousand dollars. They then found their way to the small town of San Vicente, got a room, and had sardines and beer for dinner.

One of the mules they'd stolen from Peró sported the mine's brand and word spread of the outlaws' presence. An army patrol arrived that evening to investigate. When Butch saw one of the soldiers, Victor Torres, he shot him dead. The military and villagers soon surrounded their adobe hideout, and a gun battle ensued.

In the morning the troops cautiously approached the building. "The captain entered with a soldier, and then all of us entered and found the smaller gringo [Butch] stretched out on the floor, dead, with one bullet wound in the temple and another in the arm," wrote miner Remigio Sanchez. "The taller one [Sundance] was hugging a large ceramic jug that was in the room. He was dead, also, with a bullet wound in the forehead and several in his arm."

Evidently, Butch had shot Sundance and then killed himself. The friends were unceremoniously buried on November 7 in an unmarked grave.

Or were they? ✦

SUNDANCE AND ETTA PLACE, opposite, posed at DeYoung Photography Studio before slipping off to South America. They and Butch also visited Coney Island's Luna Park, top. After arriving in South America, the outlaws took up robbery again and held up trains, like the Bolivian steam locomotive and ore car above.

CHAPTER TWO

THE MAKING OF A MOVIE CLASSIC

IT WAS A BREEZY WESTERN TRAGICOMEDY THAT EARNED TEPID REVIEWS. BUT THE SPARKLING SCRIPT AND NEWMAN-REDFORD CHEMISTRY TURNED *BUTCH CASSIDY* INTO BOX OFFICE GOLD

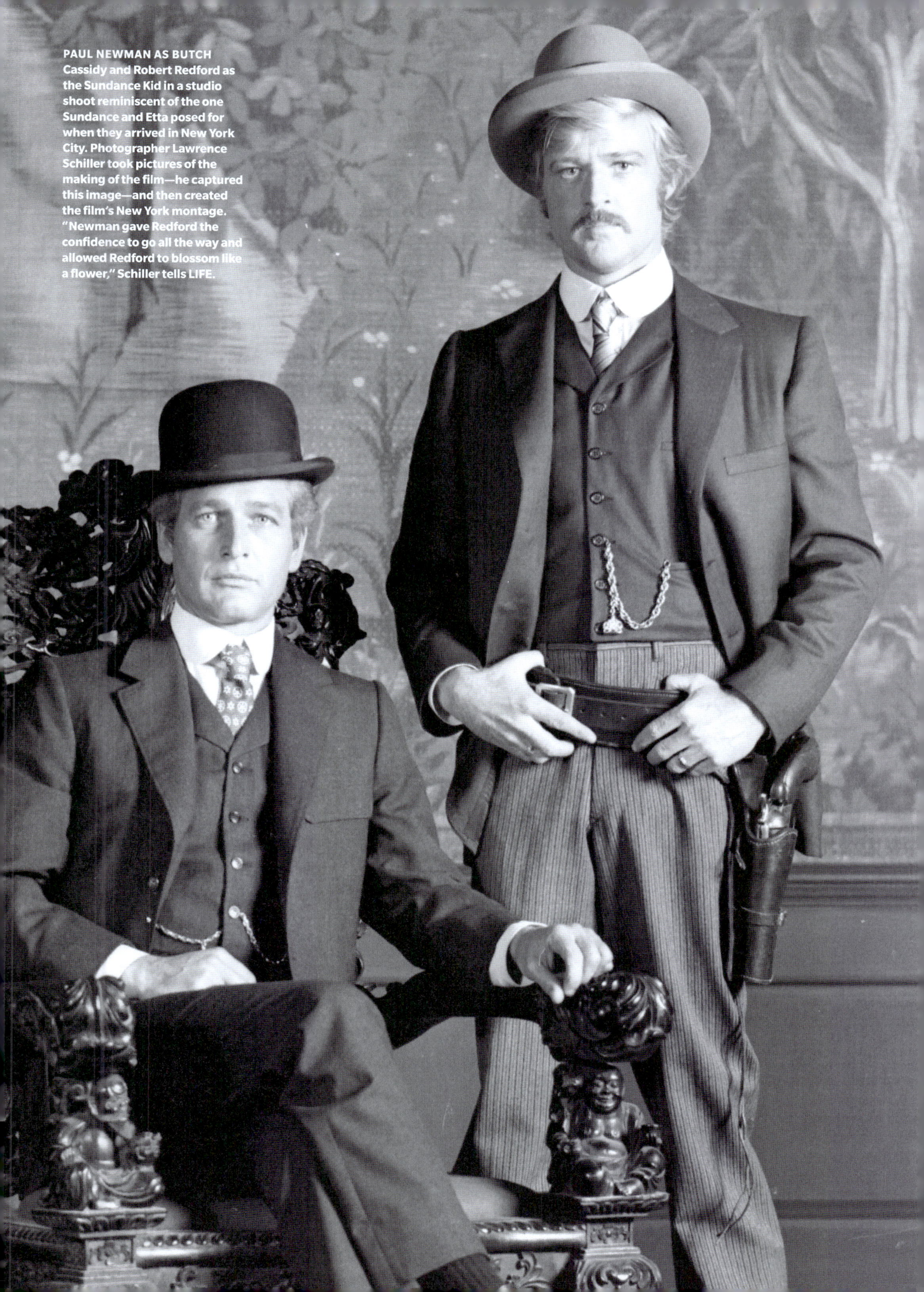

PAUL NEWMAN AS BUTCH Cassidy and Robert Redford as the Sundance Kid in a studio shoot reminiscent of the one Sundance and Etta posed for when they arrived in New York City. Photographer Lawrence Schiller took pictures of the making of the film—he captured this image—and then created the film's New York montage. "Newman gave Redford the confidence to go all the way and allowed Redford to blossom like a flower," Schiller tells LIFE.

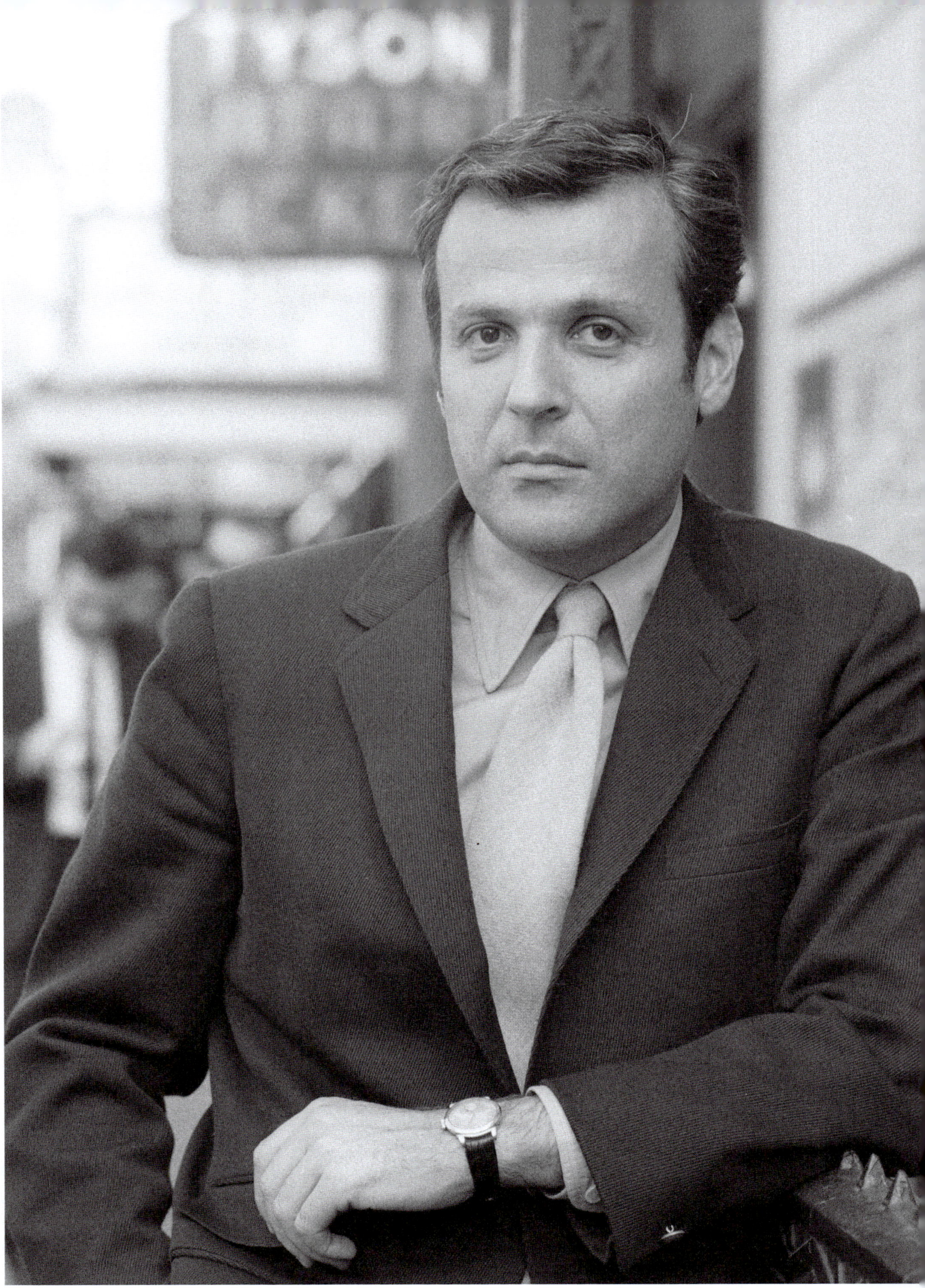

IN THE MID 1960S, THE NOVELIST WILLIAM Goldman was making a living teaching creative writing at Princeton University. His novels *Boys and Girls Together* and *No Way to Treat a Lady* had come out in 1964, and over the 1965 Christmas holiday he found that he didn't have any large writing project planned. The Chicago-born author had been fascinated since the late 1950s with the story of Butch Cassidy and the Sundance Kid—and so he decided to write a screenplay about the pair.

Goldman was taken by Butch and Sundance's exploits, intrigued by the fact that Butch reportedly didn't kill, and fascinated by the persistent rumor that they had survived the Bolivian shoot-out. Yet it was a line from F. Scott Fitzgerald's great unfinished novel, *The Last Tycoon*—"There are no second acts in American lives"—that inspired him to pursue the work. Goldman's research showed that Butch and Sundance had disproved Fitzgerald's dictum. They "ran to South America and lived there for eight years and that was what thrilled me: They had a second act," he said. "It just seems to me it's a wonderful piece of material."

This wasn't Goldman's first flirtation with Hollywood. His novel *Soldier in the Rain* had been made into a film in 1963, and Cliff Robertson got him to co-write the screenplay for 1965's *Masquerade*. Meanwhile, others had already portrayed Butch and Sundance on film. John Doucette played Cassidy and Ian MacDonald was the Kid in 1951's *The Texas Rangers*. Neville Brand played Butch twice, in *The Three Outlaws* (1956) and 1958's *Badman's Country*. Charles Bronson saddled up as Cassidy in a 1958 episode of the TV series *Tales of*

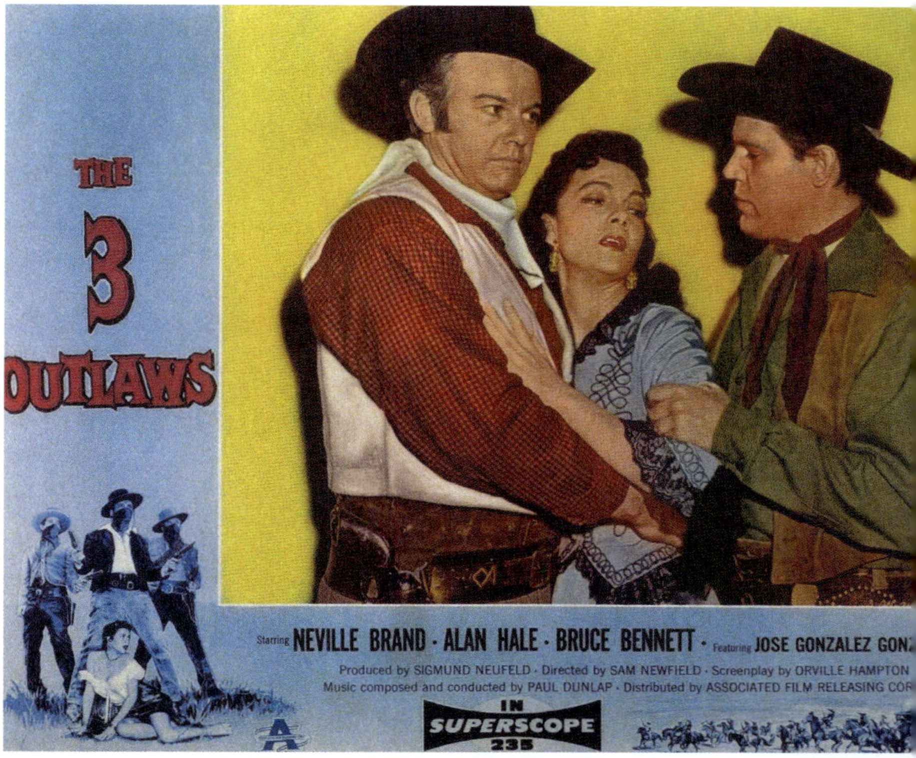

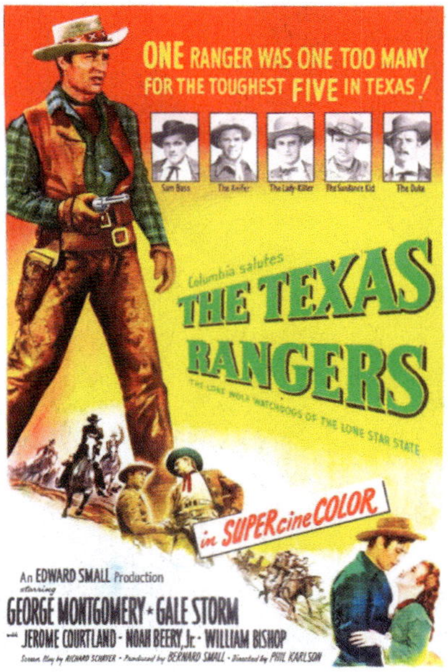

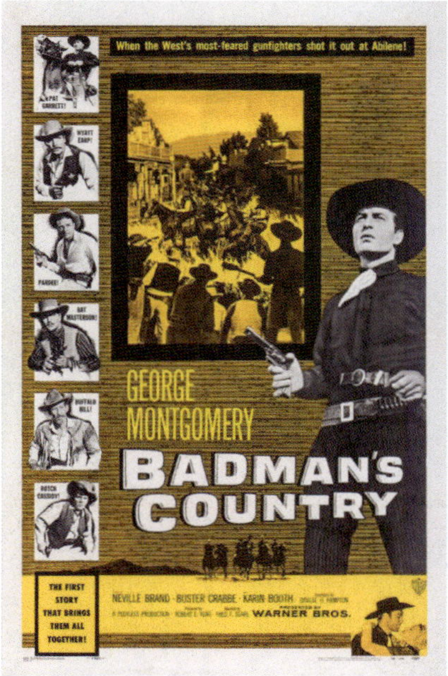

AUTHOR WILLIAM GOLDMAN, opposite, was fascinated by the legend of the outlaws and started writing his screenplay while teaching at Princeton University. Butch and Sundance have appeared in numerous Westerns, such as *The Three Outlaws, The Texas Rangers,* and *Badman's Country.*

Wells Fargo. Butch, played by Arthur Hunnicutt, even appeared in Jane Fonda's comic 1965 Western *Cat Ballou*. Meanwhile, Sundance was portrayed by Robert Ryan in 1948's *Return of the Bad Men*, by Alan Hale Jr. in *The Three Outlaws*, and by Hale's future *Gilligan's Island* castmate Russell Johnson in *Badman's Country*.

But studios showed no interest in Goldman's screenplay. One executive even scoffed at the idea of filming in South America. When Goldman replied that Butch and Sundance "went there," the studio head said, "All I know is John Wayne don't run away." Goldman tinkered with his work. He had created the script for Paul Newman's 1966 detective yarn, *Harper*, and flew down to Tucson where the star was filming the provocative Western *Hombre* to tell him the tale. He "dished it all to me, this marvelous story about the real Wild Bunch gang he was developing on spec," Newman recalled. "He said, 'This is going to be the best cowboy picture ever made.'"

But after the brief visit, Newman didn't hear anything else about the film until buddy Steve McQueen called him in November 1967 and said he had the script for a film called *The Sundance Kid and Butch Cassidy*. McQueen suggested that they make it together. "I took it home and read it," said Newman. "And of course it was wonderful. And I called McQueen up and I said, 'How much are they asking for?' And he said $350,000. I said, 'You put in $200,000 and I will put in $200,000 and we will buy it this afternoon.'"

The friends proved too slow on the draw, though. The film sold over the weekend at auction for $400,000, the highest price up to that point for a script. Goldman was also to receive a share of the film's profits. Newman figured that was it. But then 20th Century Fox chief Richard Zanuck, who had authorized the purchase, approached Newman and hitched him to the project.

Fox tapped George Roy Hill to direct. Hill had made his first mark on TV, earning four Emmy nominations, and on Broadway received a Tony nod for his direction of a stage adaptation of Thomas Wolfe's *Look Homeward, Angel*. Meanwhile, McQueen was asked about working on the film. Though he and Newman were friends, they were also professional rivals. And when McQueen learned that Newman would receive top billing, he walked away.

20TH CENTURY FOX executive Richard Zanuck (below, right, in 1965, with writer-director Hal Kanter) approved the payment of the then record $400,000 for Goldman's *Butch Cassidy* script. Steve McQueen—on the set of 1966's *Nevada Smith*—was interested in the film but backed out when he found out that Paul Newman had lassoed top billing.

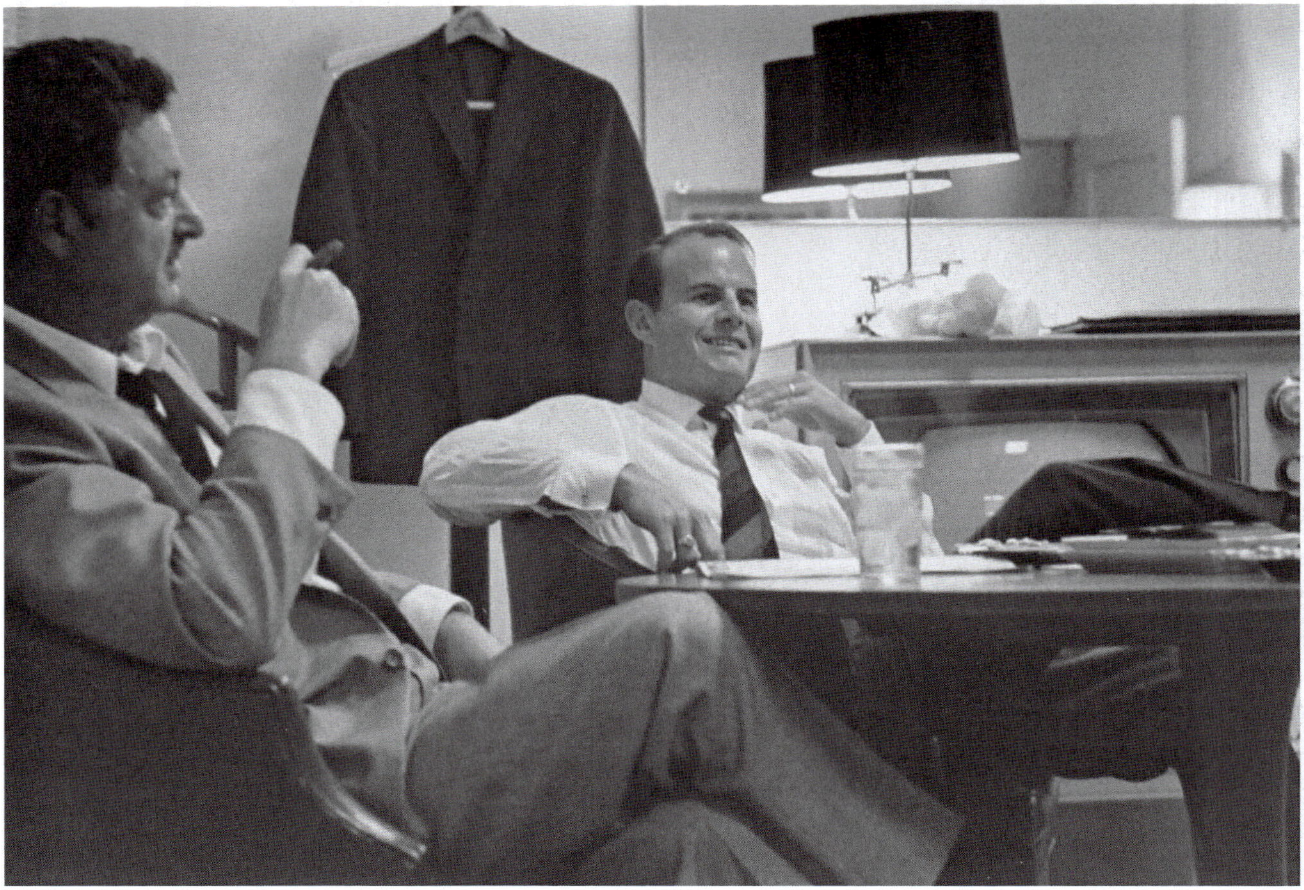

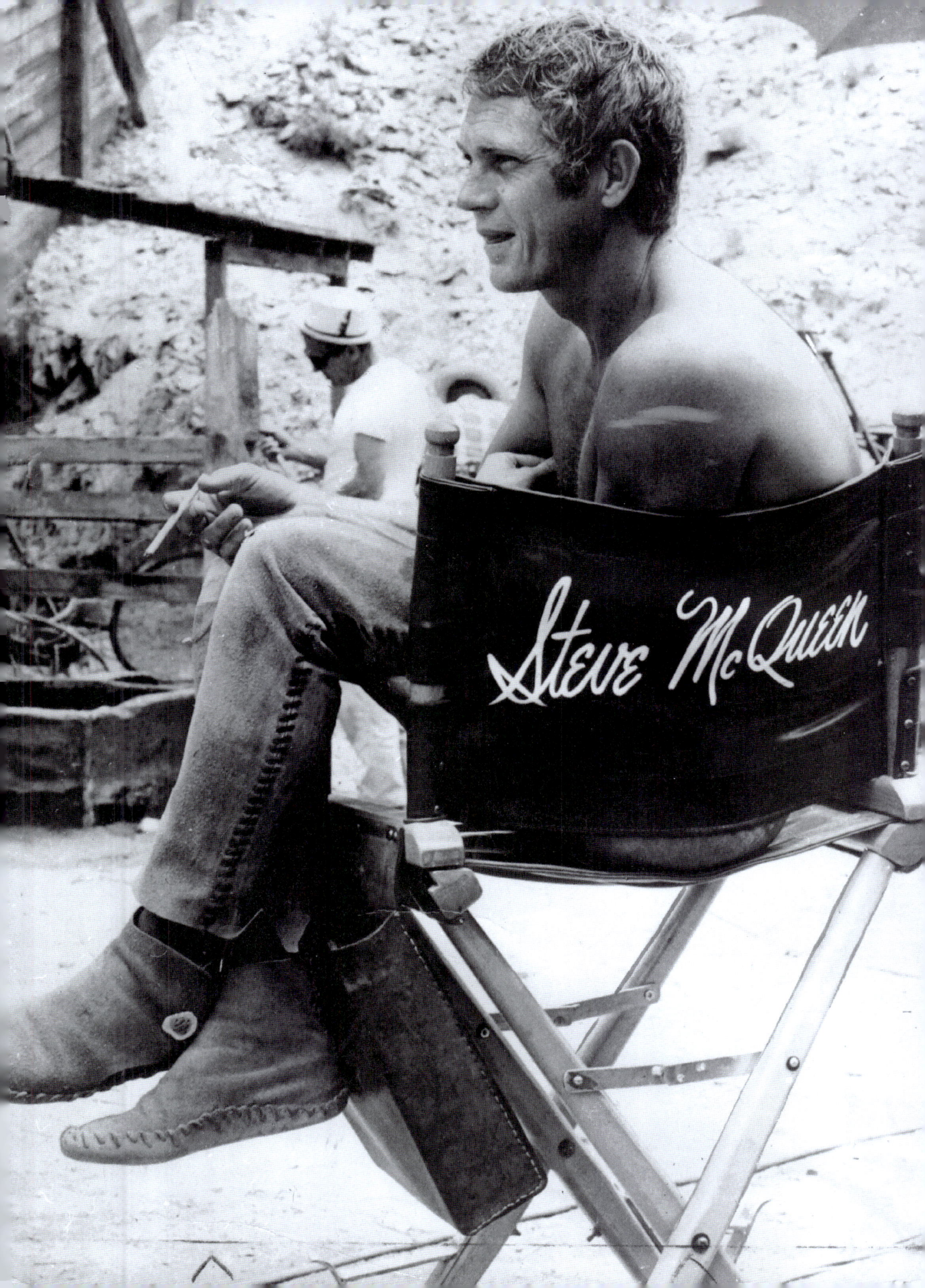
Steve McQueen

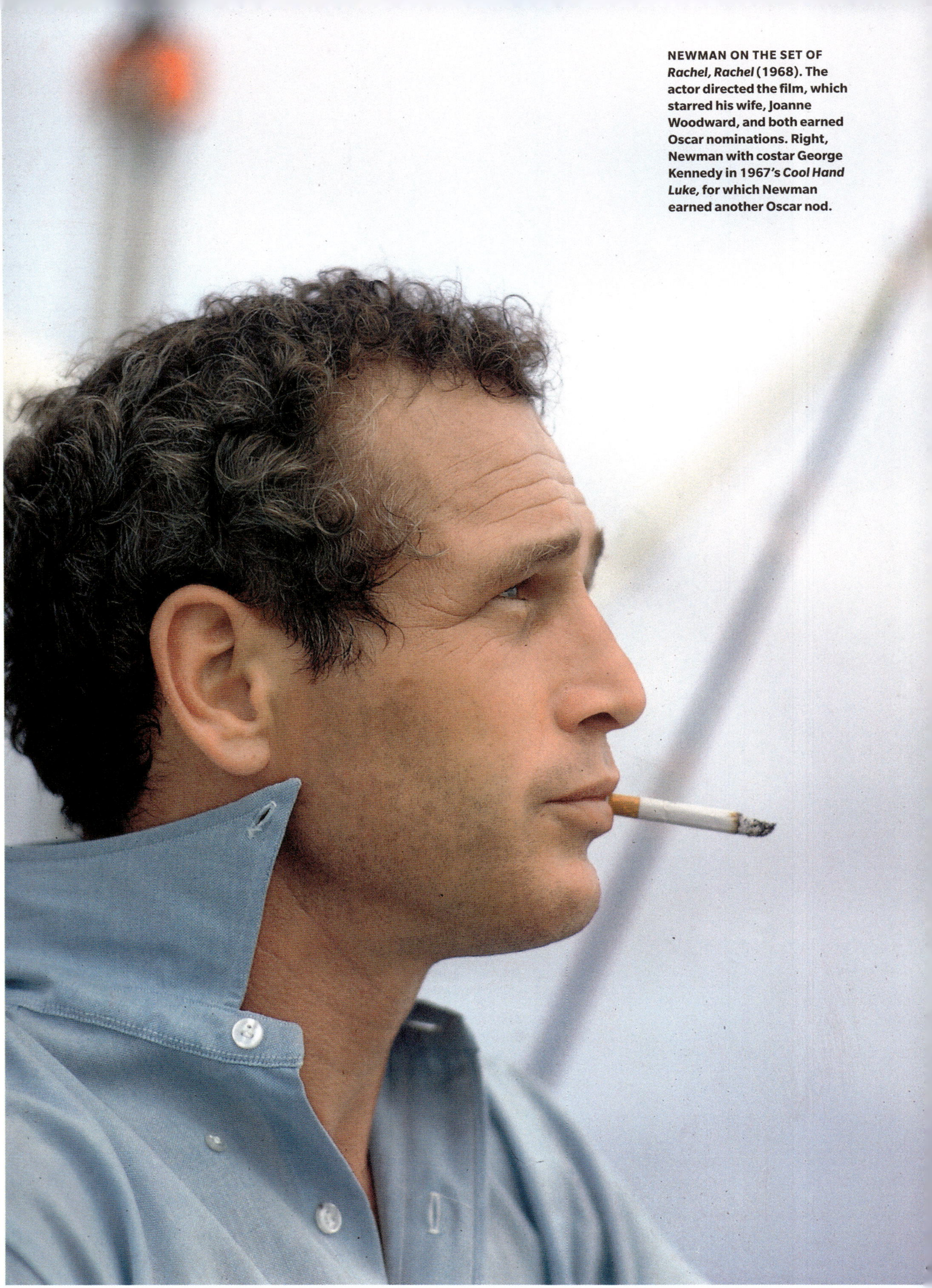

NEWMAN ON THE SET OF *Rachel, Rachel* (1968). The actor directed the film, which starred his wife, Joanne Woodward, and both earned Oscar nominations. Right, Newman with costar George Kennedy in 1967's *Cool Hand Luke,* for which Newman earned another Oscar nod.

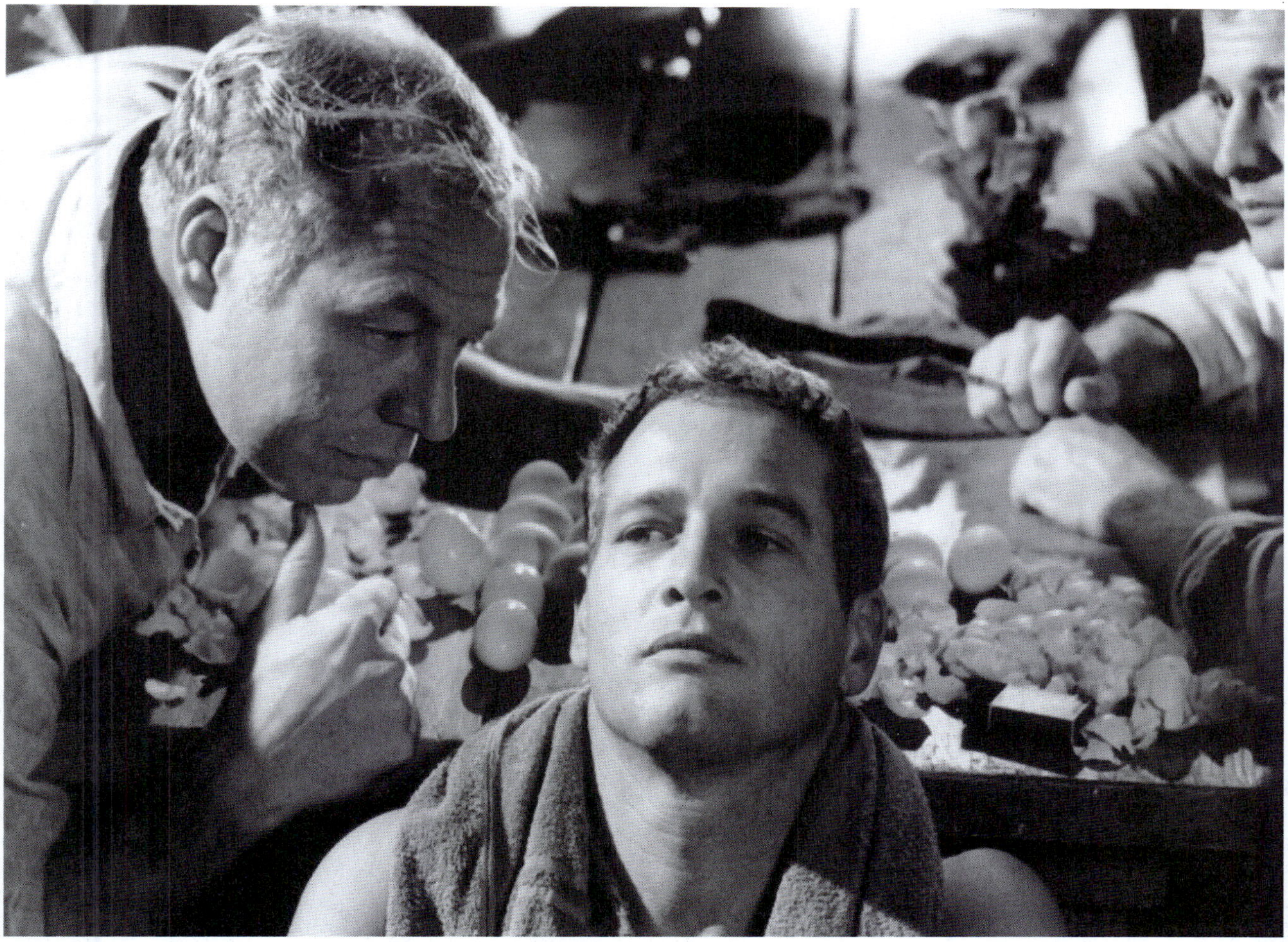

Jack Lemmon was considered, but he didn't like riding horses. Zanuck sought Warren Beatty, who had recently earned an Oscar nomination for his role as Clyde Barrow in 1967's *Bonnie and Clyde*. And the agent Freddie Fields suggested Marlon Brando.

MEANWHILE, STEPHANIE Phillips at MCA had been pushing for Robert Redford. The handsome actor had done work on *The Twilight Zone,* and Newman had seen him on Broadway in Neil Simon's *Barefoot in the Park*, a part he reprised in the 1967 film. Newman's wife, Joanne Woodward, also encouraged her husband to snag Redford for the role. But when Fields gave him the script to read, the actor blanched. "I was told almost straight away that as right as it was for me that it was a long shot because they wanted a star," Redford recalled.

But both Fields and Goldman encouraged him, and he met with Hill at Joe Allen, a popular New York theater-district restaurant. At that point the director considered Redford for the part of Butch. "To be honest," Redford told him. "I've read it and I think I'd be better as Sundance. It's the part that interests me. And from there the talk progressed . . . the more we talked, the more George came around to the idea that I should be the Sundance Kid."

WHEN STEVE MCQUEEN LEARNED THAT NEWMAN WOULD RECEIVE TOP BILLING, HE WALKED AWAY.

Hill had had a similar conversation with Newman, who saw himself as Sundance. As they talked, Hill asked him, "Why are we talking about Sundance? You're playing Butch."

"I'm Sundance," Newman replied.

"No, you're not.

"George, I was here first—I'm Sundance."

Yet that night Newman reread the script, realized that the parts were equal, and agreed to portray Cassidy.

Redford and Newman then got together for dinner, and hit it off right away. "We talked about car racing, where we liked to live, everything but the film . . . because right away there seemed to be this understanding that I would make the picture," said Redford.

And despite the studio's resistance, Hill, Goldman, Newman, and others kept on pushing for Redford. "Finally, as I understood it, they . . . kept forcing [Hill] to look at other actors and they ran out of other actors."

To ensure that Newman got the top credit, the title became *Butch Cassidy and the Sundance Kid*. Katharine Ross, who had just earned an Oscar nomination for her role as Elaine Robinson in *The Graduate* and appeared with Redford in *Tell Them*

Willie Boy Is Here, was cast as Etta Place. Redford got $150,000, which was $25,000 less than Ross and a quarter of what Newman got. Newman was also to receive a percentage of the profits.

There had been plans to call Butch and Sundance's gang the Wild Bunch after the name bestowed on them by the Pinkerton detective agency. But Warner Bros. already had in the works Sam Peckinpah's *The Wild Bunch*, about fictitious turn-of-the-century Western outlaws, so Hill decided to give Butch's gang its earlier name, the Hole-in-the-Wall Gang. To prepare for the shoot, he watched some 50 Westerns starting with the work of silent star William S. Hart. He signed up cinematographer

BUTCH IS THE AFFABLE THINKER, SUNDANCE THE BROODING, SILENT TYPE. THEIR CONTRAST AND CHEMISTRY FASCINATED REDFORD.

Conrad Hall, who had recently completed *Harper* as well as 1967's *Cool Hand Luke* with Newman, and the two men set off on scouting trips in the United States and Mexico.

The stars had two weeks of rehearsals at Fox's Los Angeles studio, and the 12-week shoot started on September 16, 1968, in Durango, Colorado. As they began, Redford, 32, and Newman, 43, were sitting together, and Newman turned to his costar: "Well, kid, how does it feel to be in your first $40 million-grosser?" It would prove to completely change Redford's life.

THEIR FILM SOMEWHAT FAITHfully follows the gang and their exploits. They take refuge in Outlaw Pass. There is a scene where Harvey Logan challenges Butch for control of the gang. They twice rob the Union

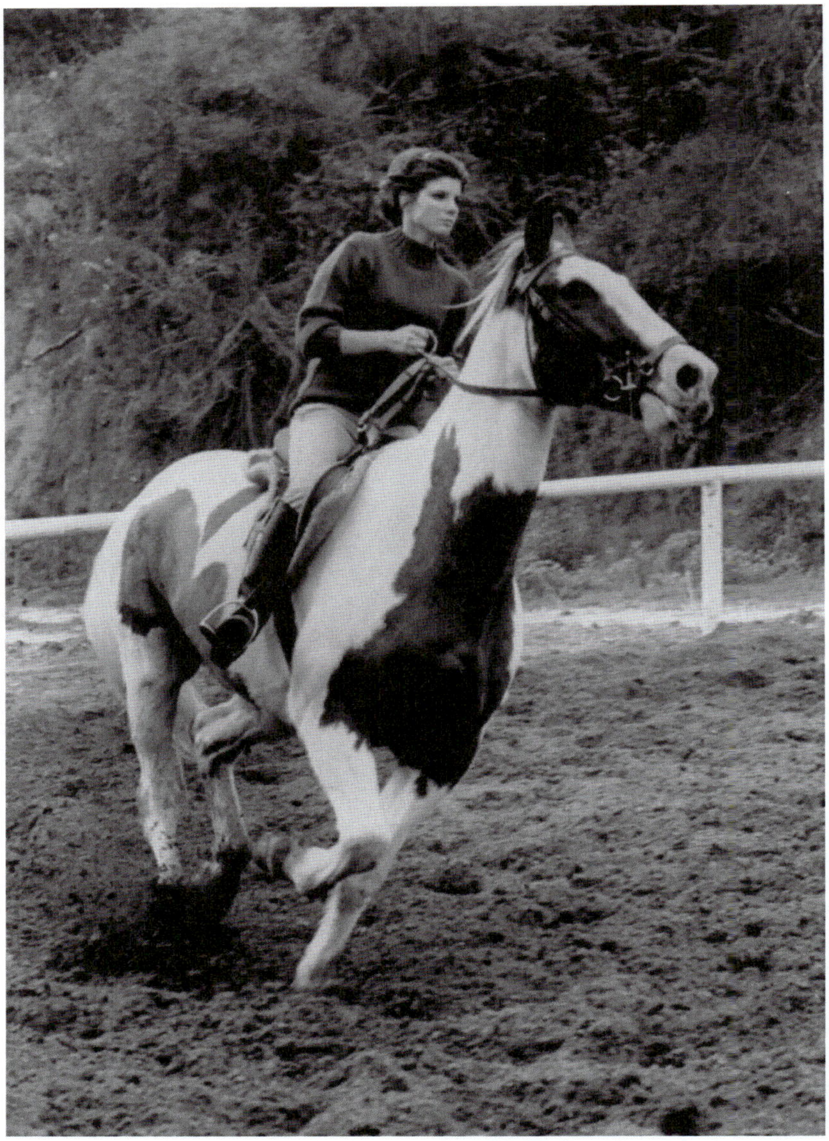

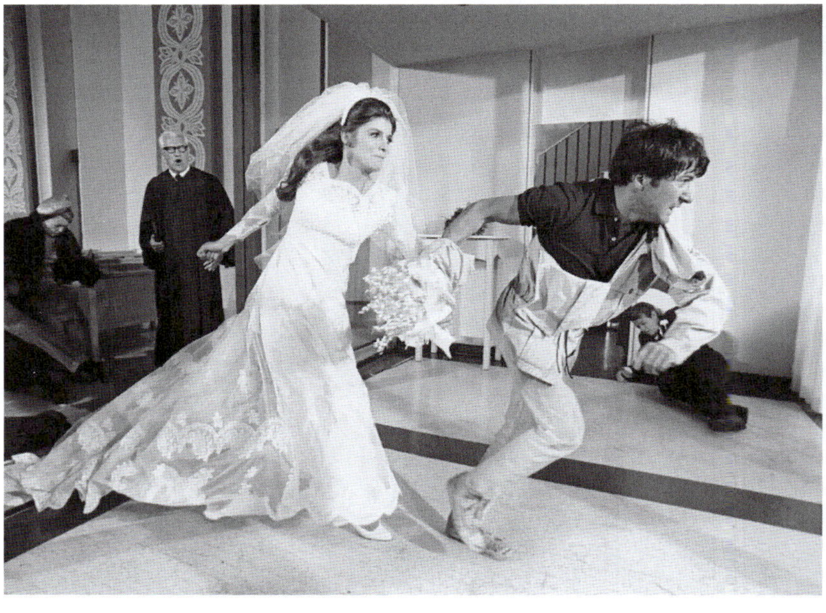

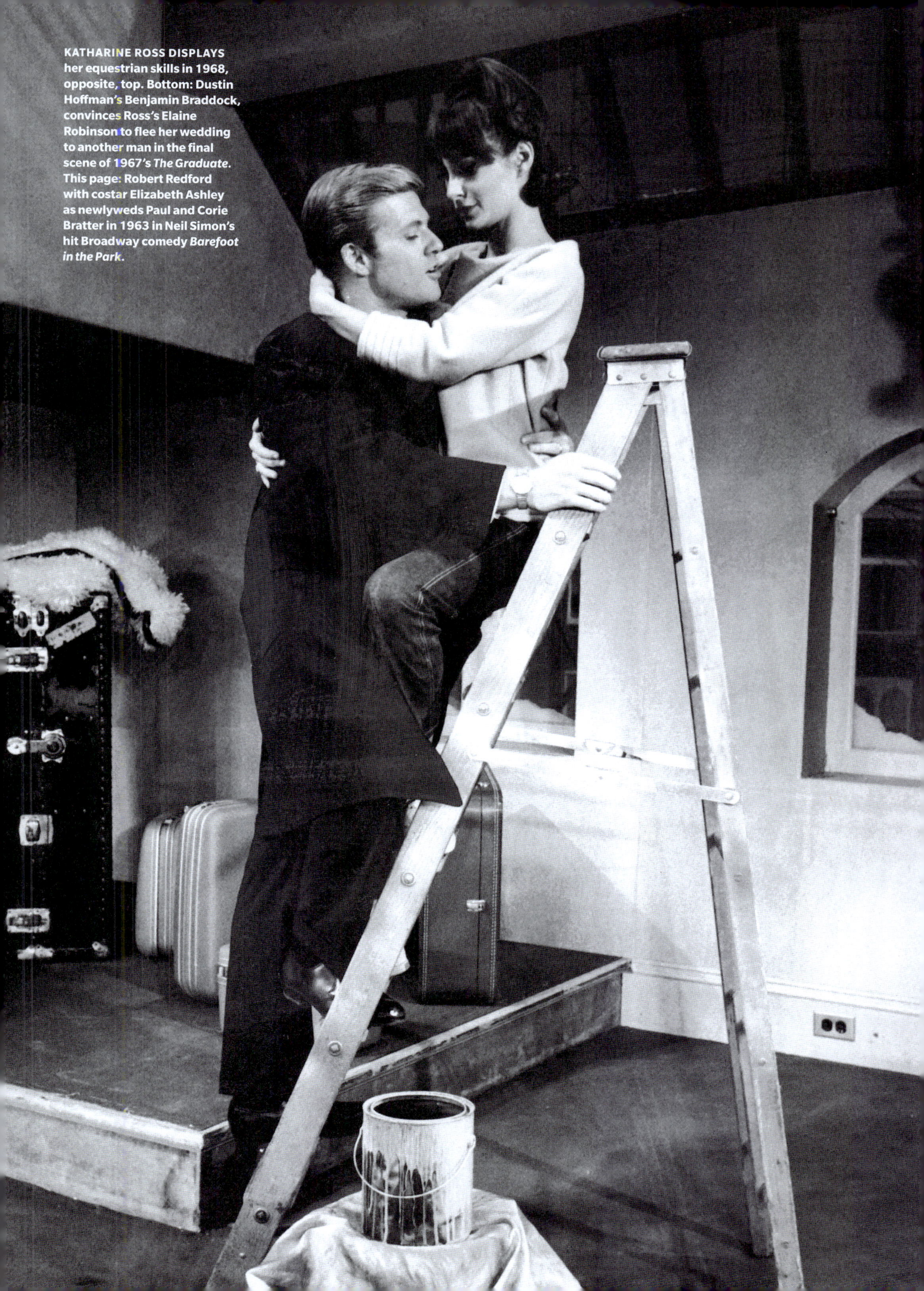

KATHARINE ROSS DISPLAYS her equestrian skills in 1968, opposite, top. Bottom: Dustin Hoffman's Benjamin Braddock, convinces Ross's Elaine Robinson to flee her wedding to another man in the final scene of 1967's *The Graduate*. This page: Robert Redford with costar Elizabeth Ashley as newlyweds Paul and Corie Bratter in 1963 in Neil Simon's hit Broadway comedy *Barefoot in the Park*.

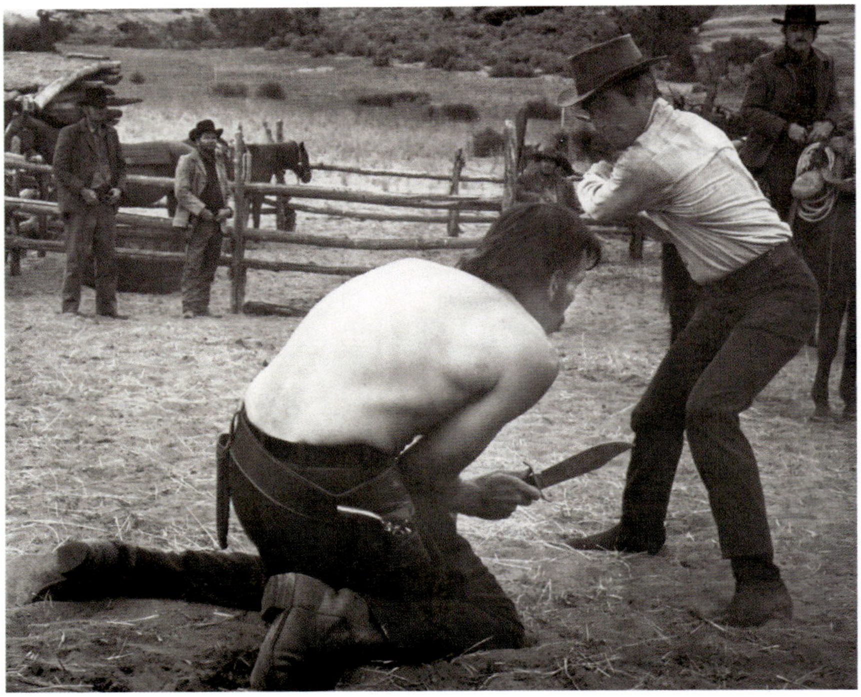

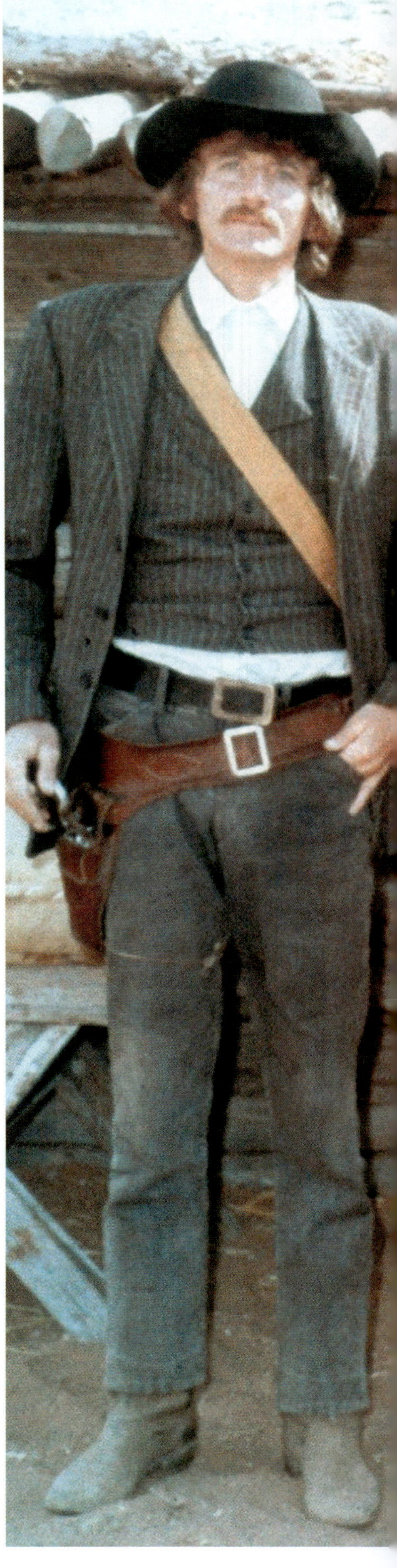

Pacific, and Butch verbally spars with Charles Woodcock. They hang out in a bordello, are chased by a posse, and ultimately head to South America. Real-life gang members include Flat Nose, played by Charles Dierkop; News Carver, played by Timothy Scott, and Logan, portrayed by Ted Cassidy.

The film, though, was not to be a Western in the shoot-em-up spirit of, say, 1960's *The Magnificent Seven*. Butch and Sundance were villains, but Goldman gave them a kinder sheen. "In our movie Butch and Sundance are lovable because they are polite, despite their mania for bank robberies and their complete incompetence," said Hill. "For the movie we make them goofballs."

Butch is the affable thinker, Sundance the brooding, silent type, as we see in the tense opening poker scene where Butch seeks to defuse Sundance's standoff with a rival player who has accused him of cheating. "He is aloof. He's a loner," Redford said of Sundance. "Somewhat sullen. And to the outsider he is a very distant kind of guy, maybe even a bit schizoid."

It was the contrast and chemistry between the characters that fascinated Redford. "I was interested more than anything in the relationship between the two guys. I thought it was unique. Fun. Direct. You see a lot more warmth."

The outlaws' bond reflected one the stars quickly developed as they found they were kindred spirits who enjoyed the outdoors, liked to drink and gossip and play jokes. "Bob and Paul consciously established a relationship that was excellent," said Hill, who noted that that "included Redford having to laugh at all of Newman's god-awful jokes." Their bond made it hard for Ross, 28, though, who as Etta is the focus of a love triangle. "Every comedy, you have to have the straight guy . . . It was frustrating for me," she admitted. "When everybody is laughing you want people to laugh at you too, or with you."

And just as the title characters

CONTINUED ON PAGE 40

WHEN BUTCH FIRST ARRIVES back at the Hole-in-the-Wall camp, Harvey Logan, played by Ted Cassidy (above), challenges him for control of the gang. After asserting that there are no rules in a knife fight, Logan quickly loses. Right: The Hole-in-the-Wall Gang's all here: from left, Timothy Scott as News Carver, Redford as Sundance, Cassidy as Logan, Newman as Butch, Dave Dunlop as an unnamed gunman, and Charles Dierkop as Flat Nose.

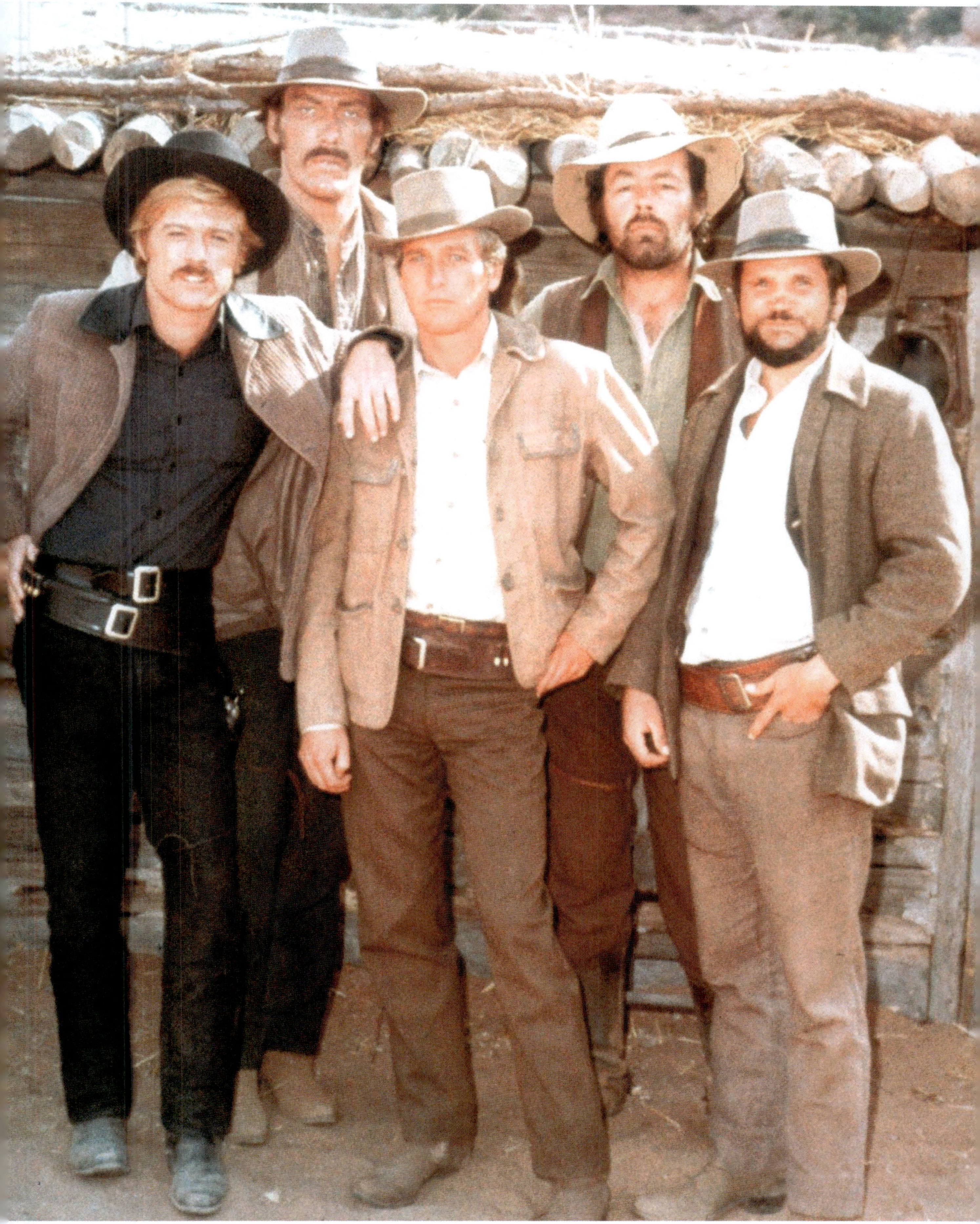

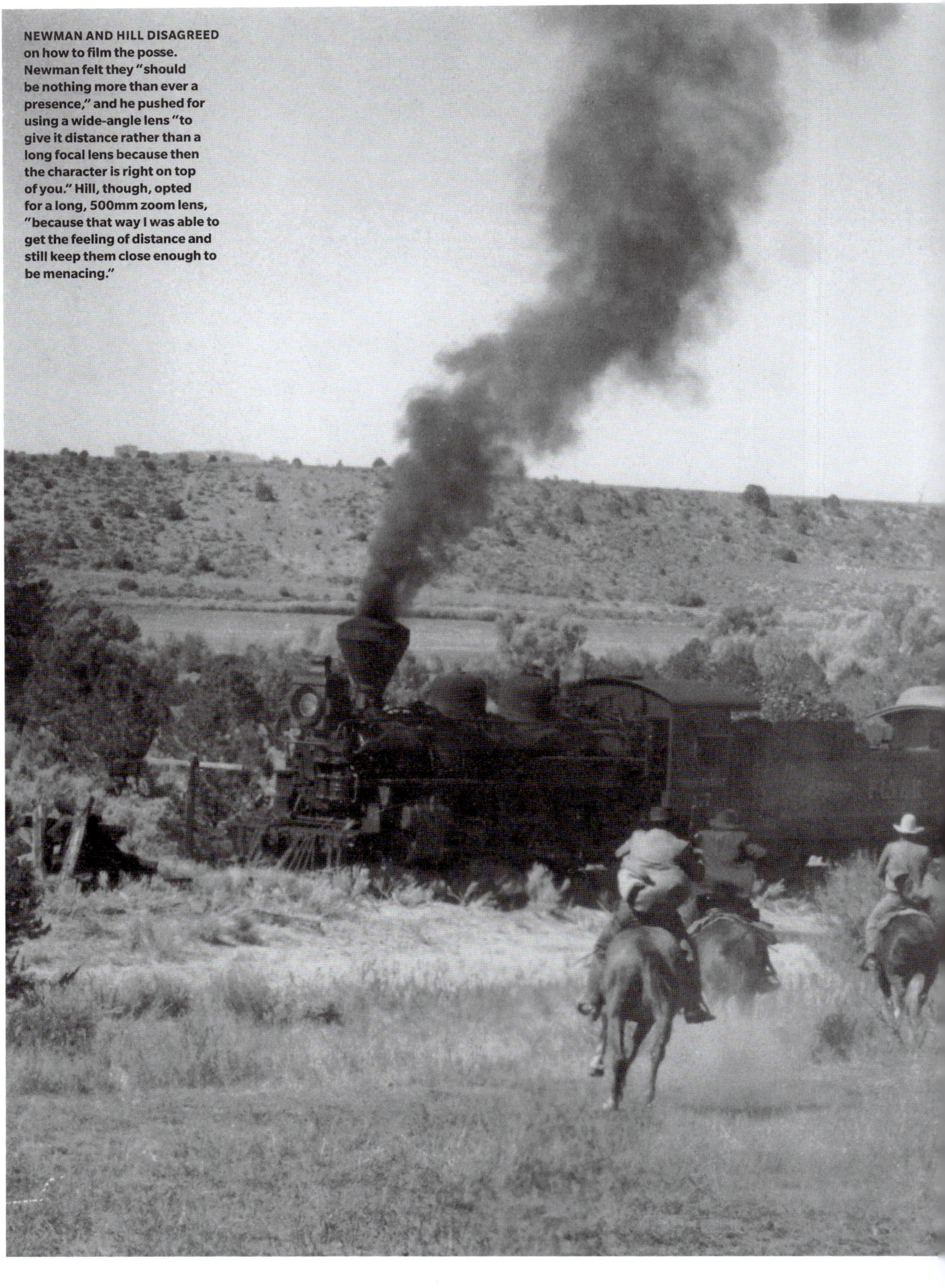

NEWMAN AND HILL DISAGREED on how to film the posse. Newman felt they "should be nothing more than ever a presence," and he pushed for using a wide-angle lens "to give it distance rather than a long focal lens because then the character is right on top of you." Hill, though, opted for a long, 500mm zoom lens, "because that way I was able to get the feeling of distance and still keep them close enough to be menacing."

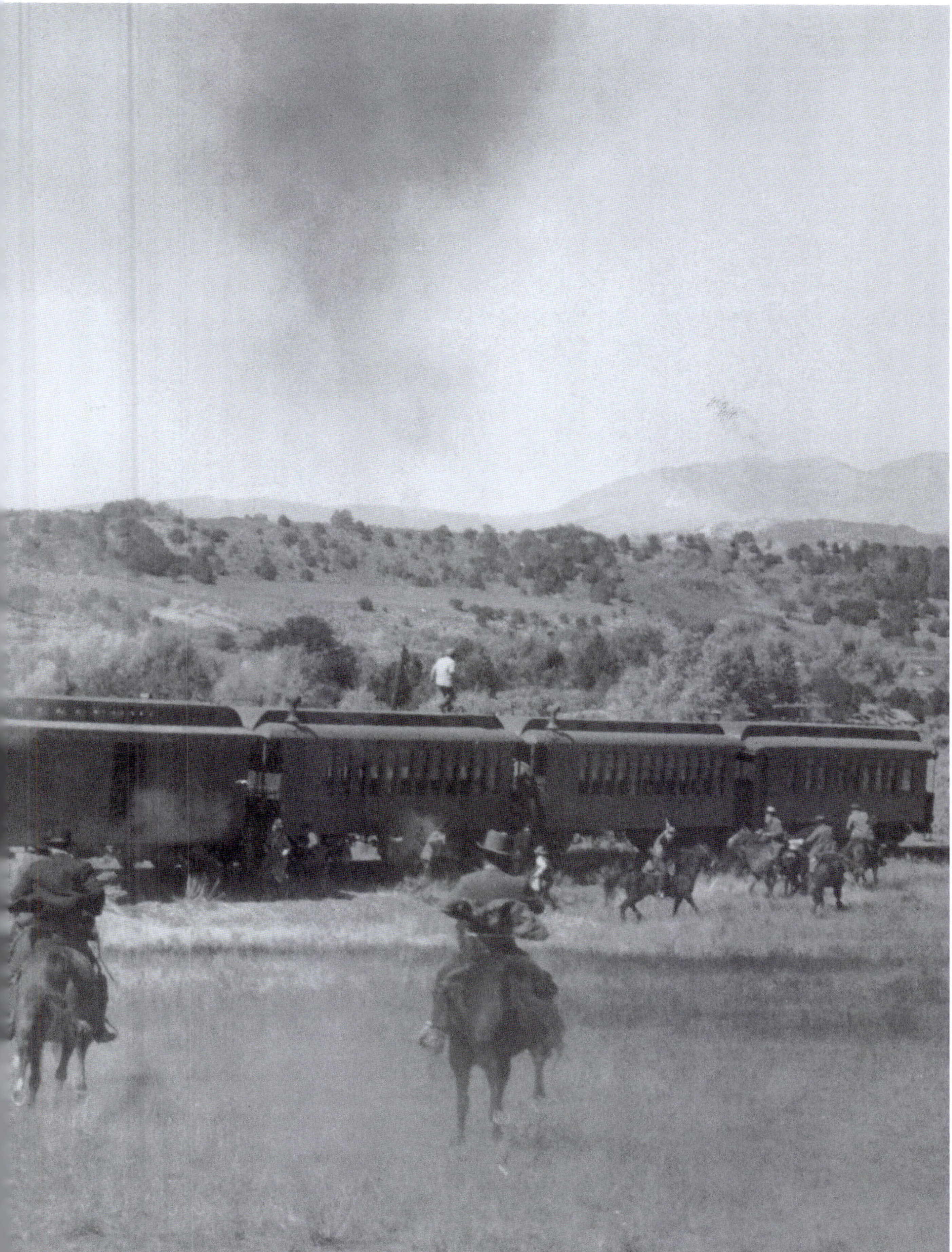

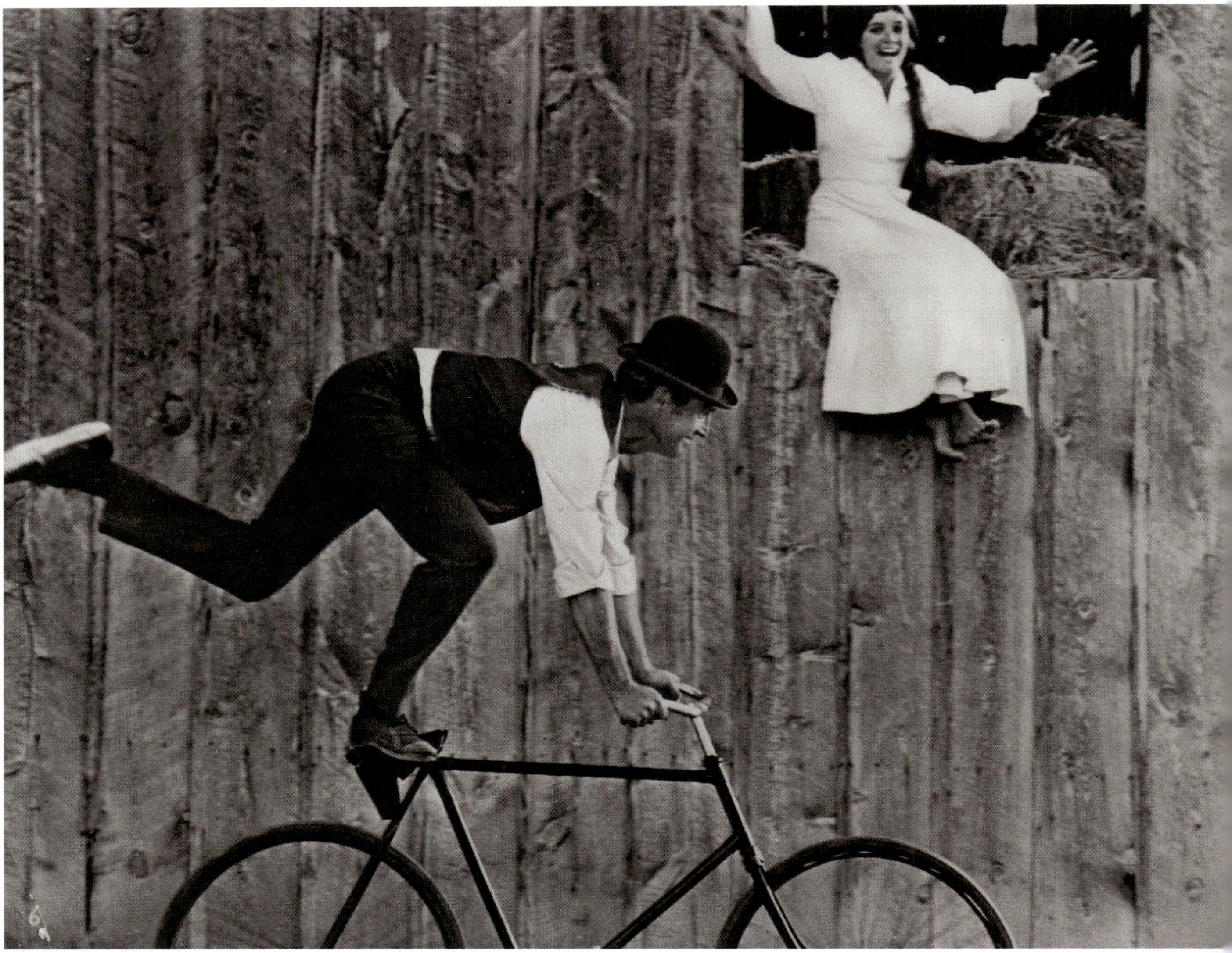

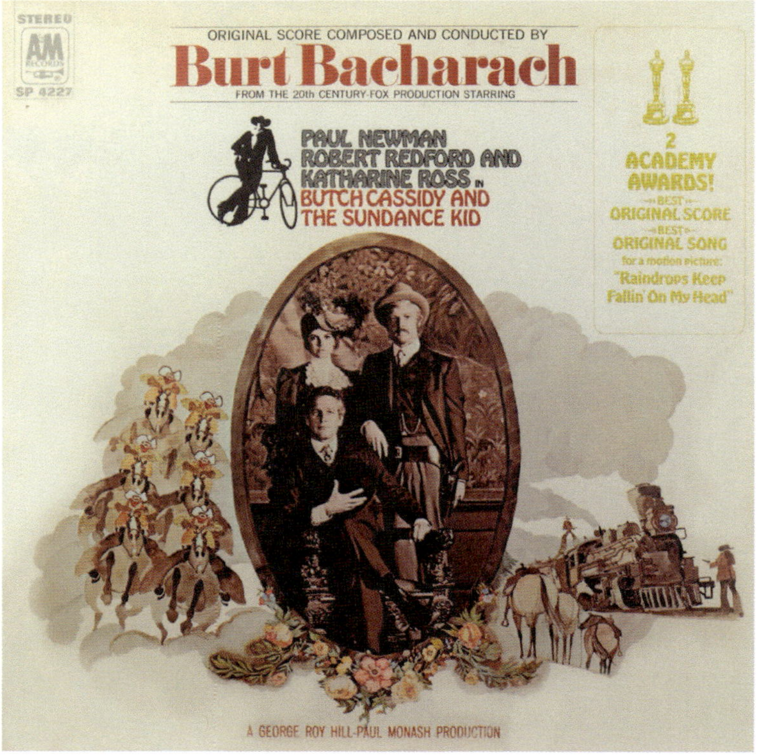

DIRECTOR GEORGE ROY HILL USED MUSIC sparsely in the film. One of *Butch Cassidy's* most memorable scenes has Newman and Ross clowning on a bicycle to Burt Bacharach and Hal David's pop tune "Raindrops Keep Fallin' on My Head," sung by B.J. Thomas. A stuntman was originally hired to perform the scene, but he complained that the antique bicycle wouldn't hold up. When Newman rolled by on it doing tricks, Hill fired the man on the spot.

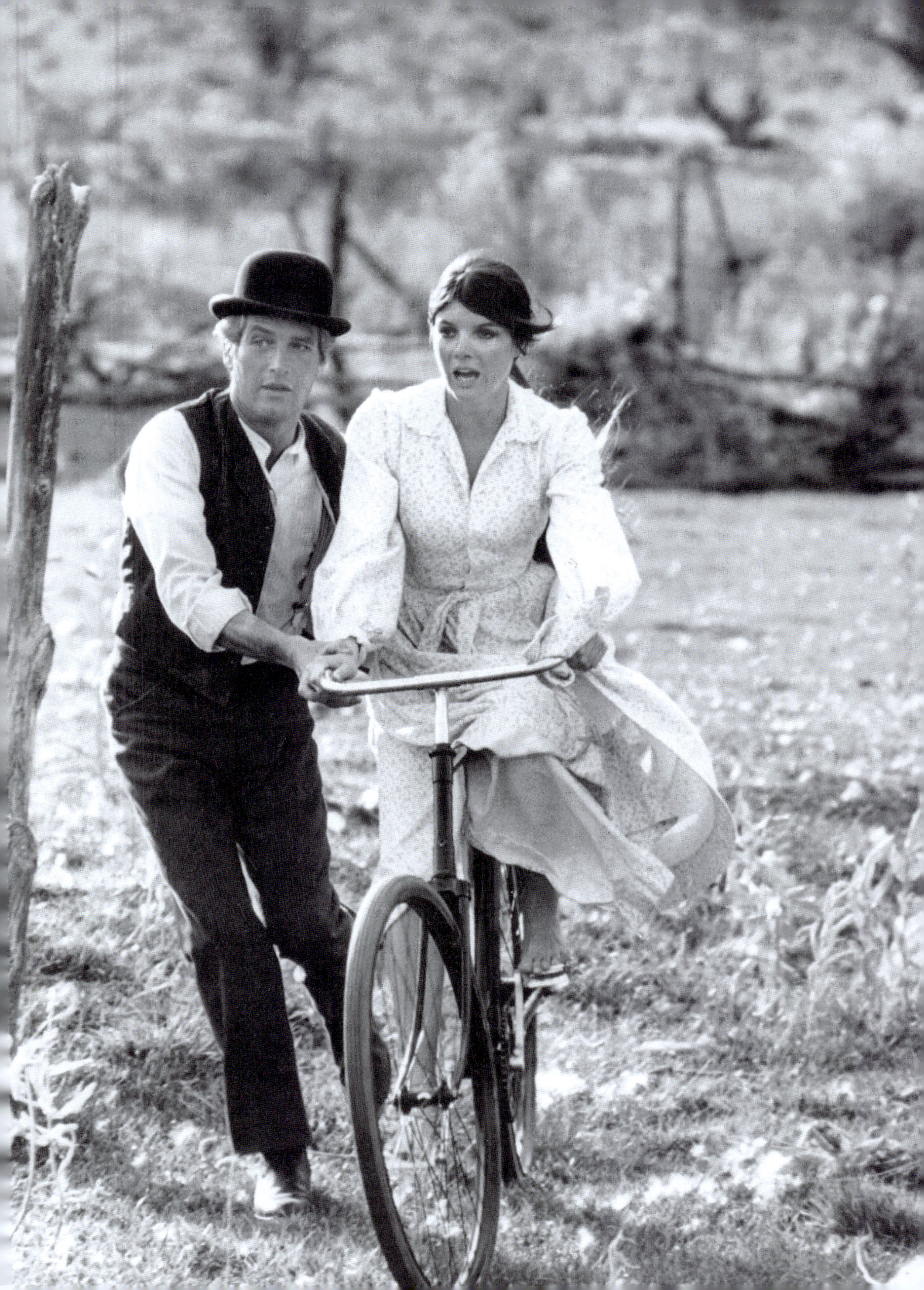

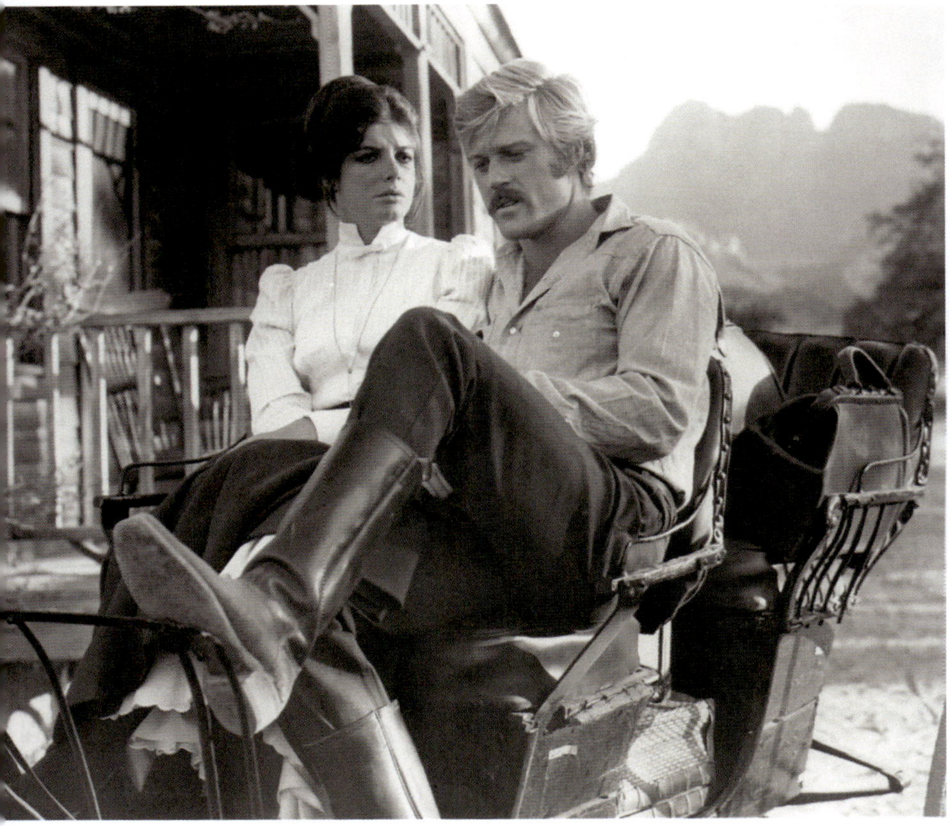

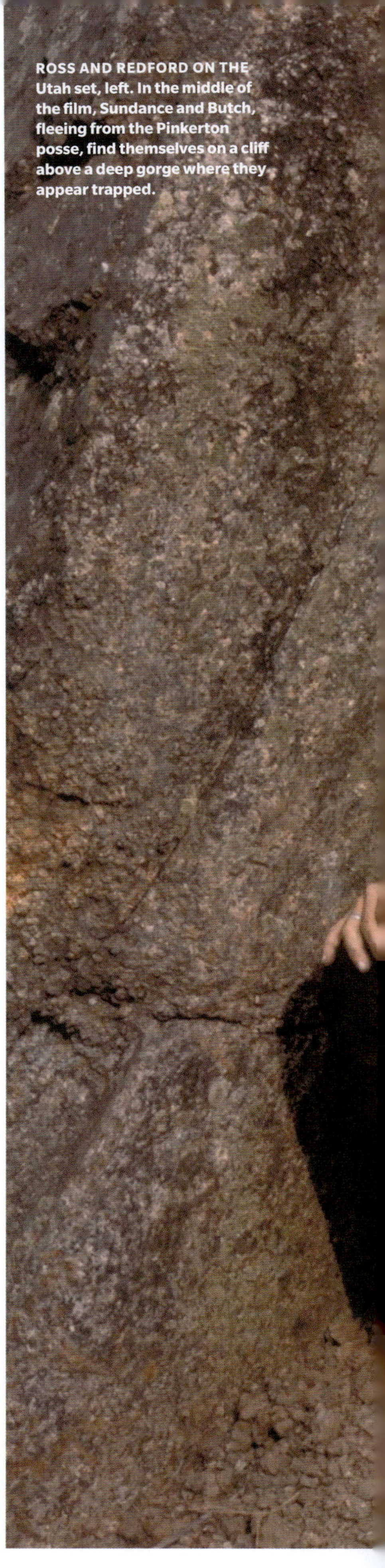

ROSS AND REDFORD ON THE Utah set, left. In the middle of the film, Sundance and Butch, fleeing from the Pinkerton posse, find themselves on a cliff above a deep gorge where they appear trapped.

CONTINUED FROM PAGE 34

differ, so too did Newman and Redford's approaches to acting. "Newman will talk a scene to death," said Hill. "Redford would just stand there and squirm during all the intellectualizing." This became evident as soon as they began filming. On the first day of shooting the company was set up outside the Union Pacific's express car. Newman, who appeared relaxed in rehearsals, began questioning how to play his part and struggled to find the right rhythm for his character.

His initial confusion is not surprising, since there were discussions from the start about whether the film would be a comedy or a drama. Quickly, though, the comedic feel won out, and that clearly comes across during the two Union Pacific scenes. George Furth, who would appear in 1974's *Blazing Saddles* and later find success as a Broadway playwright—portrays the messenger Woodcock, who finds himself in the unenviable position of being inside the train the Hole-in-the-Wall boys blow up. As the gang pours into the demolished car, the jokey Butch tells him that whatever the railroad "is paying you ain't enough."

HILL ASKED THE CINEMATOGRAPHER TO INFUSE THE FILM WITH DESATURATED COLORS.

For that segment, Hill had found just the right period train to use. Similarly he strove for an authentic, washed-out look for the film, and asked Hall to infuse it with desaturated colors. The cinematographer achieved that effect by overexposing film two or three stops. Hall also worked with backlight, stirred up dust, and wafted smoke in many shots to give scenes a hazy look. Even so, there is plenty of footage in the film that extols the rich lushness of the open land. Hill likewise hired Edith Head, the legendary costume designer who worked on more than 1,000 films and had won seven Oscars (she would win her eighth for 1973's *The Sting*), to give the stars a relaxed, trail-worn look. Hollywood hairstylist Jay Sebring, meanwhile, did Newman's hair.

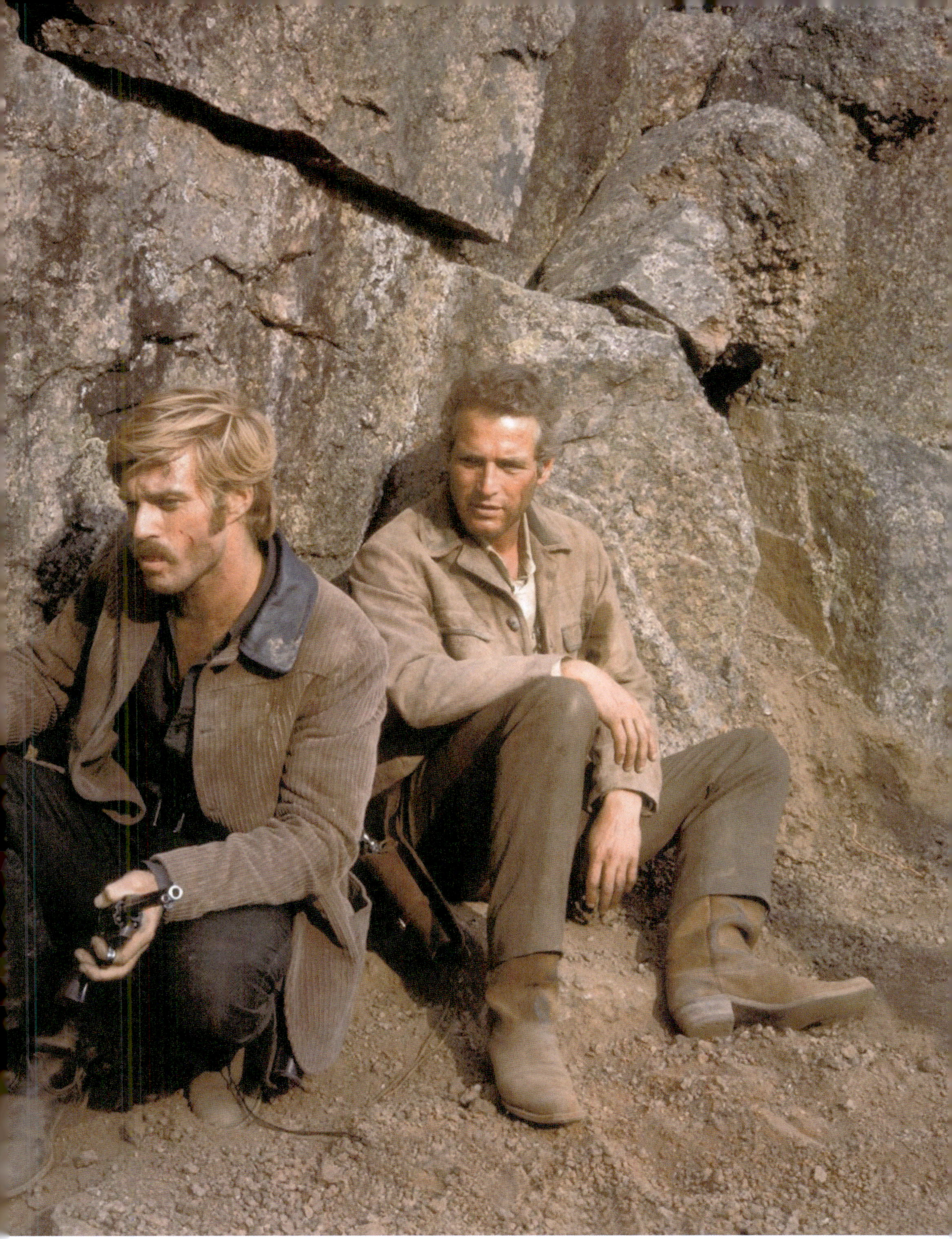

AS A FORMER MARINE MAJOR who had piloted planes during World War II and the Korean War, Hill commanded the shoot like a battalion. With a staff of 165 and the cost of $30,000 to $35,000 a day, he had his crew working 16-hour days. But while the filming had a regimental pace, the set had a relaxed feel. Newman and Redford brought their families, and there was, according to Redford's son Jamie, "incessant talk, gags, and laughs." The two stars also drove up with their cars. Newman had his Volkswagen Beetle souped up with a Porsche engine. He was fascinated by auto racing, and recently started lessons in preparation for his Indy 500 film, *Winning*. Redford, who was also a Porsche aficionado, pulled up in his rare Porsche 904 GTS. According to Fox publicist Francis Feighan, "the testosterone in the air was overpowering."

There was a clear fellowship, with good-natured ribbing going around. Redford had a habit of showing up on set 10 to 15 minutes late, causing Newman to keep repeating to him, "Punctuality is the courtesy of kings," a motto that Joanne fashioned for Redford on a framed sampler. There were also plenty of pranks. When Redford said he could fence, the others sought to lure him into a bet to test his ability. Thankfully, Redford heard from one of Newman's daughters that "they're going to do something bad to you," and quickly backed out.

But while the two stars playfully sparred, there was a growing tension between Newman and Hill. They argued about scenes, technique, even the sort of lenses to use. "I thought George was terribly rigid when we first started rehearsing," said Newman. "They both have this habit of pointing with their index fingers when they argue," recalled Redford, "and during one major, uh, discussion, they were both pointing and their fingers crossed, liked locked swords. Hilarious. Everybody cracked up."

Eventually, they worked out their differences. And though Hill learned to bend, the former military officer bristled when people did things without his approval. As they filmed, Ross had become involved with cinematographer Hall. One day when Hall only had four cameramen for his five cameras, he let Ross handle one. "It was the last shot of the day," recalled Ross, who hadn't appeared in the film yet. "[Hill] said, 'I want to talk to you when we get back to the motel.' The end result was that I was banned from the set except for when I was working... That incident or that action haunted me for the rest of the film."

While they filmed, Hill invited Butch's sister Lula Parker Betenson to visit. Officials at Fox hoped that she would help promote the film, and Newman came up to her at a lunch break when they were shooting the scene where Logan—played by the towering Ted Cassidy, who is best remembered as Lurch on the TV series *The Addams Family*—tries to take control of the gang. When Newman saw Betenson, he flashed his famous grin and said, "Hi, I'm Butch." The 84-year-old looked at him and said, "I'm sure glad it's you playing Butch. My brother was a real fine boy." Newman, Redford, and Hill then quizzed her about her famous sibling.

Ross's first scene was shot in Grafton, Utah, at a deserted Mormon community. In the film, Etta is presented as a teacher. The crew converted an adobe church into a schoolhouse and built a house for her so they could shoot both outside and inside during

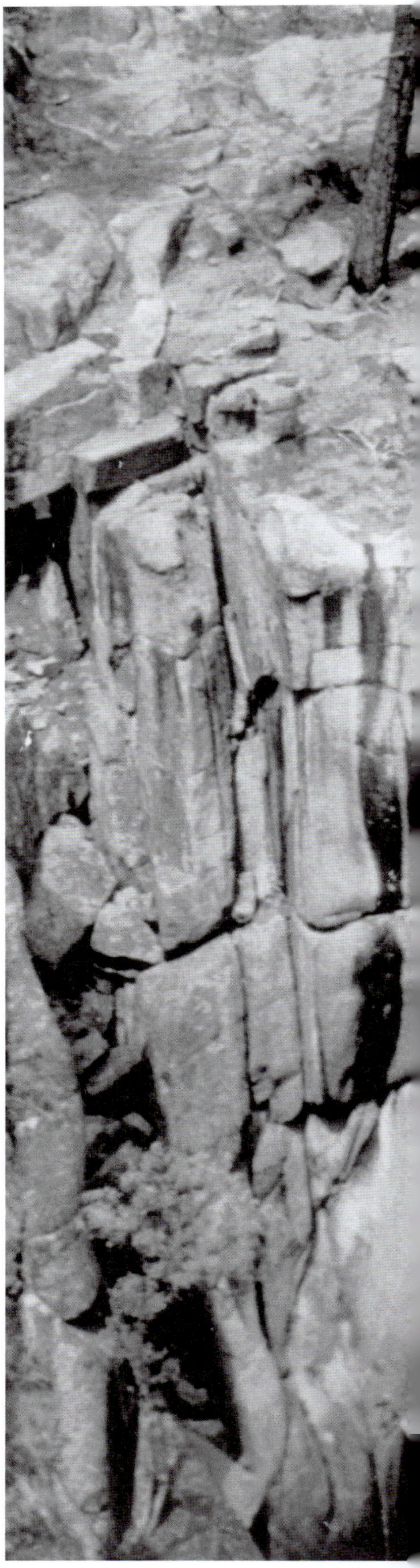

AFTER THE SUNDANCE KID reluctantly admits that he cannot swim, the men have no choice but to make the plunge into the river below. Cinematographer Conrad Hall shot the scene in two parts. In the first, Redford and Newman appear to jump from the cliff, yet actually land on a scaffold built just below the ledge. The actual plummet was then filmed using two stuntmen.

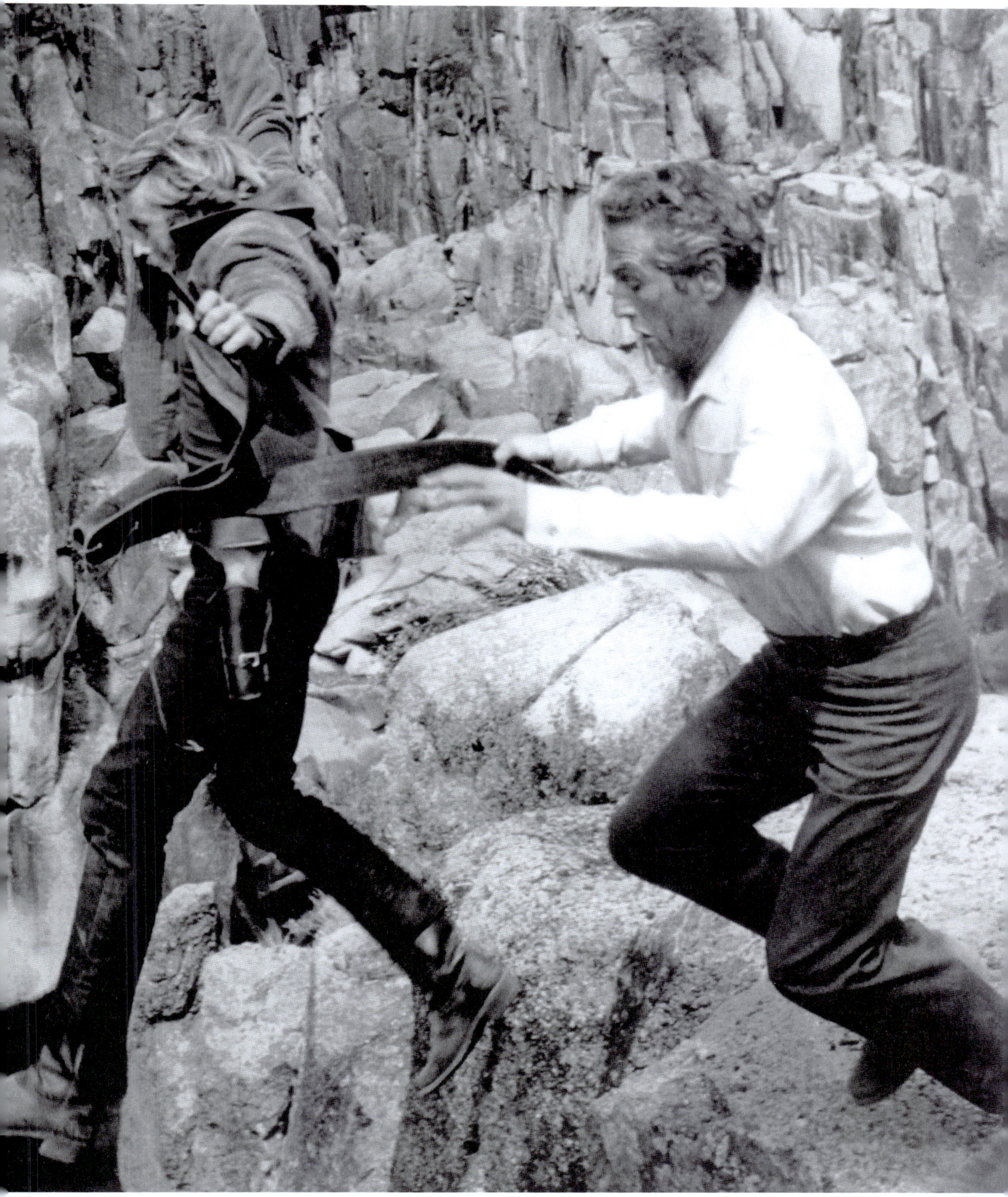

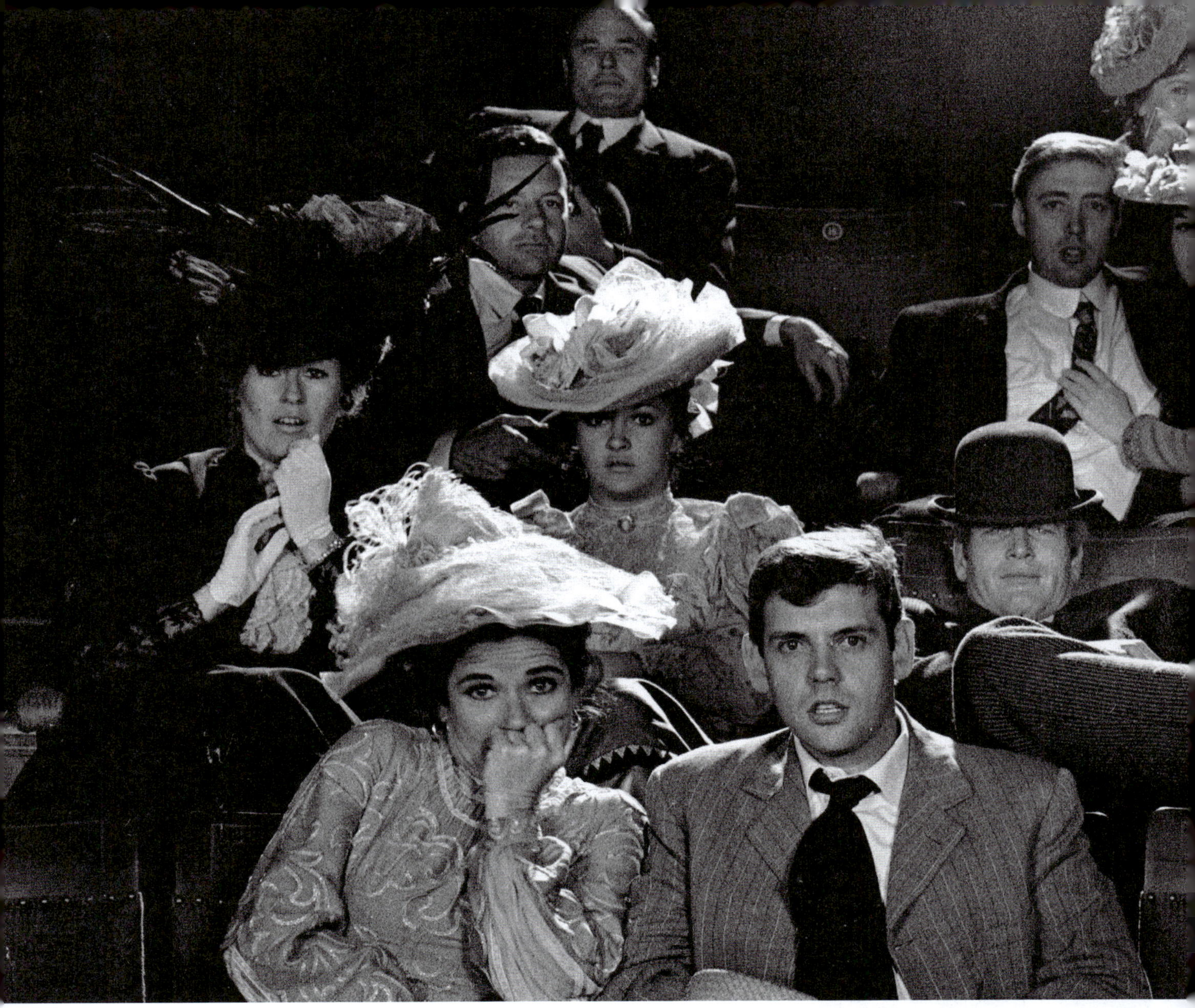

the scene where Butch and Etta ride a bicycle, which, as Butch jokes, represents "the future." The segment was added at the last minute to create a romantic triangle, and Hill had hired a stuntman to do the scene. Yet as the man tried to explain to Hill that the old-fashioned bike was too rickety to hold up, the daredevil Newman rolled by standing on it. Hill fired the stuntman. Despite her earlier problems with Hill and the discomfort of riding on top of handle bars, Ross enjoyed filming the scene. "It was a lot of fun," she said. "I enjoyed those parts the most."

Not a fan of music played over dialogue, Hill made the unusual decision to make the bicycle sequence one of a series of wordless musical interludes. For it, Hill nixed the idea of a traditional Western score. Producer John Foreman suggested pop music, and the filmmakers tried out Simon and Garfunkel's "The 59th Street Bridge Song (Feelin' Groovy)." But after viewing a rough cut, Hill contacted Burt Bacharach, who had co-written the Oscar-nominated song "What's New Pussycat?" To write music for the sequence, Bacharach watched Newman and Ross roll by over and over again on his Moviola machine, and with lyricist Hal David composed "Raindrops Keep Fallin' on My Head."

TO FILM THE BOXCAR EXPLOSION, THE CREW CONSTRUCTED A TRAIN CAR OUT OF BALSA WOOD SO THERE WOULD BE MINIMAL INJURY.

A few special effects had to also be created. To film the boxcar explosion, the crew constructed a train car out of balsa wood so that when the dynamite blew up there would be minimal injury. Not wishing to have to repeat the shot, Hall set up four cameras, constructing wooden bunkers for the men in the closest ones. He then had each cameraman run his camera at a different speed.

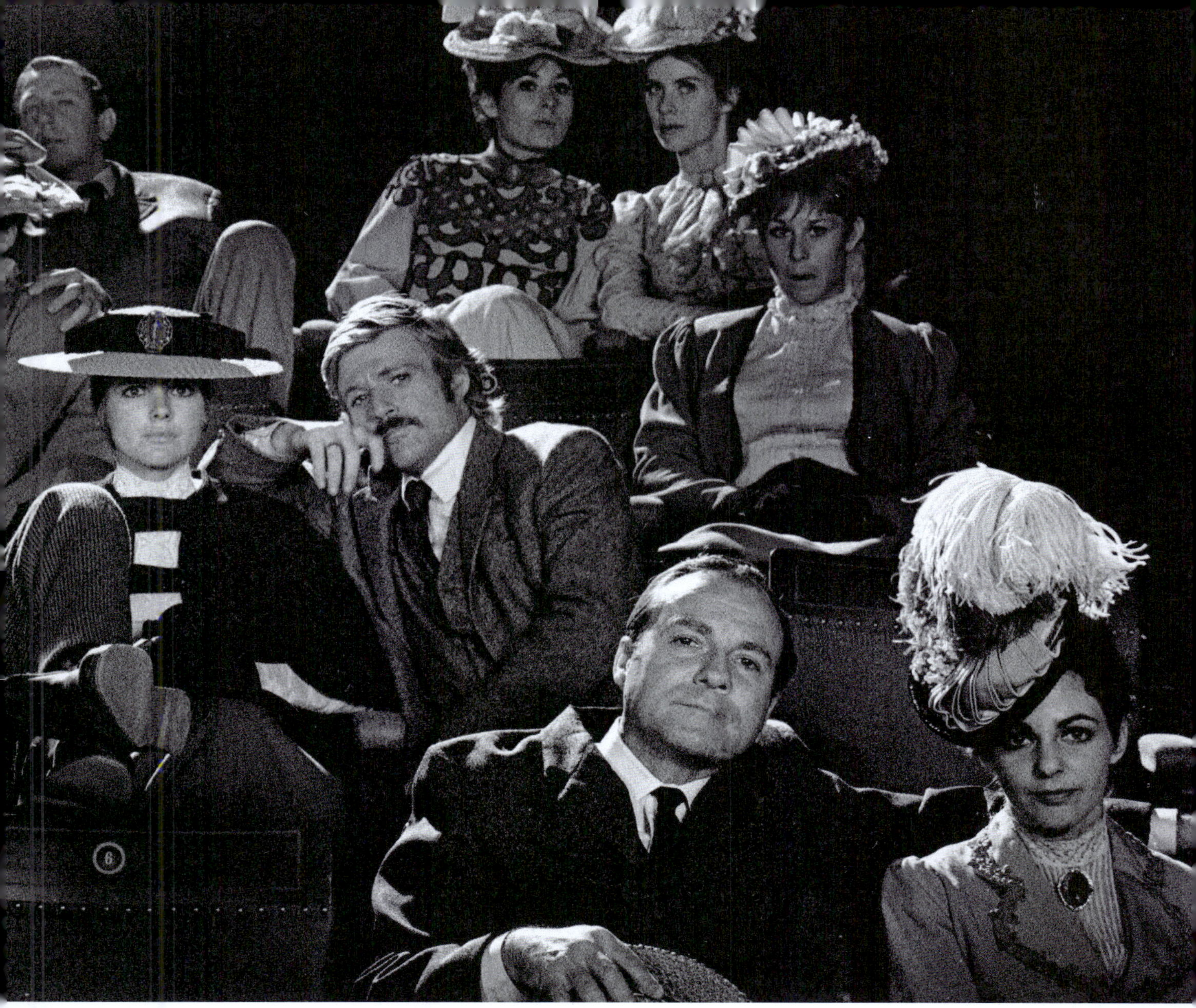

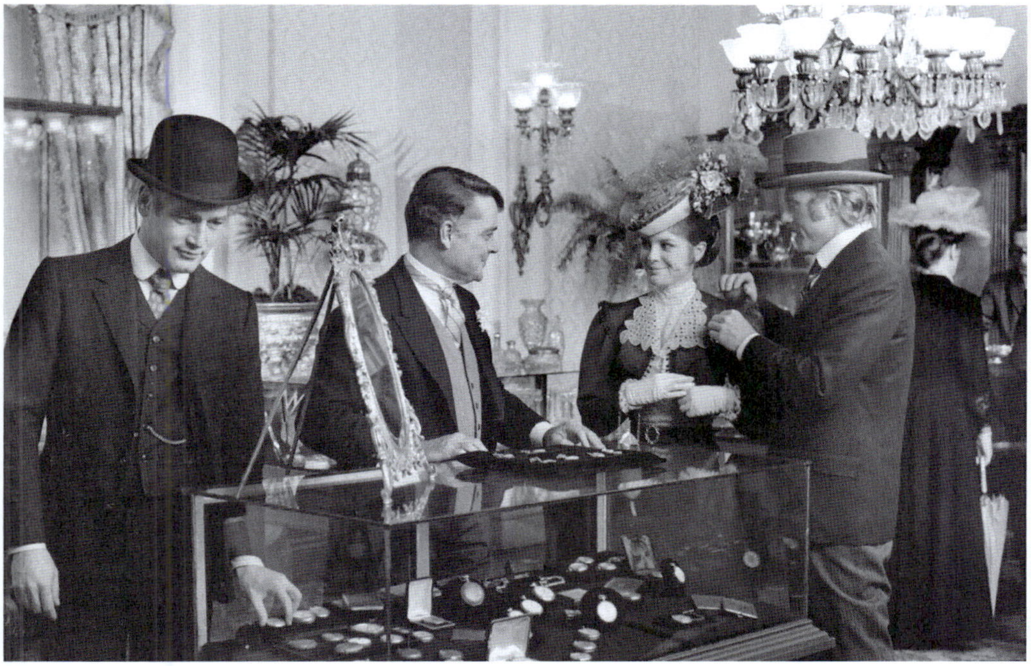

IN NEW YORK CITY, THE TRIO take in entertainments not available in Outlaw Pass, including a moving picture show and a stop in a jewelry store. In real life, they went to Tiffany's, where Sundance bought a $150 gold lapel pendant watch for his lady friend and a stickpin for himself, while Butch paid for a gold watch.

"You have to over crank an explosion otherwise it will be too fast on film," said Hill. "We didn't want to take this shot over again."

As Butch and Sundance view their handiwork after setting up the dynamite, Butch says, "Well, that oughta do it." The fuse is lit, and the two are immediately knocked down and covered with debris, prompting Sundance to deadpan, "Do you think you used enough dynamite there, Butch?" The explosion caused the money from the safe to shoot into the air, and to create that sequence, Hall set up large fans and had the crew feed fake money over them so it would seem to fly around in the wind.

THE FAMOUS BICYCLE SEGMENT WAS ADDED AT THE LAST MINUTE TO CREATE A ROMANTIC TRIANGLE.

It is after that that the Pinkerton super posse arrives. To accommodate the scene, a special boxcar three feet taller than a standard car had to be constructed. And to give the illusion of agents charging out of the train, crew members positioned ramps on both sides so stunt riders could gallop up one and then pour out the other.

The gang is clearly outnumbered, and instead of fighting, they flee. Butch and Sundance seek help from the sympathetic Sheriff Ray Bledsoe (Jeff Corey,

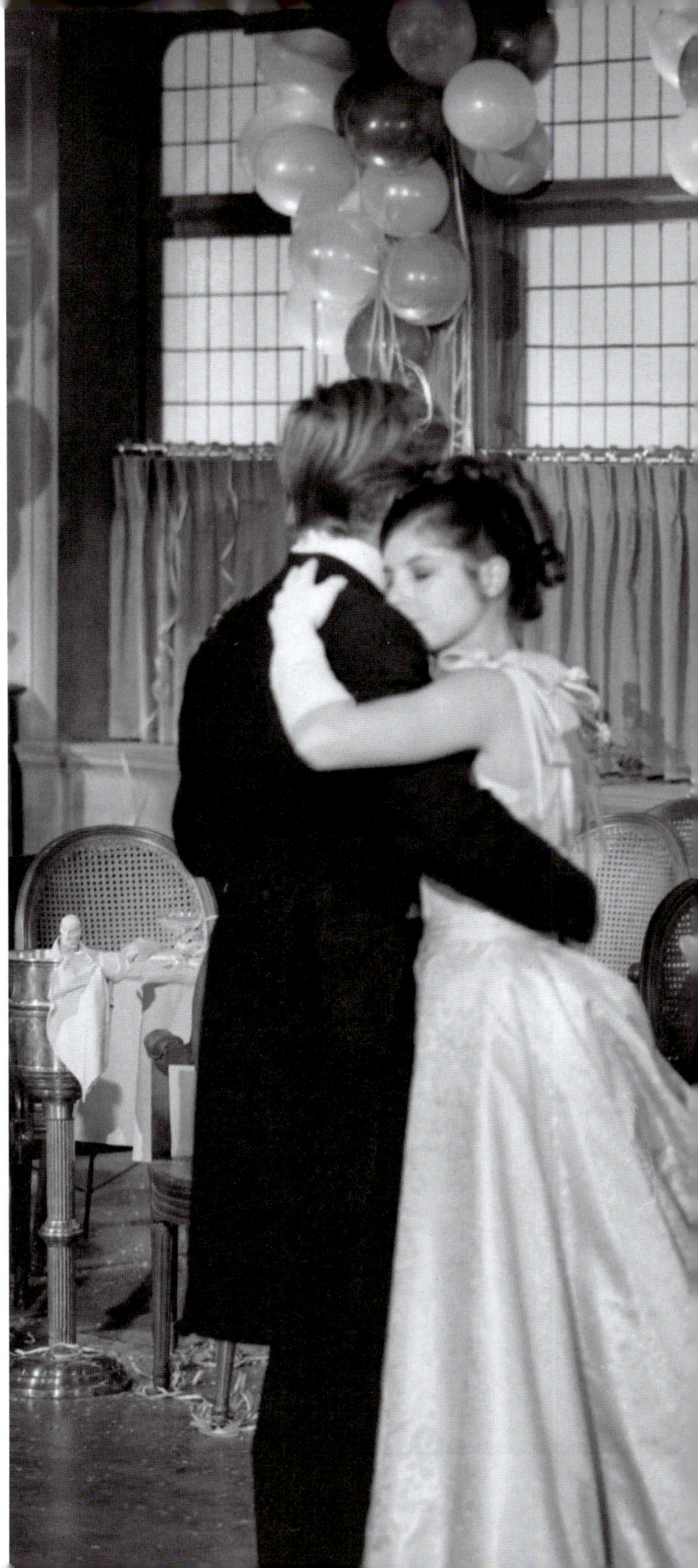

HAVING AVOIDED THE POSSE, Butch and Sundance collect Etta, slip off to New York, and then in fin-de-siècle style sail first class by steamship to South America. The scene was part of photographer Lawrence Schiller's montage for which he had sets built.

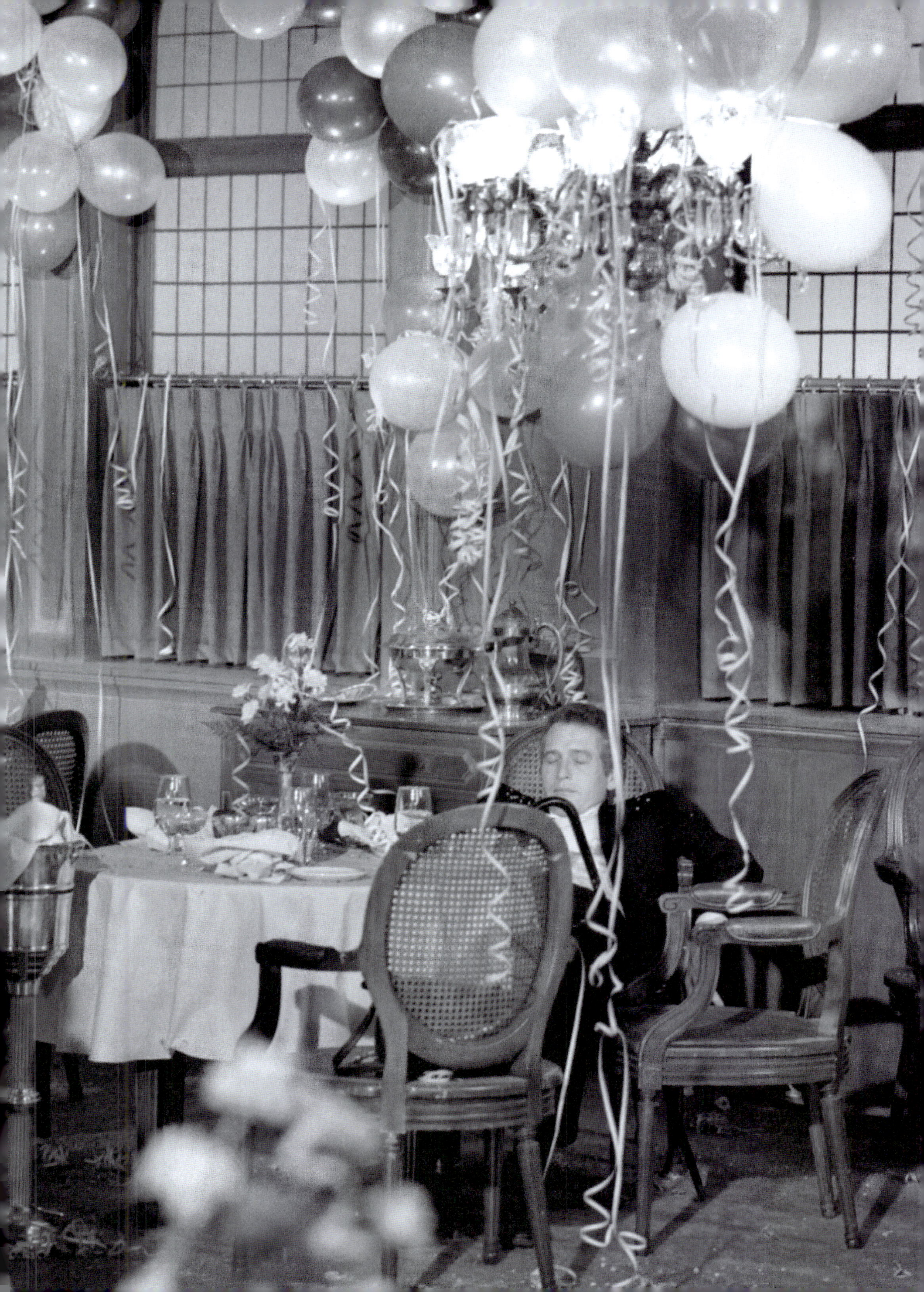

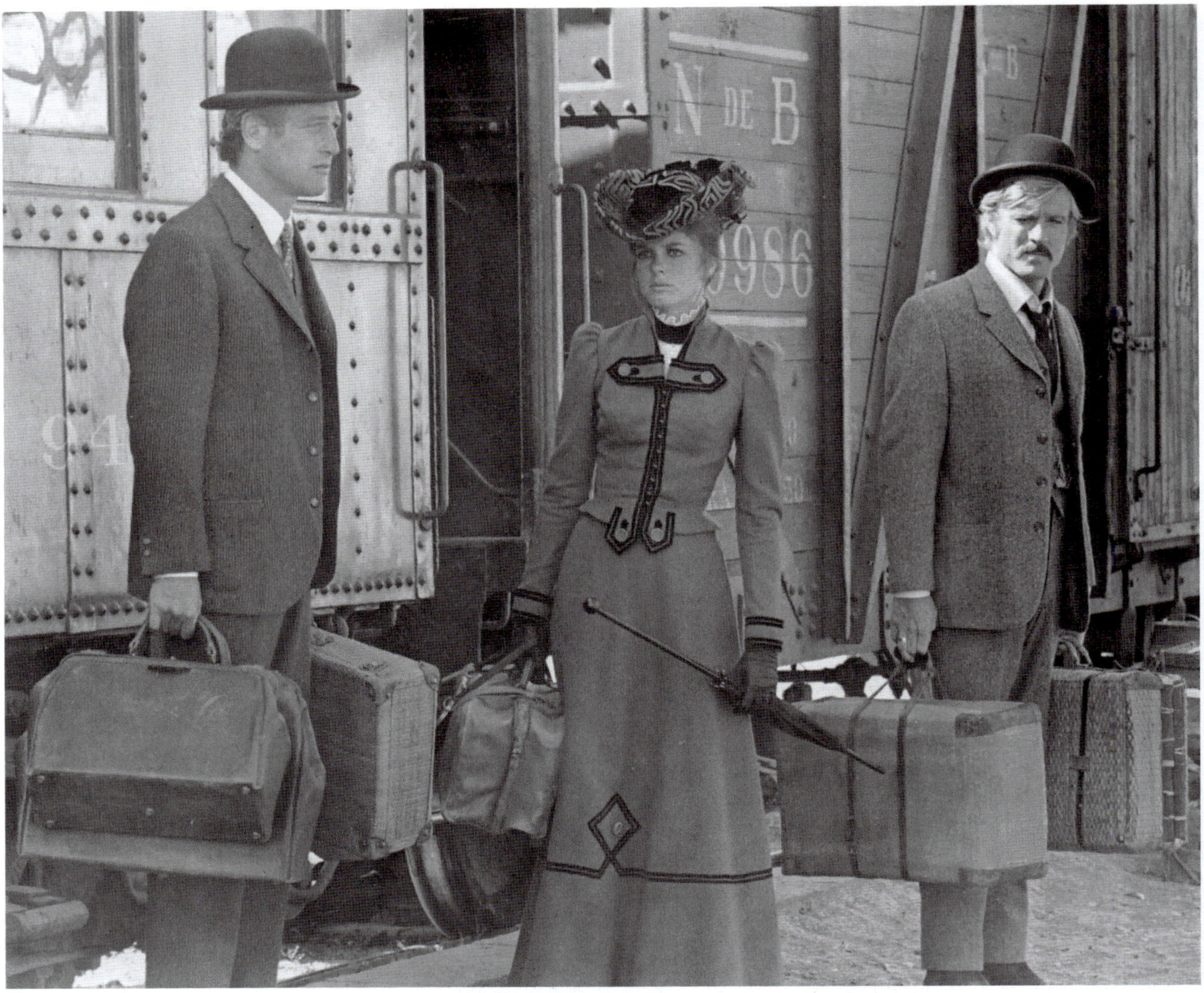

who also appeared in that year's *True Grit*). Upset that the outlaws showed up at his door, an irate Bledsoe sums up the change that has come to the West when he tells them, "There's something out there that scares you, huh? But it's too late. You know you should have let yourself get killed a long time ago while you had the chance . . . It's over. Don't you get that? Your times is over, and you're gonna die bloody, and all you can do is choose where."

Bledsoe is quite prescient. The outlaws cannot shake the law on their tail or the approaching modernity that Butch quips about when he shows Etta the bicycle. There is no way back for them. Finding themselves trapped on the edge of a cliff shortly thereafter, they have no other choice but to jump into a river and abandon their old lives.

For that scene, the water along the Animas River Gorge in Durango proved too shallow to leap into, so Hall shot the segment in two parts. The crew constructed a platform with a mattress-cushioned ledge set six feet below the cliff, onto which Newman and Redford jumped. The actual leap and plunge was then shot a few months later at the Fox Studio Ranch in Malibu. Lenwood Ballard "Bill" Abbott—who headed the studio's special photographic effects and would rack up four Academy Awards during his career—had glass plates painted to look like the Durango cliffs. The cameramen then positioned the glass in front of the camera, filming through it to give the impression of towering rock faces, as two stuntmen leaped from a 70-foot crane set just out of the camera's view. As they plummet from what appears to be the ledge, the camera pans down to where Hall had set outboard motors to stir up the water and simulate rapids.

"YOUR TIMES IS OVER, AND YOU'RE GONNA DIE BLOODY," SHERIFF RAY BLEDSOE (JEFF COREY) TELLS BUTCH AND SUNDANCE.

SAFE FROM THE POSSE, Butch, Sundance, and Etta head to South America. Before leaving the country, they visit New York City. For that segment, they wanted to film on Fox's New York street set of the upcoming *Hello Dolly!* but studio chief

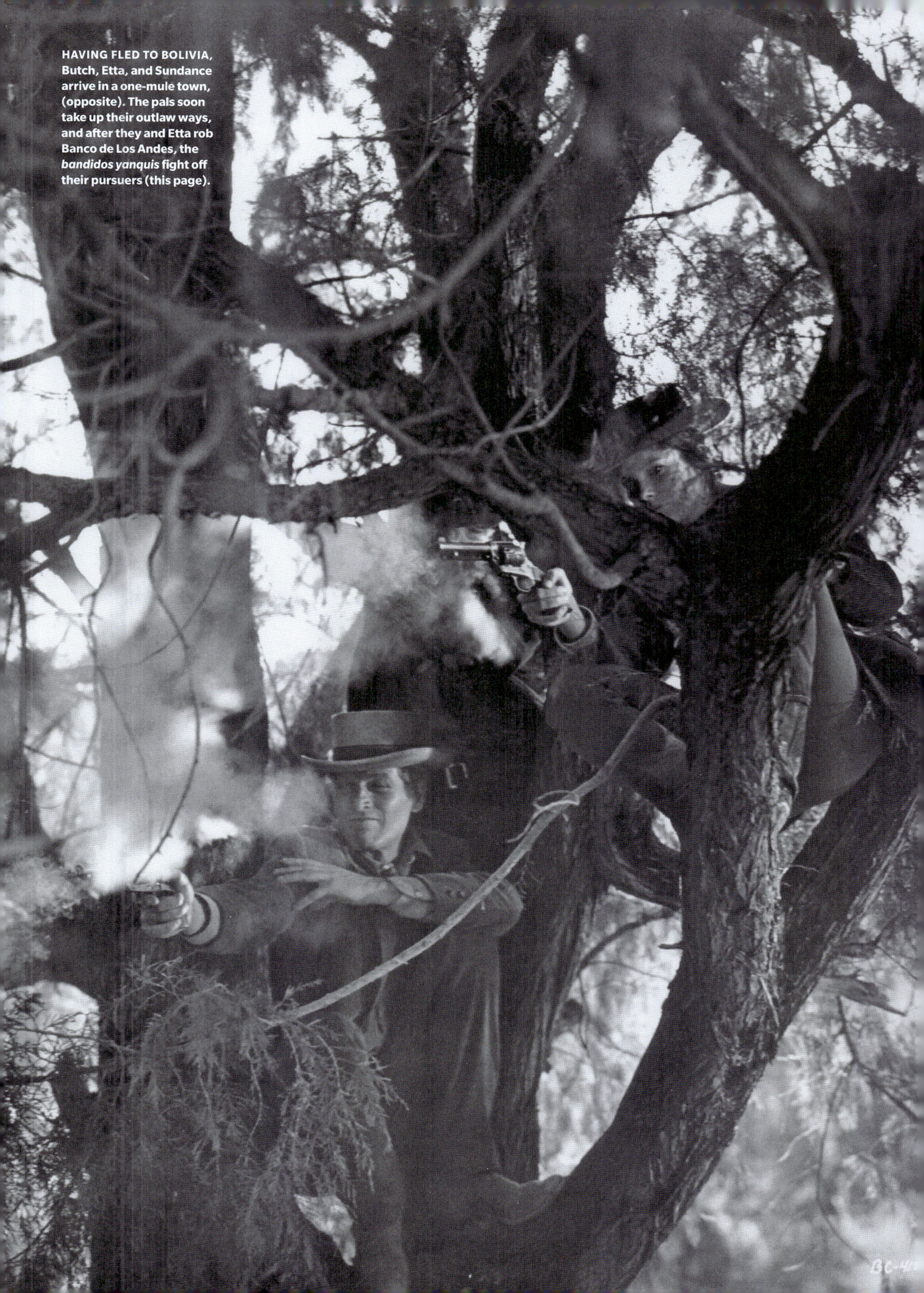

HAVING FLED TO BOLIVIA, Butch, Etta, and Sundance arrive in a one-mule town, (opposite). The pals soon take up their outlaw ways, and after they and Etta rob Banco de Los Andes, the *bandidos yanquis* fight off their pursuers (this page).

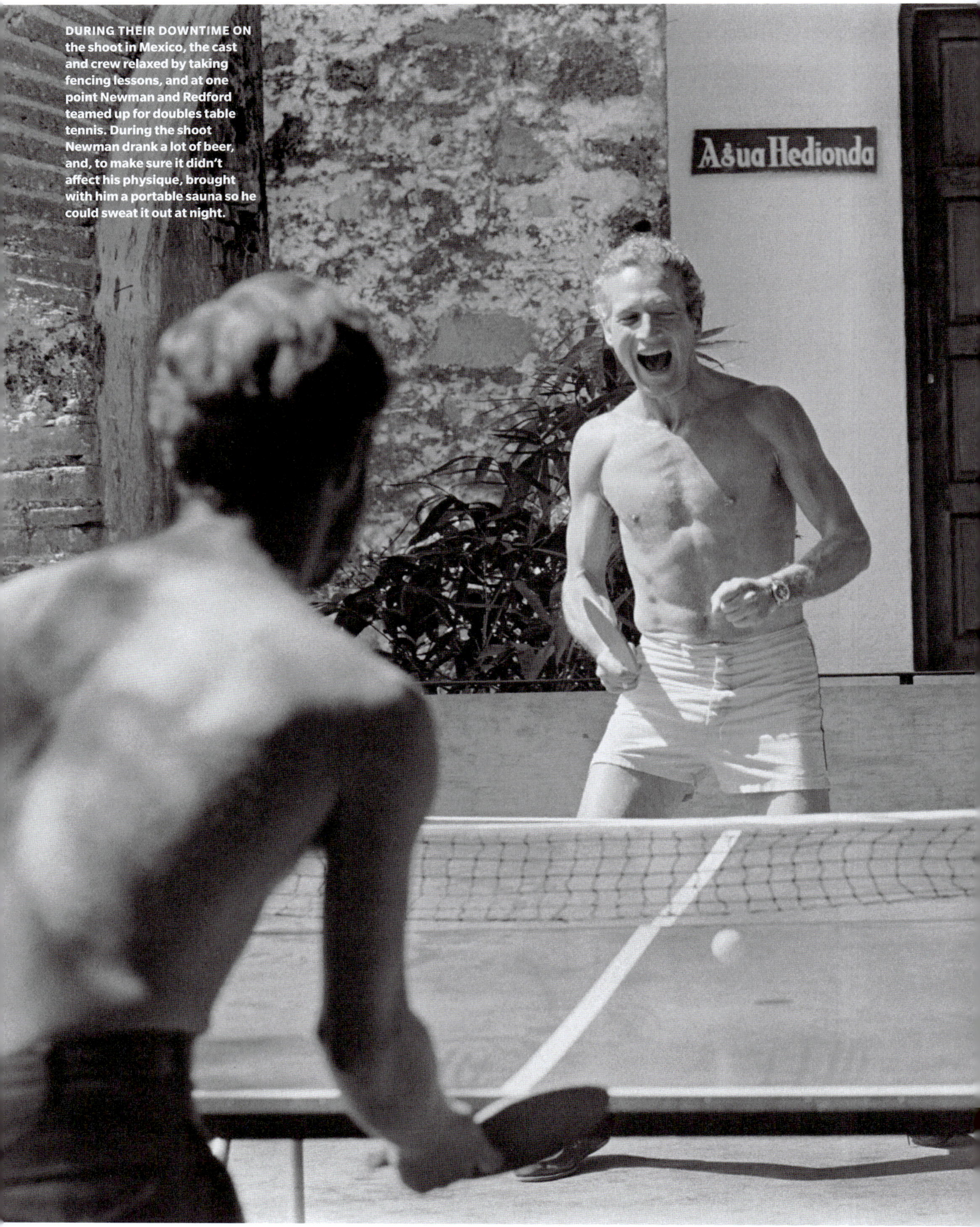

DURING THEIR DOWNTIME ON the shoot in Mexico, the cast and crew relaxed by taking fencing lessons, and at one point Newman and Redford teamed up for doubles table tennis. During the shoot Newman drank a lot of beer, and, to make sure it didn't affect his physique, brought with him a portable sauna so he could sweat it out at night.

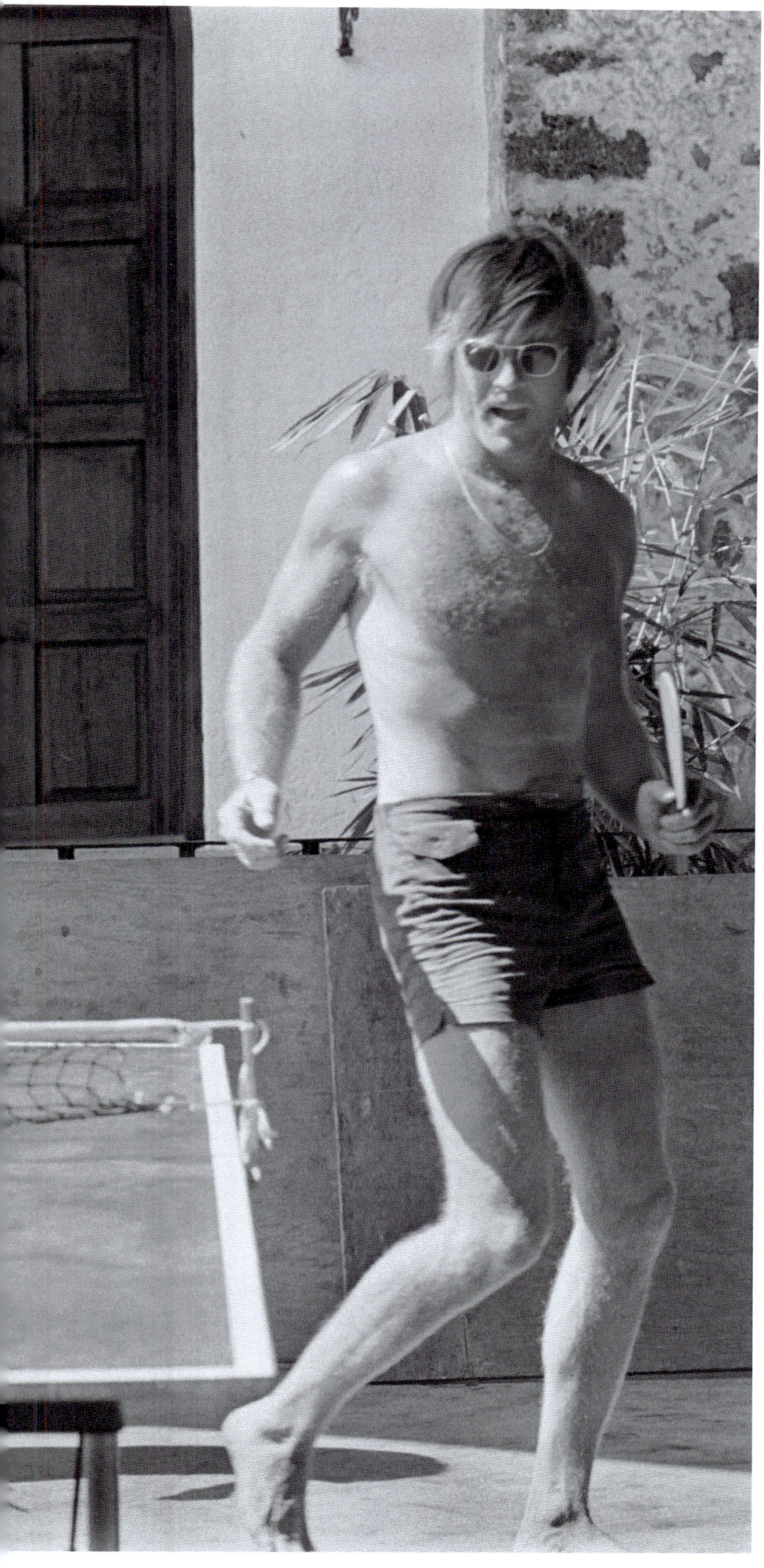

Richard Zanuck didn't want the public to see the sets before that film opened. It was then decided to turn Butch, Sundance, and Etta's New York visit into the film's second musical sequence by having photographer Lawrence Schiller create what looked like old photographs of the city. Newman, Redford, and Ross dressed up in costumer Head's turn-of-the-century outfits and posed on the *Hello Dolly!* streets. Their images were then cut and pasted onto old period photographs, printed in sepia, and shot on an animation stand.

When the action moved south of the border, the cast and crew spent time in Cuernavaca and Taxco, Mexico, where Newman and Redford happily drank beer and played table tennis. For one bank robbing scene, which became the third musical interlude, Ross dresses as a man and the three *bandidos yanquis* end up in a tree firing pistols. "Isn't that a pretty sight," Butch laughs as they drive away their Bolivian pursuers. "Well, we are back in business, boys and girls, just like the old days." But it is not to be. Sensing the end is near, and learning that the boys don't want to go straight by farming or ranching, Etta decides to leave. The men then head to their (apparent) deaths.

IT WAS DECIDED TO TURN BUTCH, SUNDANCE, AND ETTA'S NEW YORK VISIT INTO THE FILM'S SECOND MUSICAL SEQUENCE.

The final Bolivian scene was shot in Tlayacapan, 16 miles east of Cuernavaca. Hill and Hall chose the town's market for the gunfight; on the Sunday before the filming, Hill set out with second unit director Michael Moore and art director Philip Jefferies and planned the whole sequence shot by shot. To offer the actors cover during the

CONTINUED ON PAGE 58

THERE WERE REGULAR BREAKS in filming as cinematographer Conrad Hall waited for the perfect light, and during one time-out Newman took a seat on one of the more deadly looking props. Opposite: Redford prepared for the final shoot-out in the Bolivian town square.

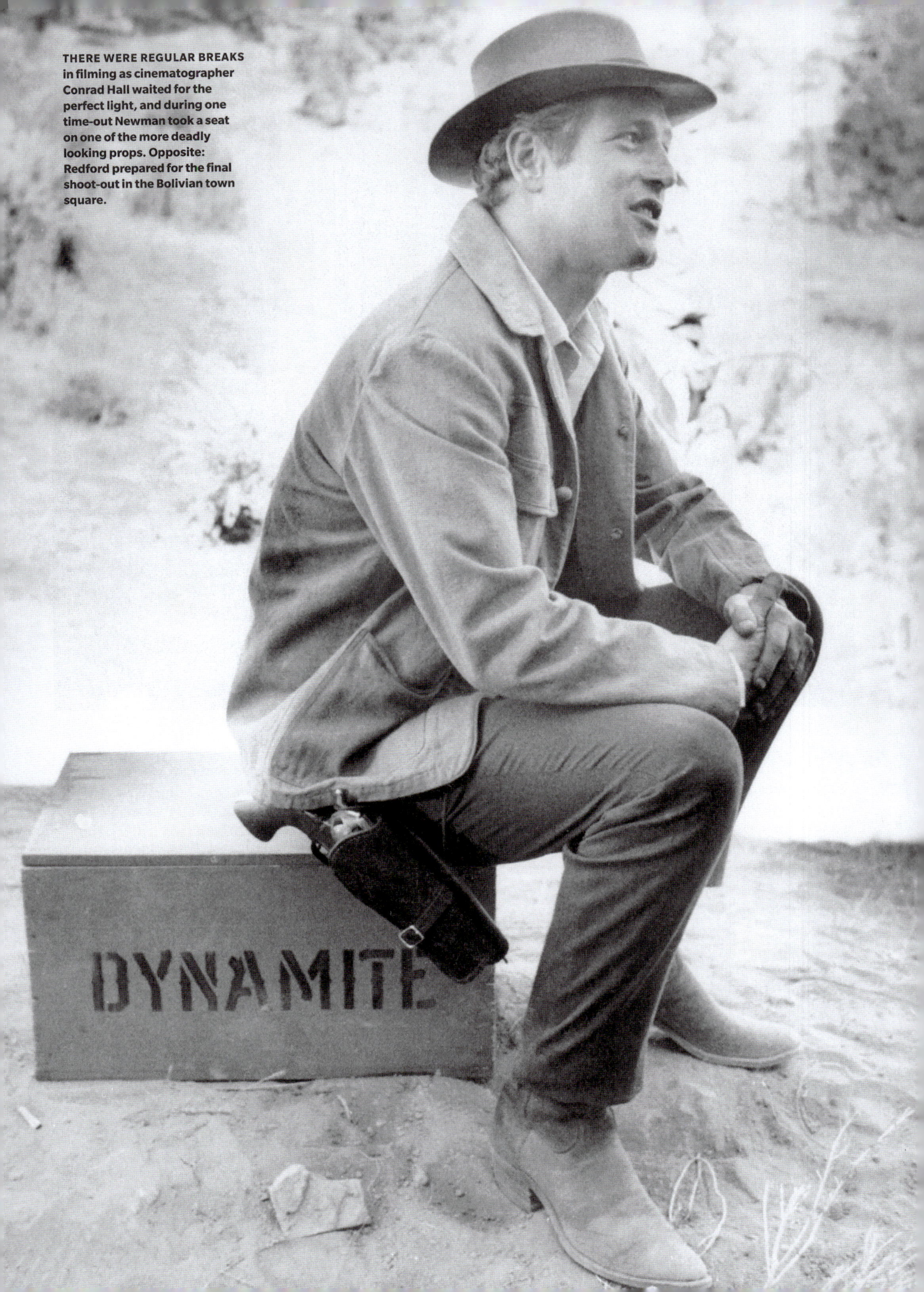

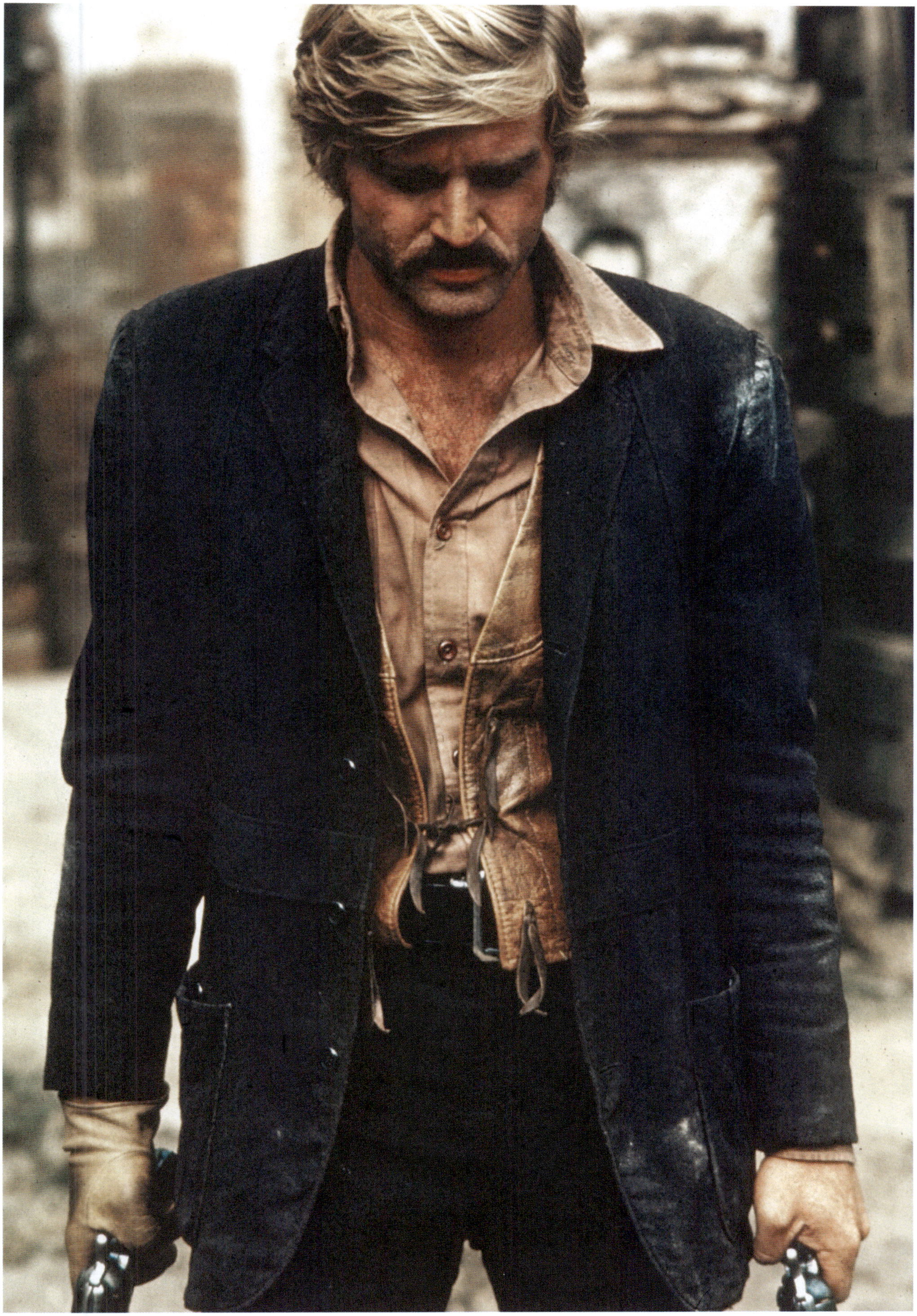

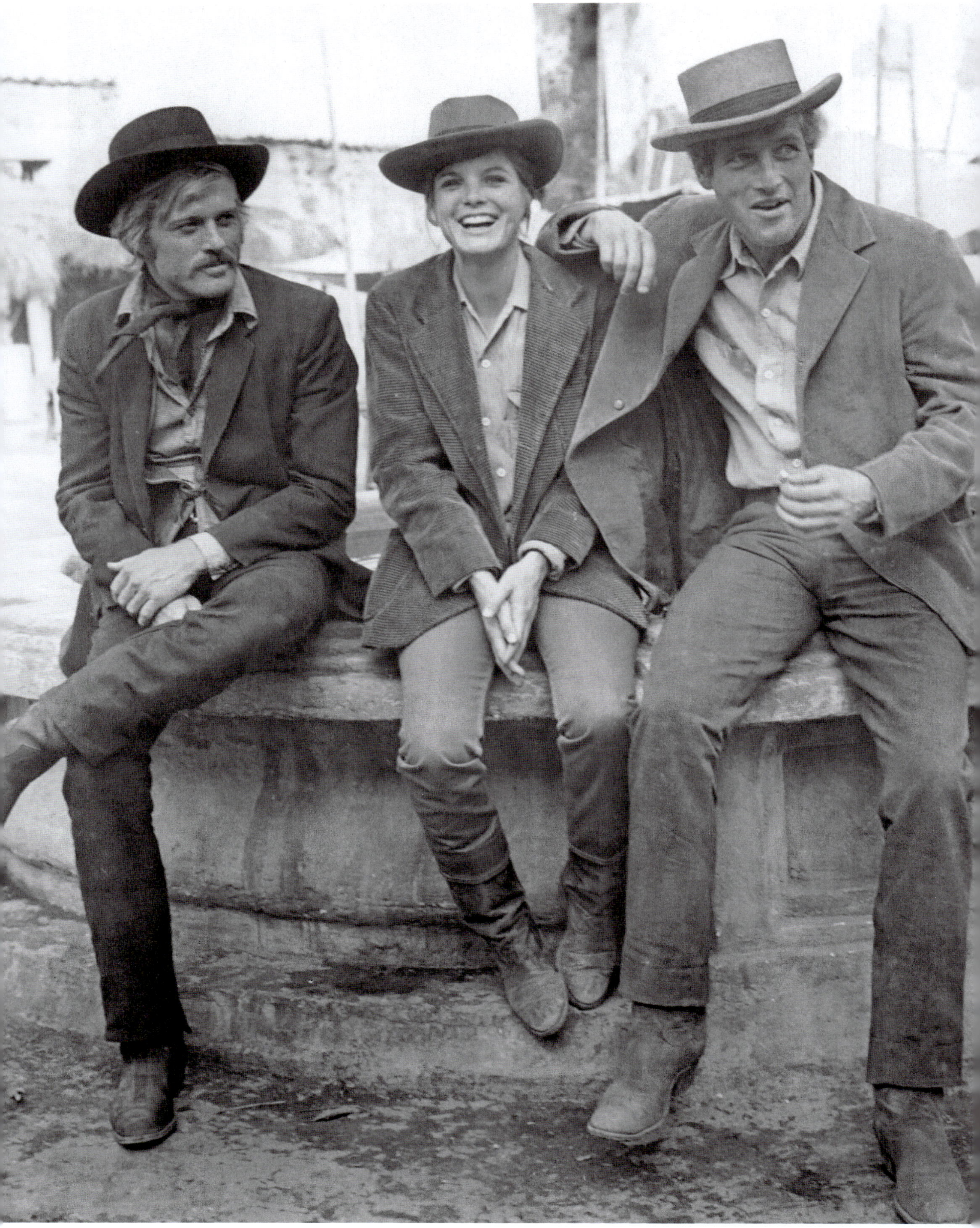

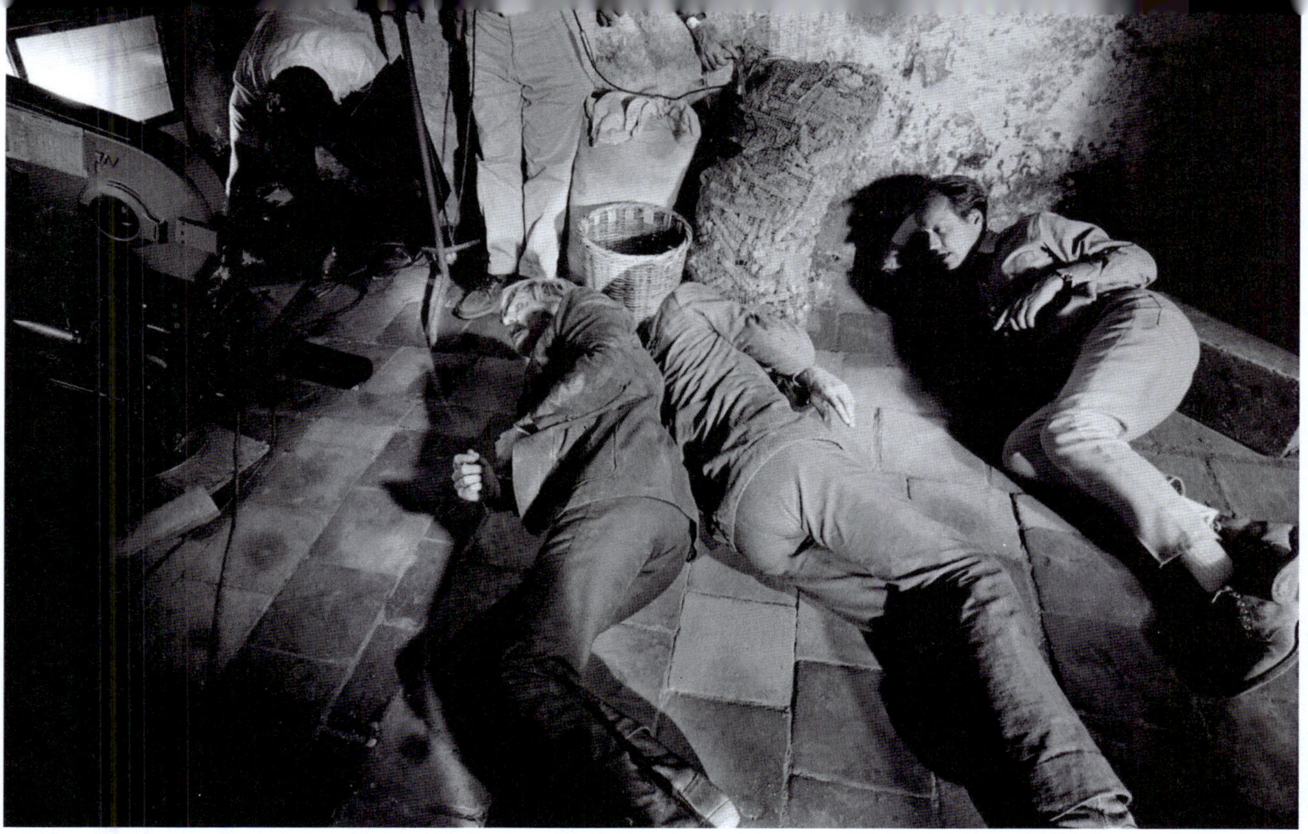

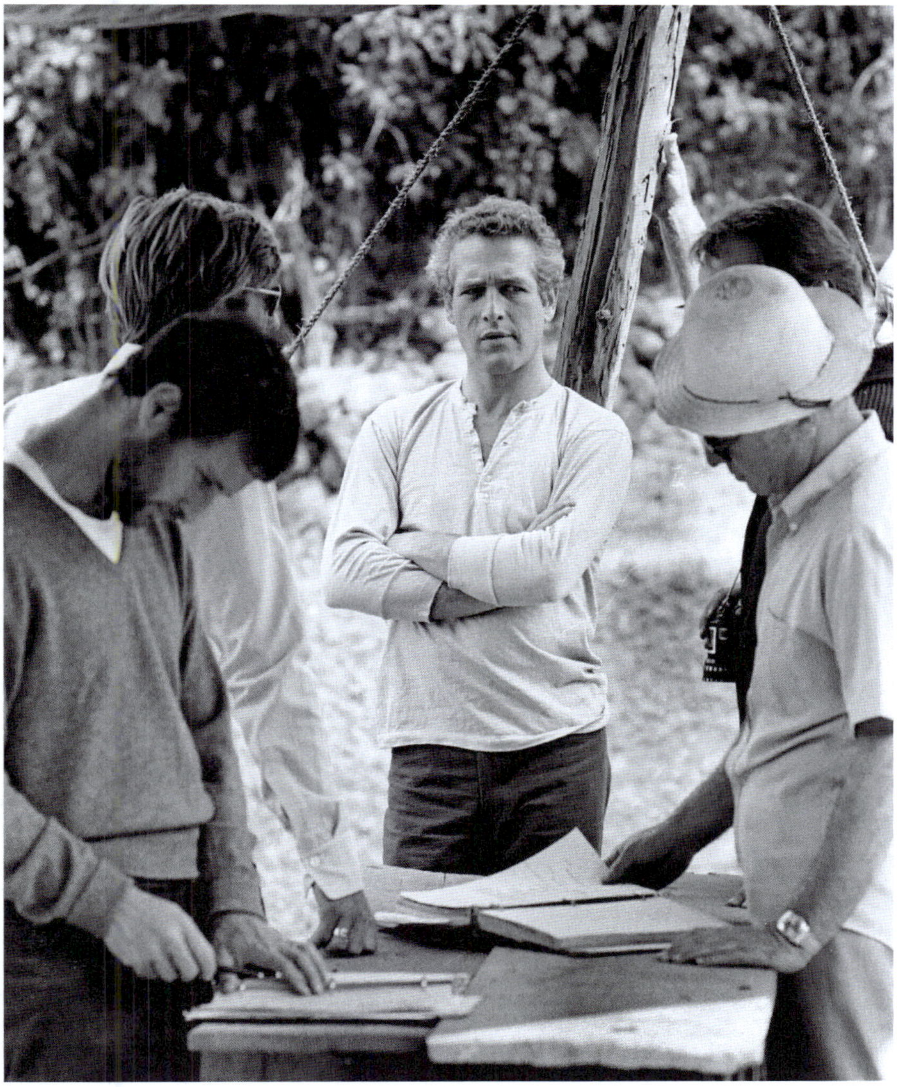

REDFORD, ROSS, AND Newman, opposite, take a break from the scene in which Etta joins the boys to rob a Bolivian bank. Above: Director Hill, right, discusses the final gunfight scene with Newman and Redford. Left: Redford, Newman, and crew members brainstorm during the planning for a take.

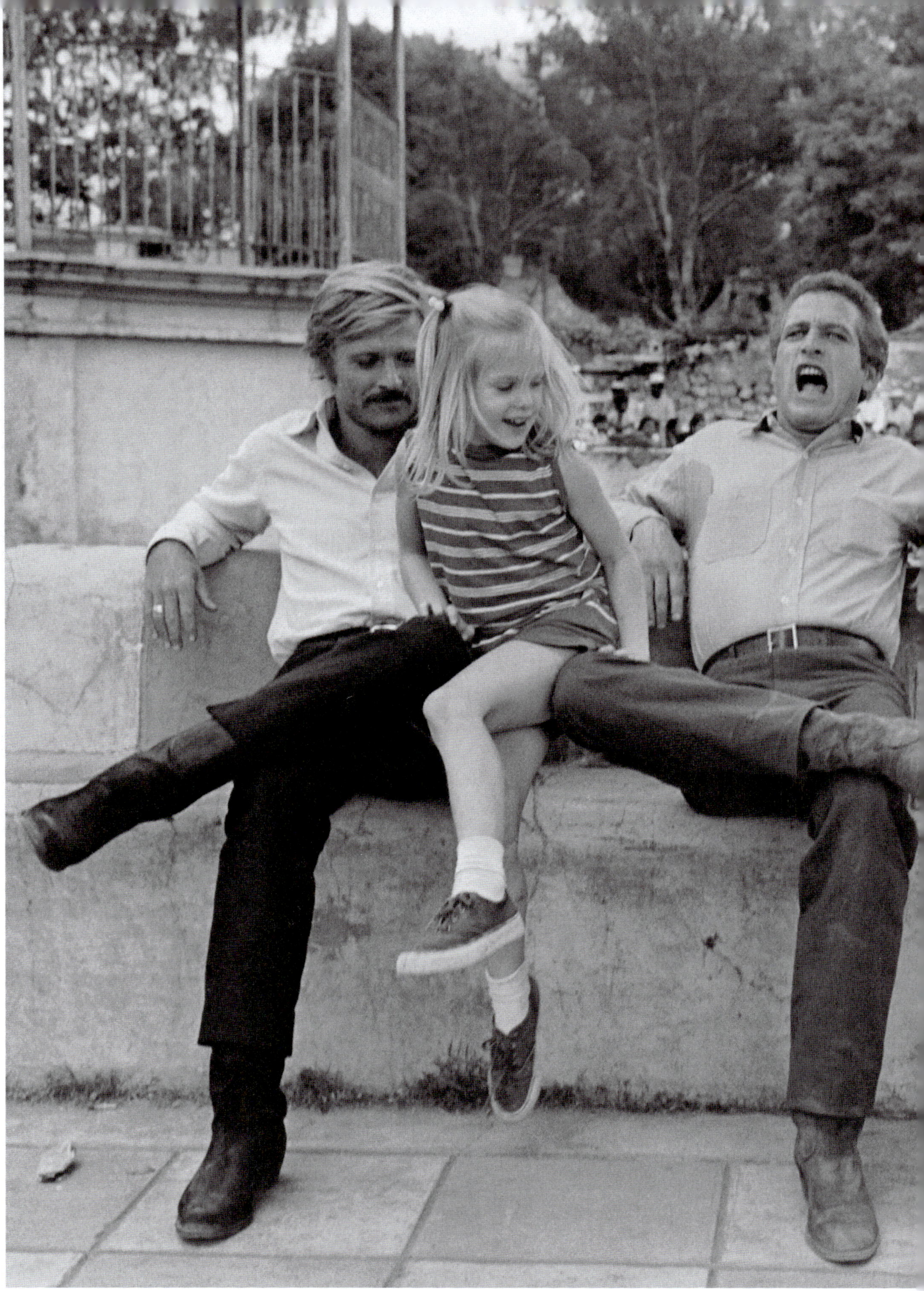

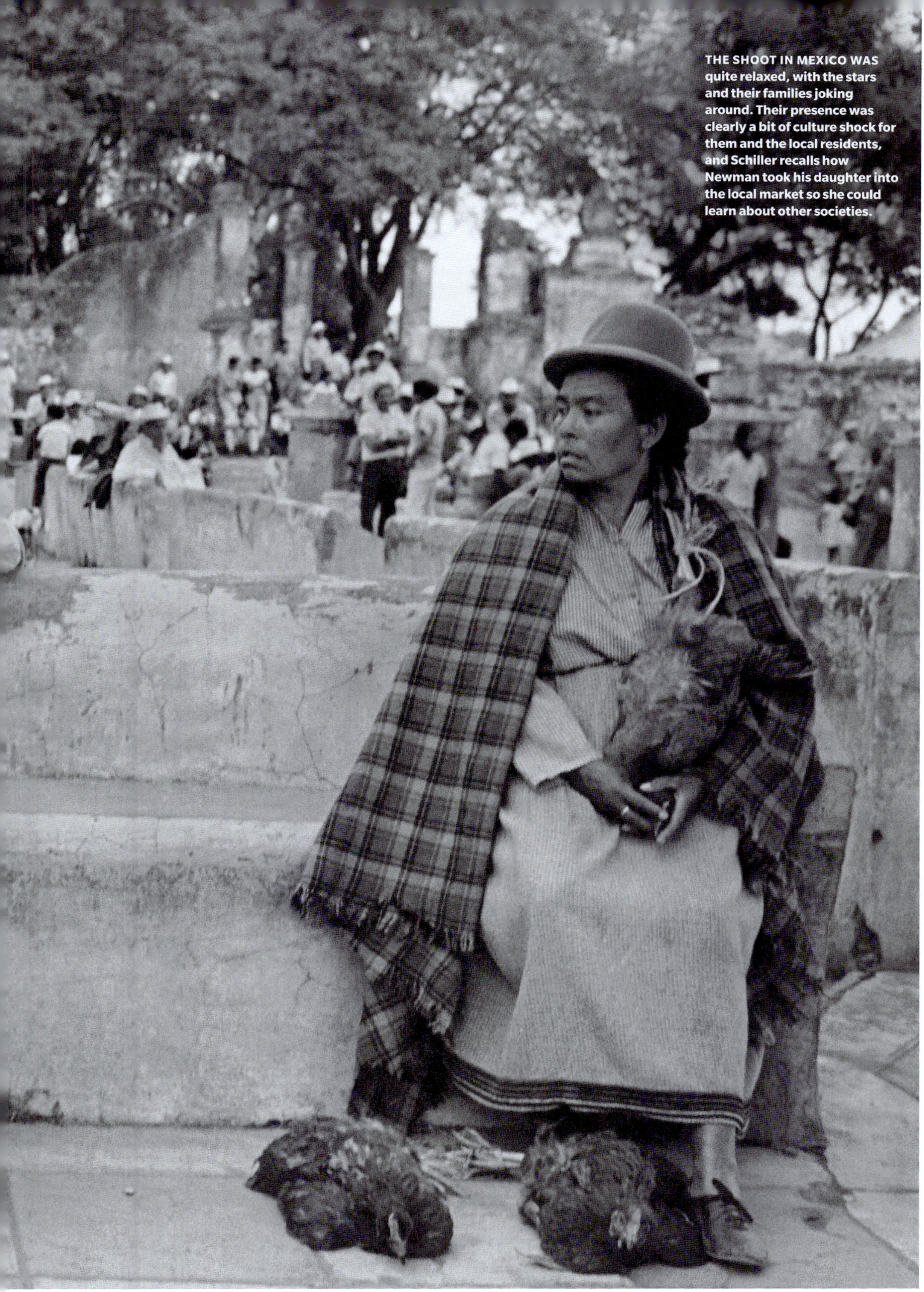

THE SHOOT IN MEXICO WAS quite relaxed, with the stars and their families joking around. Their presence was clearly a bit of culture shock for them and the local residents, and Schiller recalls how Newman took his daughter into the local market so she could learn about other societies.

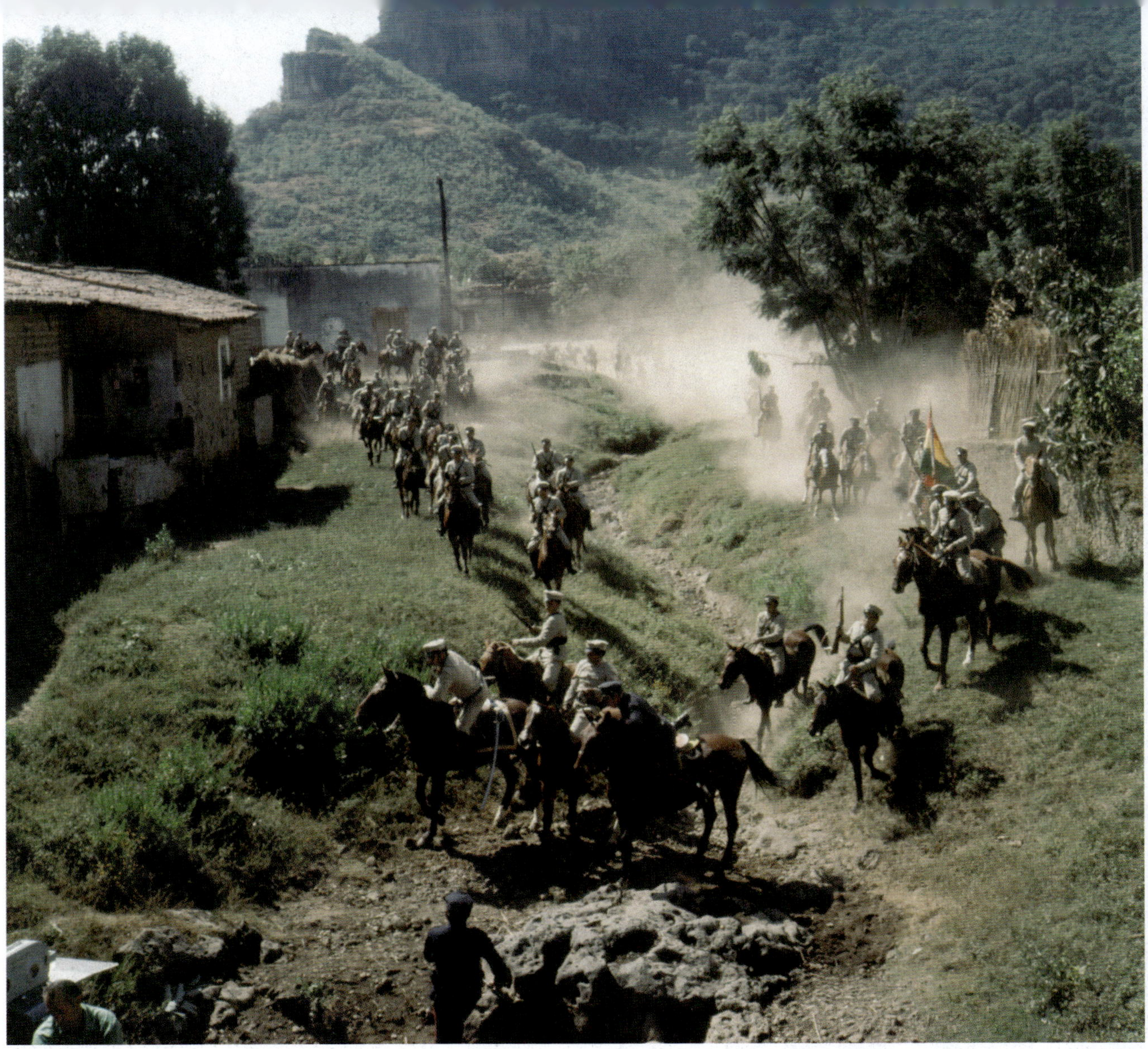

CONTINUED FROM PAGE 51

shoot-out, the crew turned the square into a market place. They set up hitching posts for horses and mules, along with stalls loaded with clothes, produce, baskets, and clay jugs to give the scene color as well as numerous spots for Butch and Sundance to dive behind and hide in. They then planted charges in walls, wired tables for simulated gunshots, and spread out the crew with air guns to shoot dust and blood pellets.

To make it appear more realistic, Hill staged it so that as Butch and Sundance take cover, they have to stop and reload their weapons, though in Sundance's final bursts of fire he shoots off about 18 rounds from his two six-shooters before taking refuge with Butch in a building. Badly wounded, the men huddle inside. Though injured, they continued their bantering, a painful balancing of humor and hope as they discuss going to Australia. Sundance then places a gun in Butch's bloody hand, and the two head out.

AWARE OF THE MYTH THAT THE OUTLAWS DIDN'T PERISH, HILL ENDED THE FILM JUST BEFORE THE MOMENT OF THEIR DEATHS.

Well aware of the story that the outlaws did not really perish in Bolivia, Hill decided to end the film just before the moment of their deaths. "I wanted to take them right up to the point of their being killed and freeze frame and make them a part of the still photograph of the scene in the same sepia color that we used in the New York stills." To do that, he brought Bill Abbott down from Los Angeles. Hall first filmed from the overlooking roof as Butch and Sundance charge from the door. Then, on the same spot, Abbott quickly set up an 8 x 10 still camera, using the large-format camera to shoot a high-resolution image of the whole set with no one on it, so the building's shadows matched the final take. Then back in the studio they froze the 35mm action, took the last frame, bled out the color so it was sepia-toned, pasted the image of the two outlaws onto a blowup of the picture, and rephotographed it on an animation set.

Pulling back, it shows Butch and Sundance frozen in celluloid history. ✦

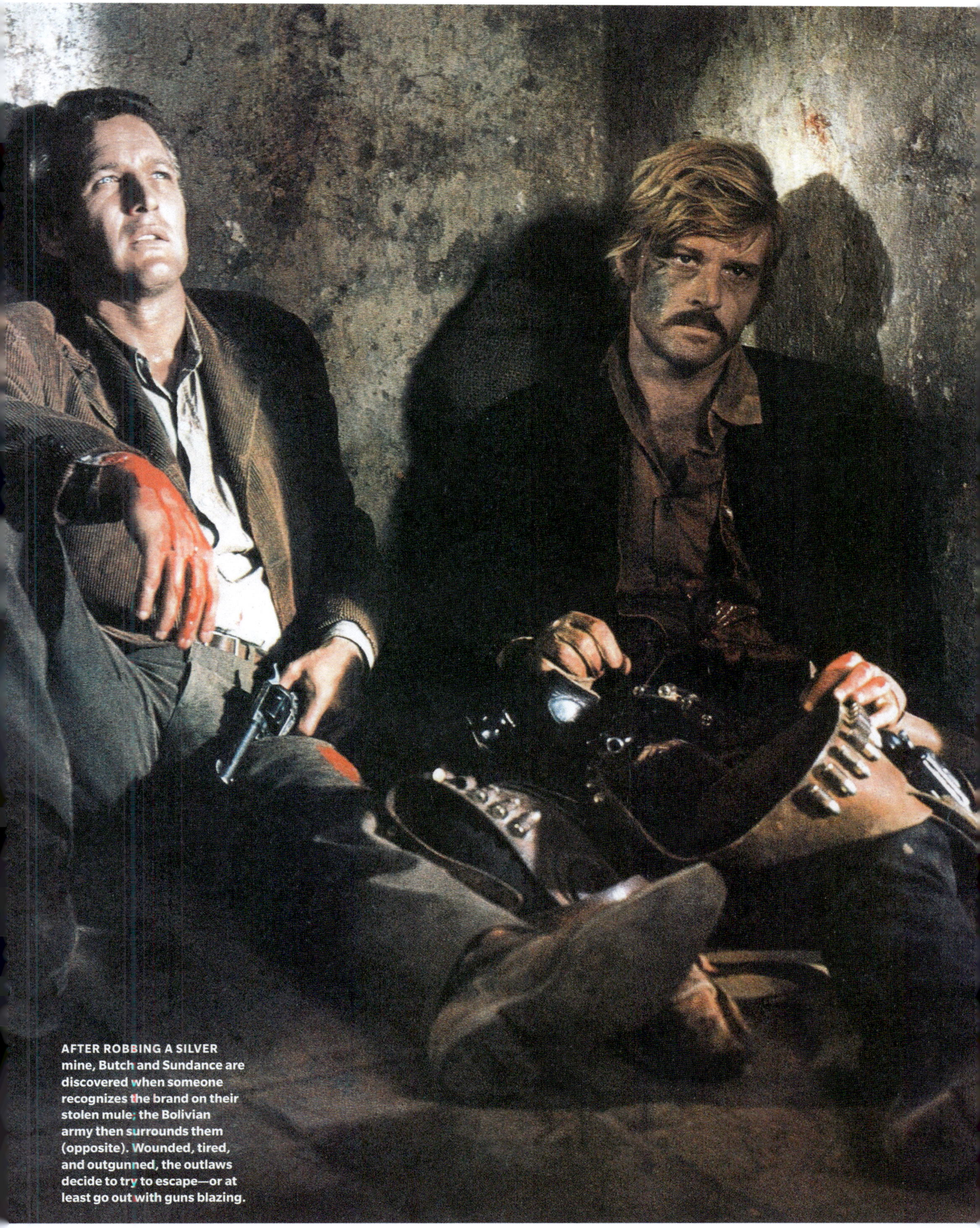

AFTER ROBBING A SILVER mine, Butch and Sundance are discovered when someone recognizes the brand on their stolen mule; the Bolivian army then surrounds them (opposite). Wounded, tired, and outgunned, the outlaws decide to try to escape—or at least go out with guns blazing.

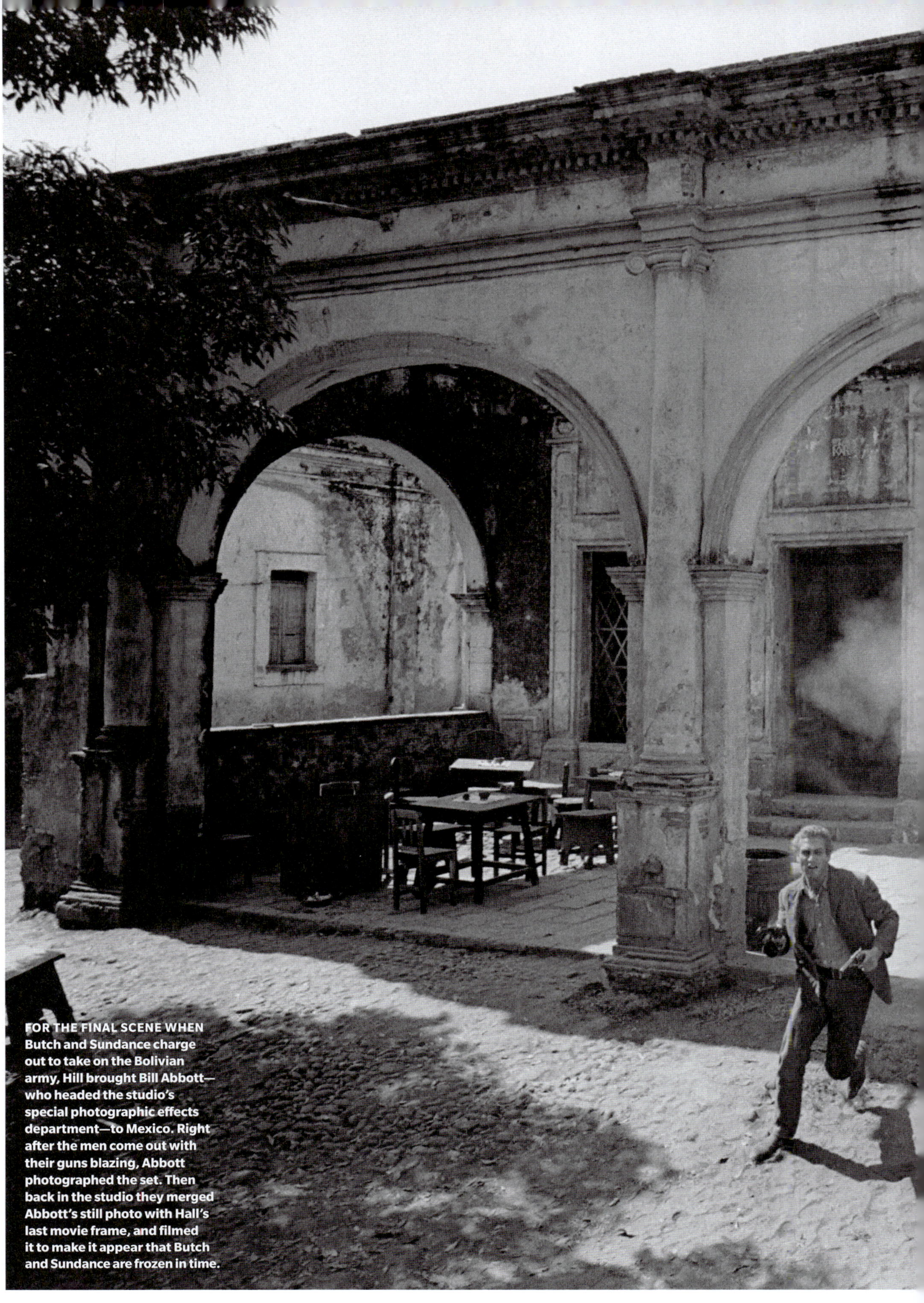

FOR THE FINAL SCENE WHEN Butch and Sundance charge out to take on the Bolivian army, Hill brought Bill Abbott—who headed the studio's special photographic effects department—to Mexico. Right after the men come out with their guns blazing, Abbott photographed the set. Then back in the studio they merged Abbott's still photo with Hall's last movie frame, and filmed it to make it appear that Butch and Sundance are frozen in time.

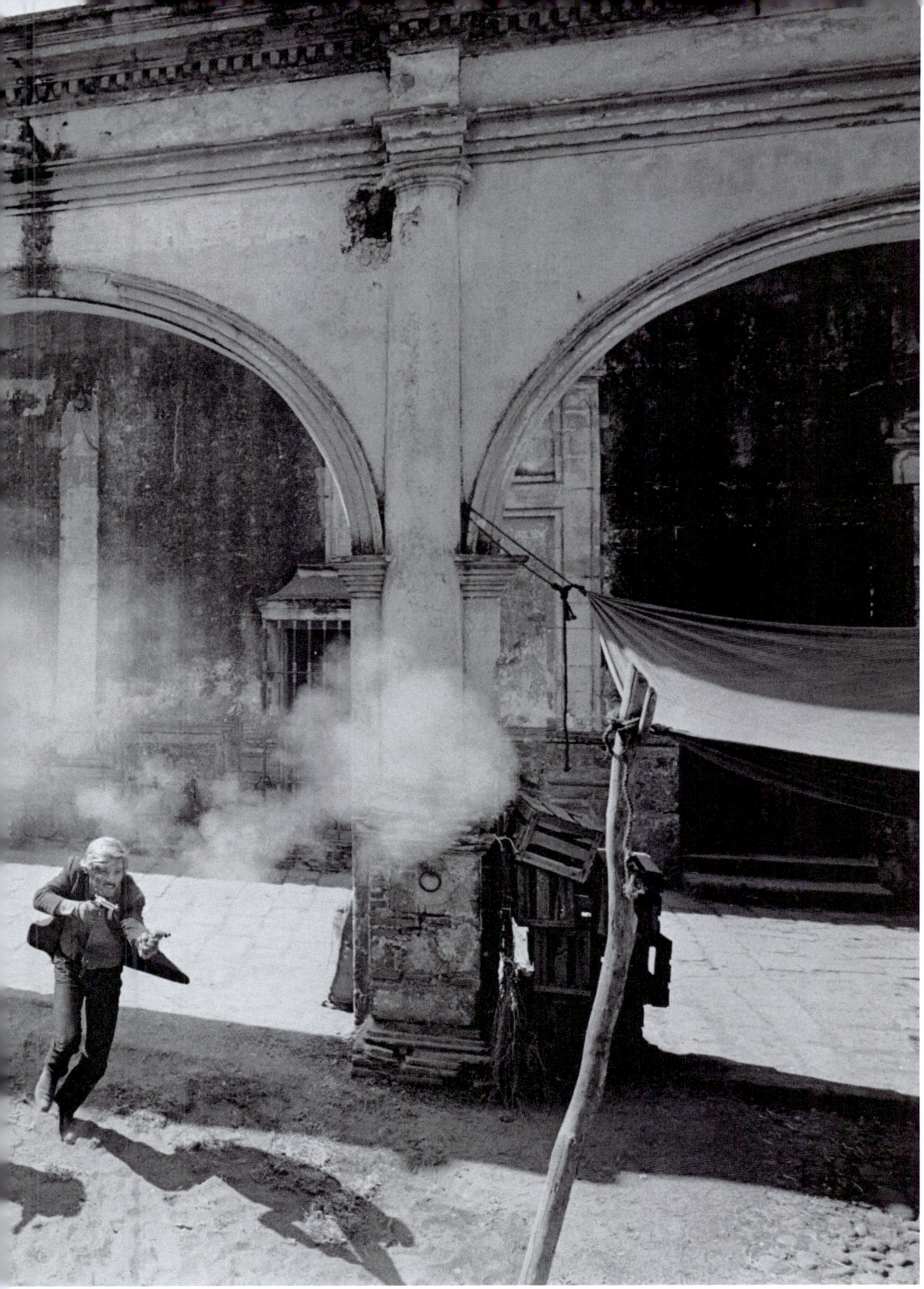

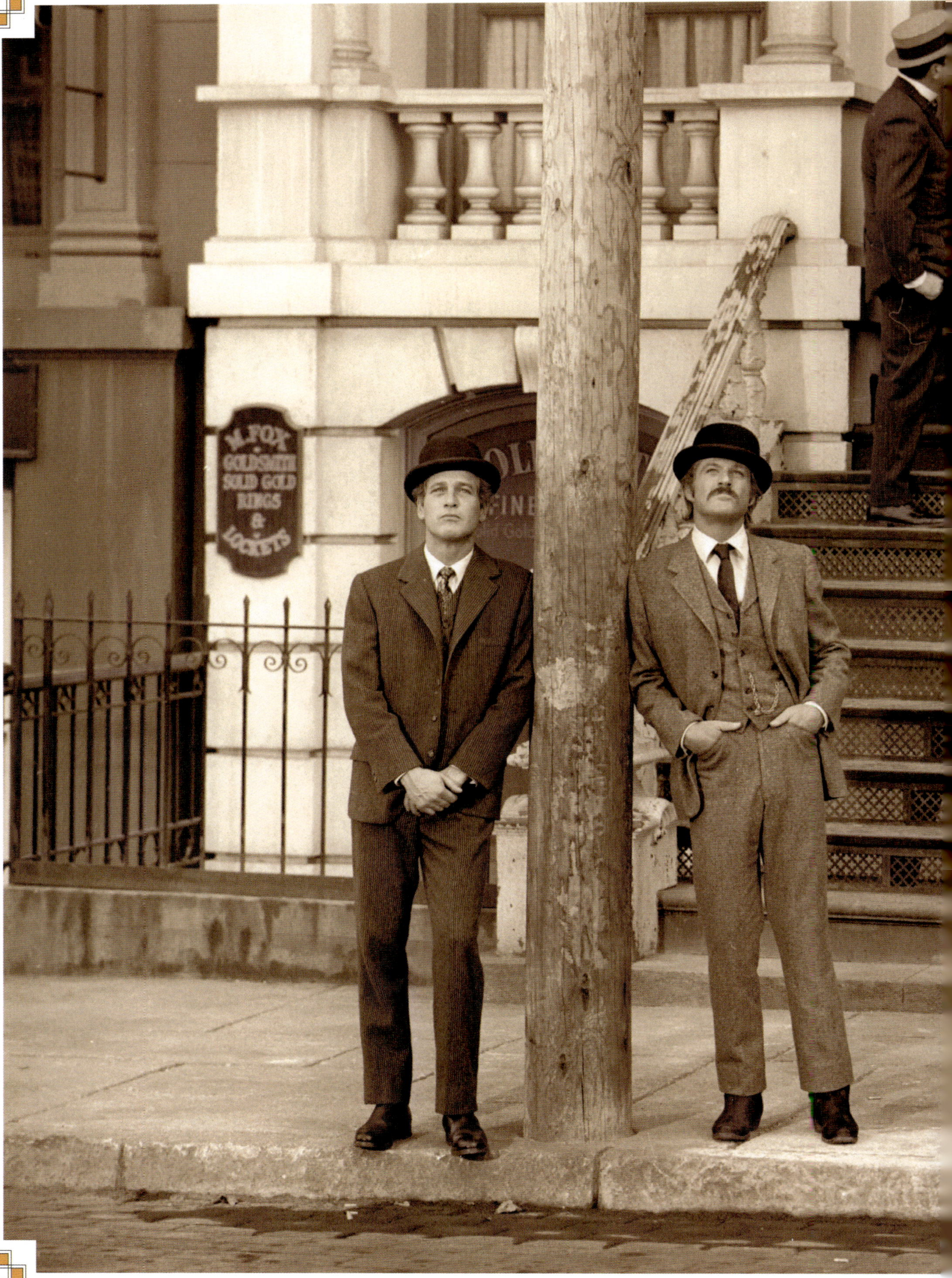
M. FOX
GOLDSMITH
SOLID GOLD
RINGS
&
LOCKETS

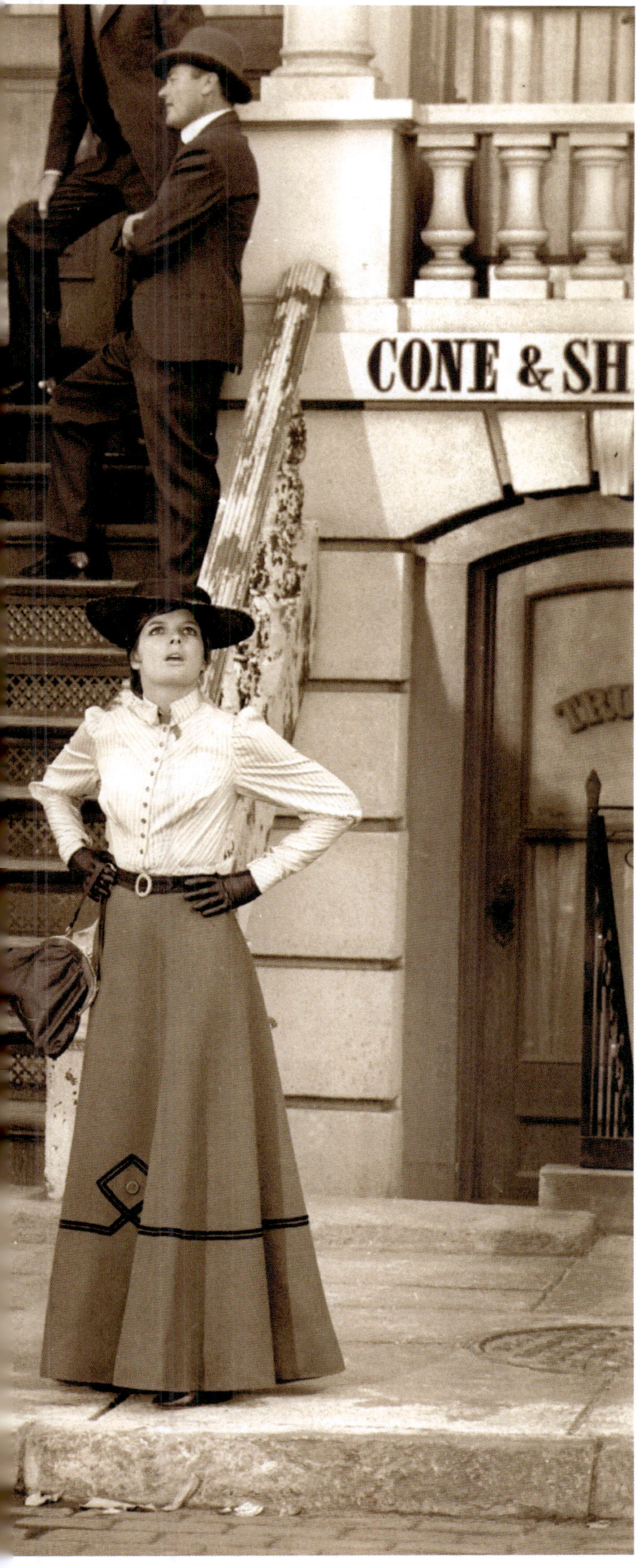

Urban Cowboys

LAWRENCE SCHILLER'S STYLISH ON-SET PHOTOS CAPTURED THE OUTLAWS' SOJOURN IN NEW YORK CITY

LAWRENCE SCHILLER HAD EARNED A living making photographs for LIFE and other publications, as well as for movie studios. He had gotten to know Paul Newman, who said, "Why don't you start shooting motion pictures?" Schiller recalls working on the *Butch Cassidy* set and saying to Newman, "There's something wrong with this script." Butch, Sundance, and Etta moved too fast to Bolivia, Schiller thought. The film should include a photo montage to explain their activities. Producer John Foreman liked the idea and Fox president Richard Zanuck gave the production access to the sets for *Hello Dolly!* while producer Paul Monash let them use those of the TV series *Peyton Place.* Schiller photographed the stars. Some images he printed unaltered. Others he superimposed onto period photos. He then filmed the segment. While *New York Times* critic Vincent Canby was no fan of *Butch Cassidy,* he praised Schiller's "lovely five-minute montage." What follows is a collection of images, some rarely seen, from that shoot.

WITH ACCESS TO SETS FOR *Hello Dolly!* Lawrence Schiller shot Newman, Redford, and Ross in a series of New York City street scenes.

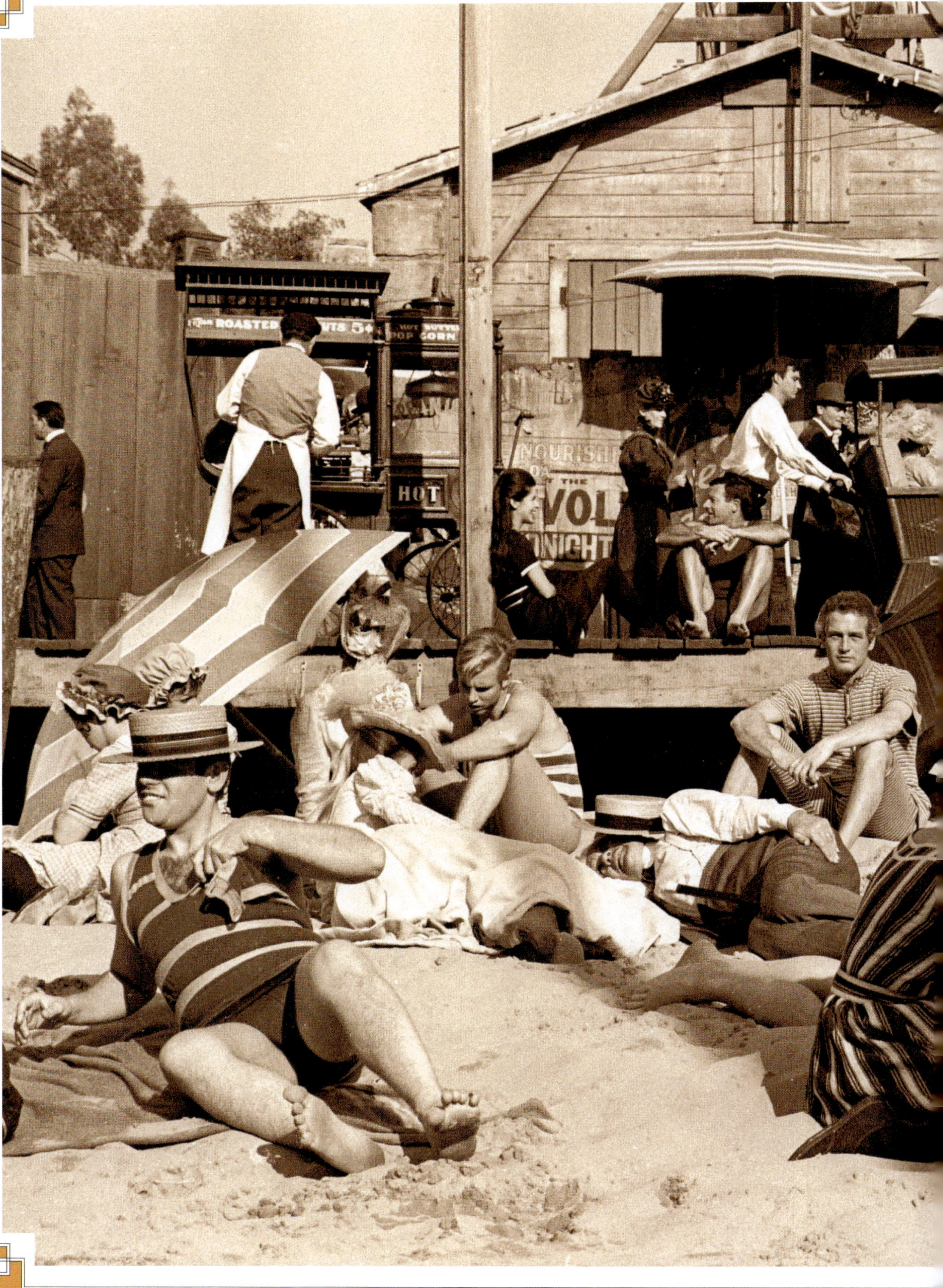
ROASTED
POP CORN
HOT
NOURISH
VOL
NIGHT

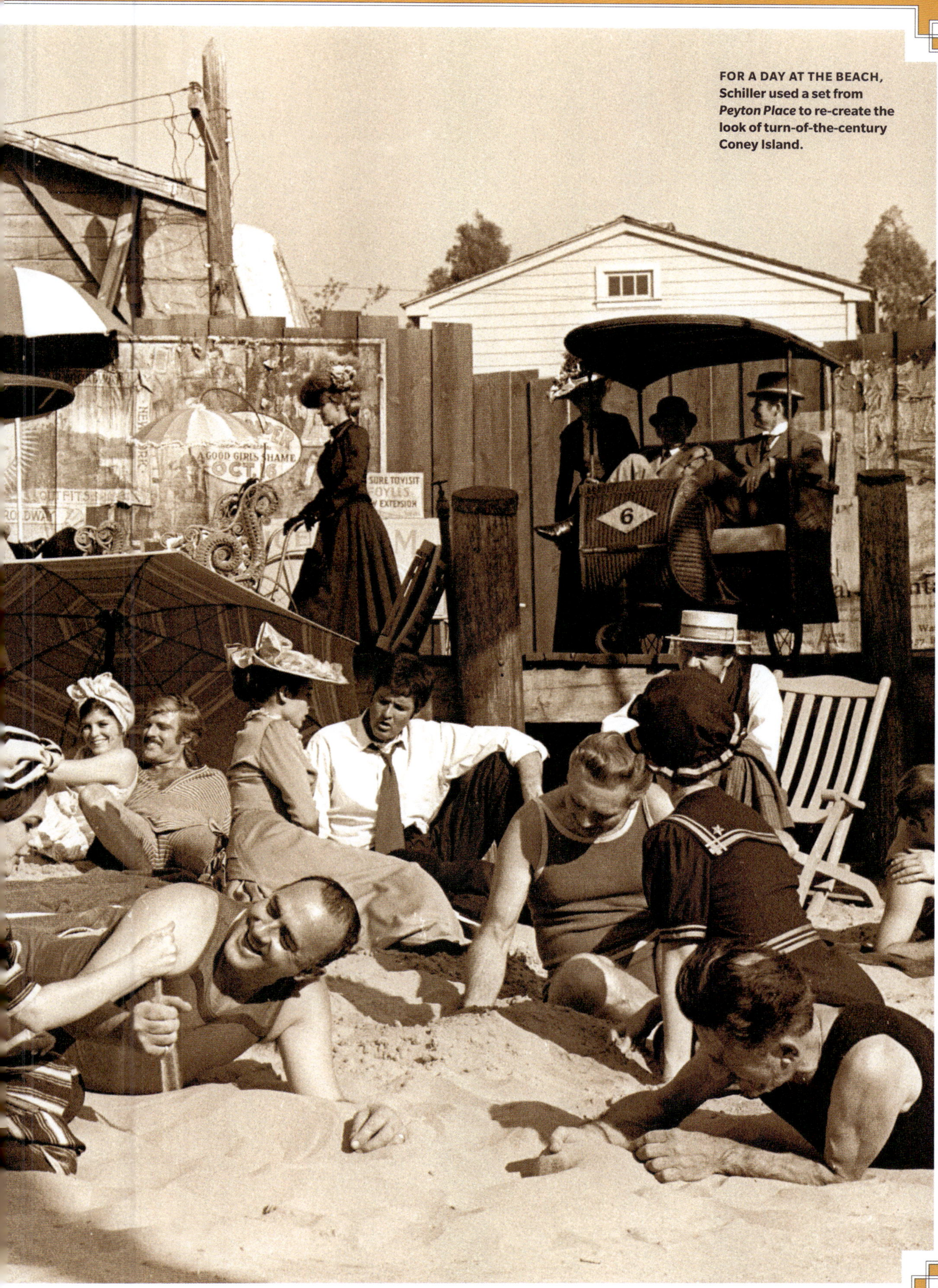

FOR A DAY AT THE BEACH, Schiller used a set from *Peyton Place* to re-create the look of turn-of-the-century Coney Island.

WITH A $250,000 BUDGET, Schiller had sets built and used backdrops to photograph Etta and Butch at the Brooklyn beach, and Butch, Etta, and Sundance rowing on Central Park's lake.

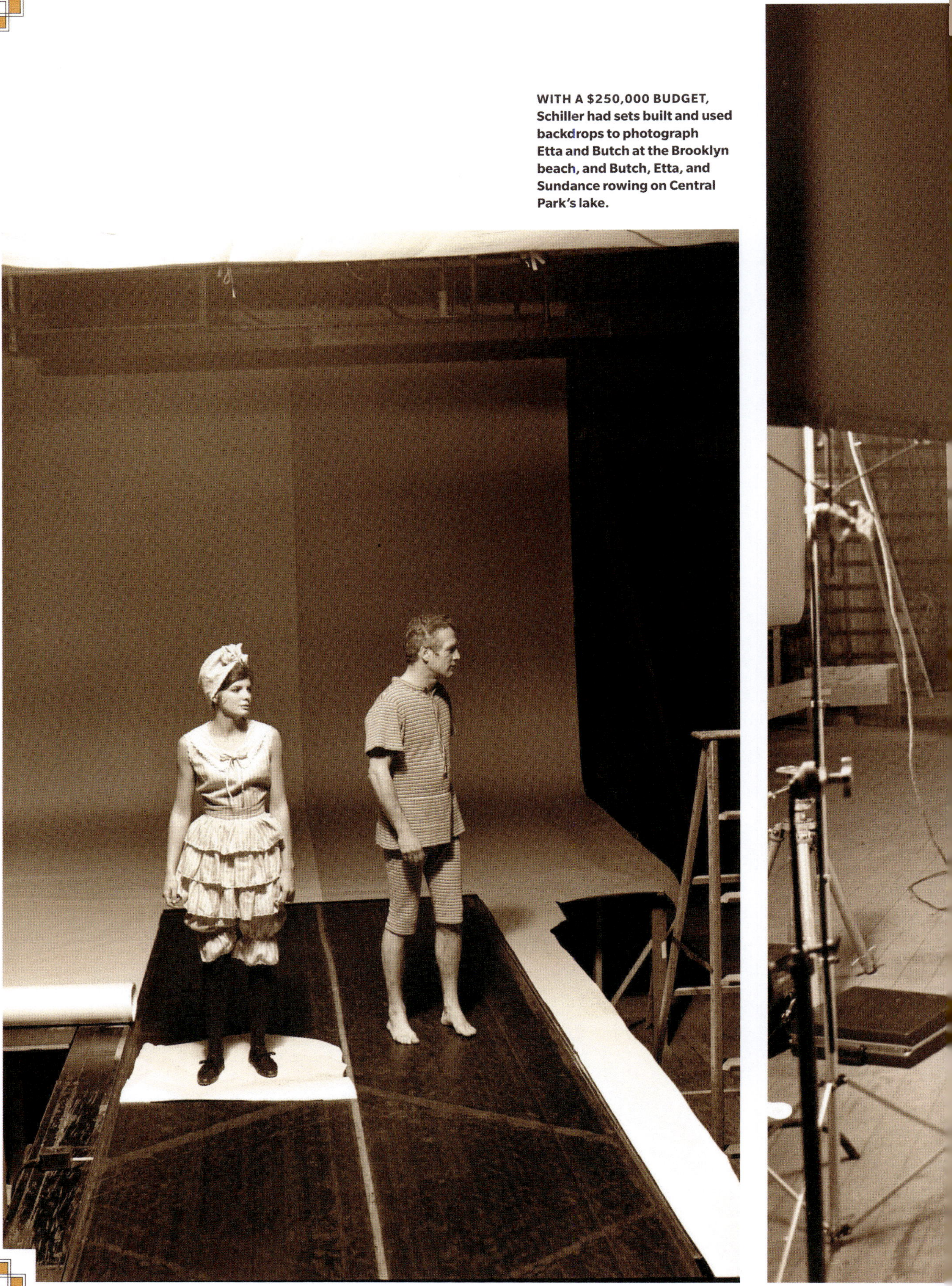

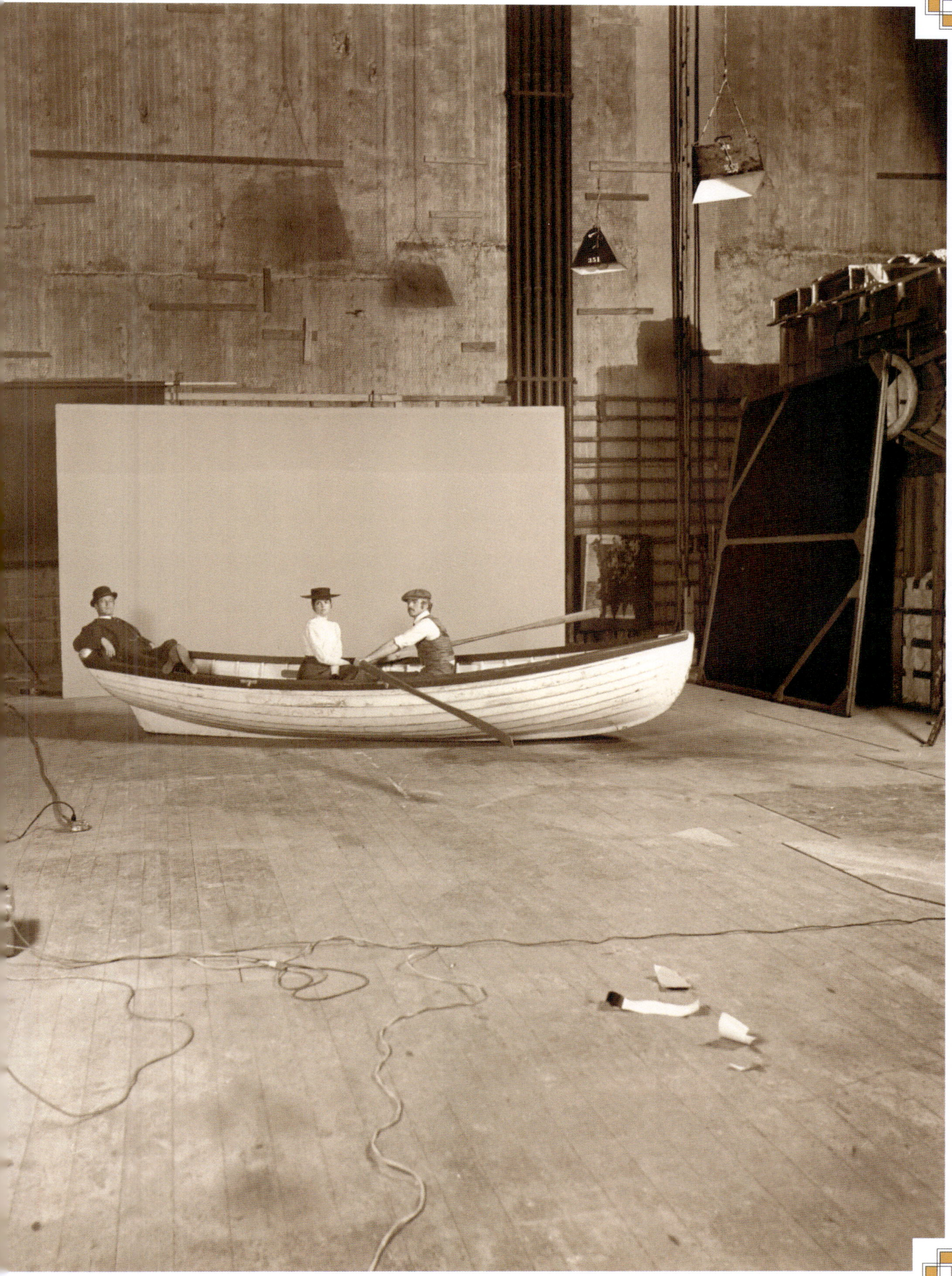

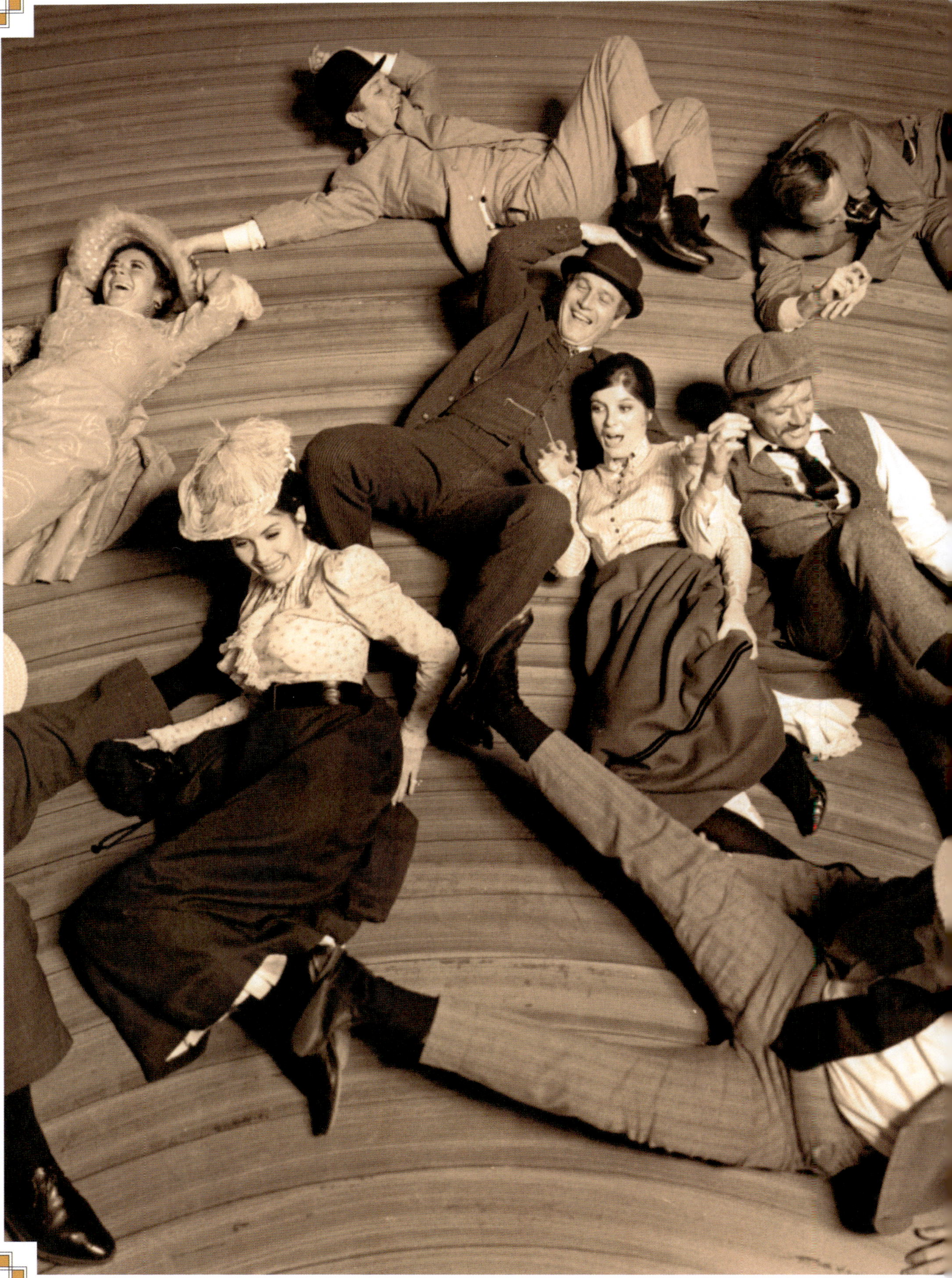

SCHILLER USED PLYWOOD TO re-create the Human Roulette Wheel at Steeplechase Park's Pavilion of Fun, left, and had the trio take a look at the newfangled horseless carriage, below, which proved to be all the rage at the turn of the century.

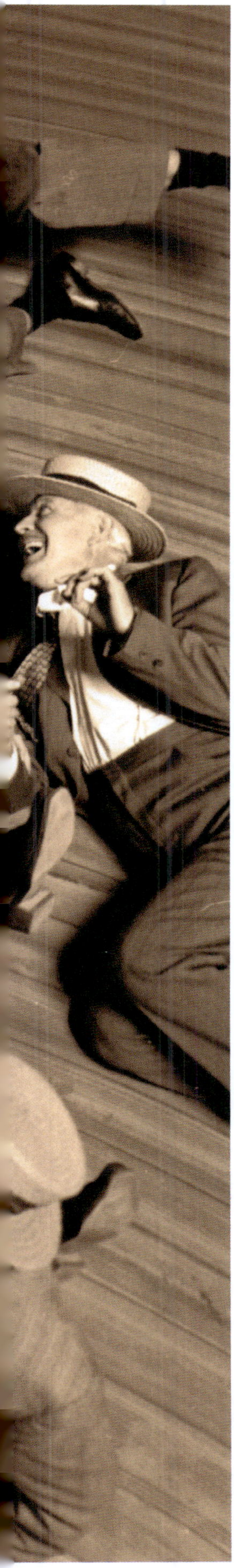

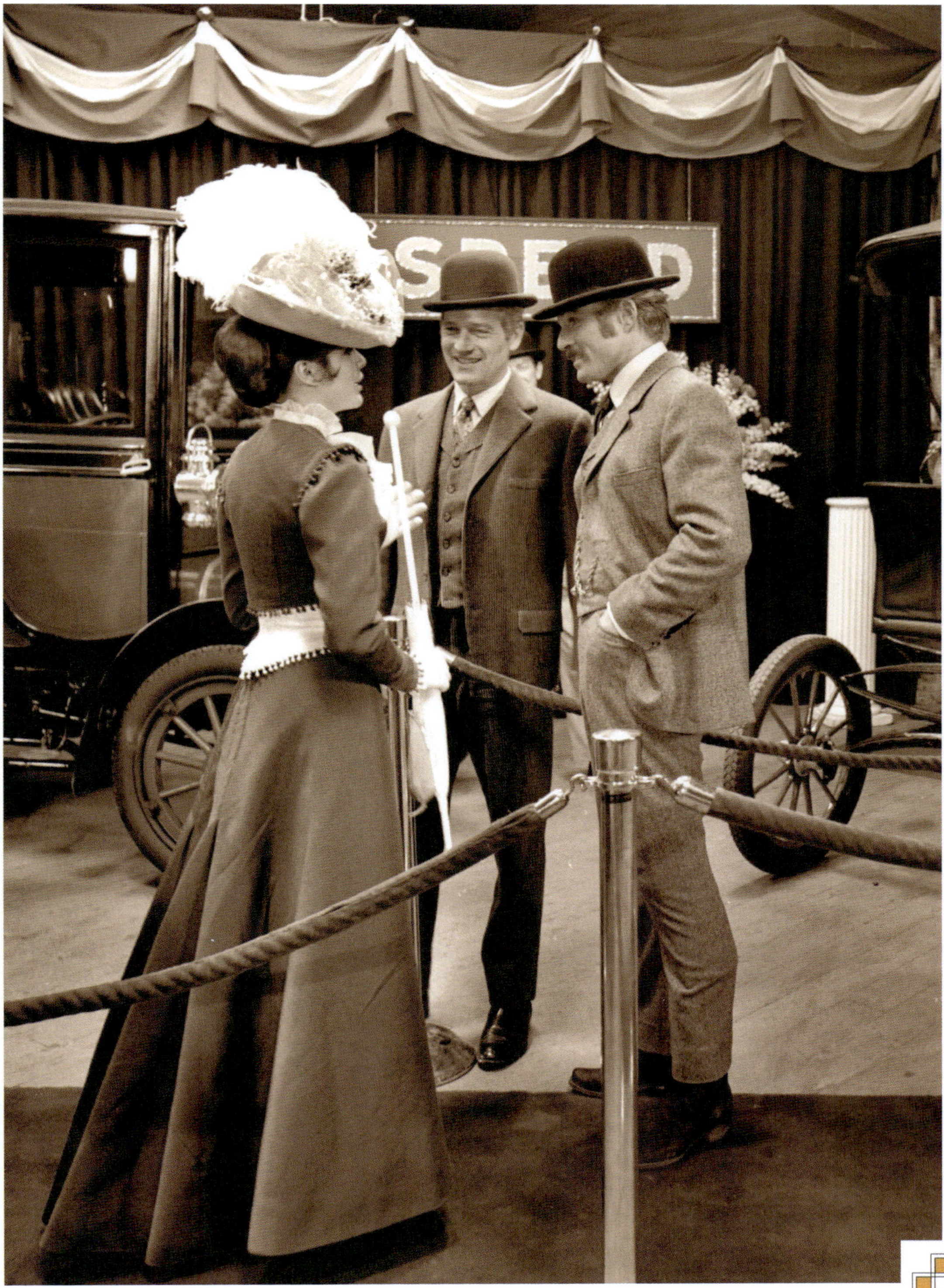

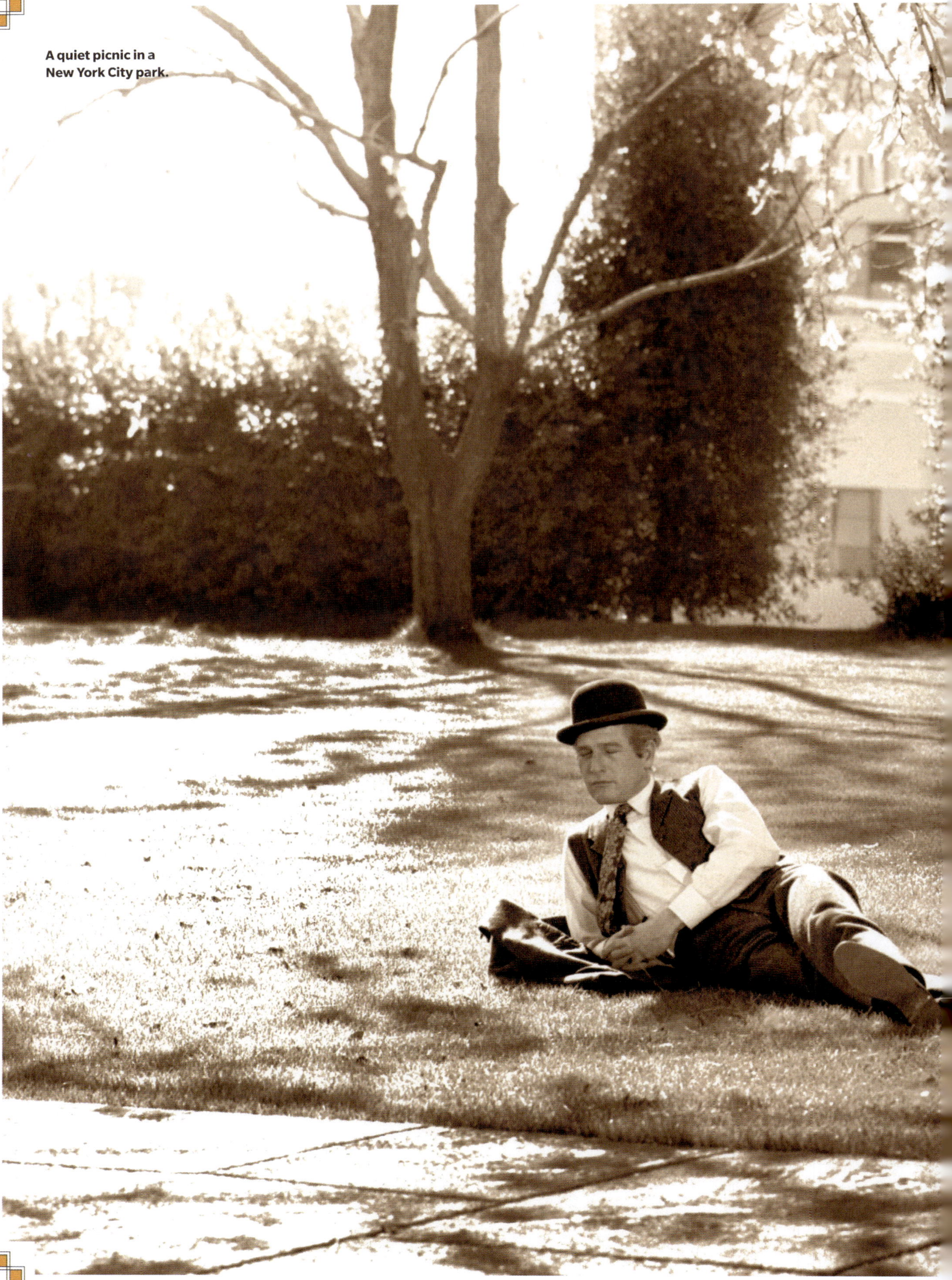

A quiet picnic in a New York City park.

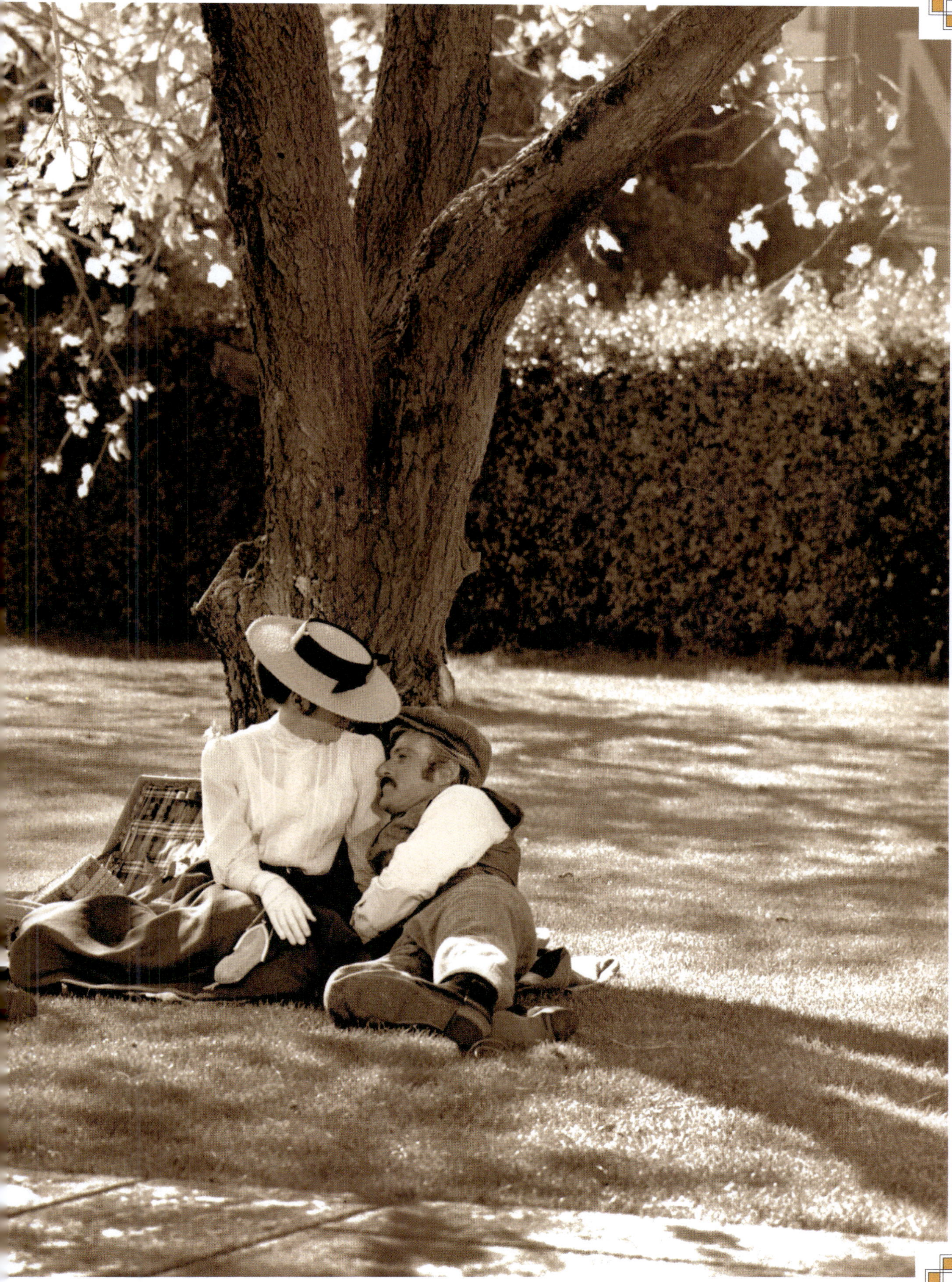

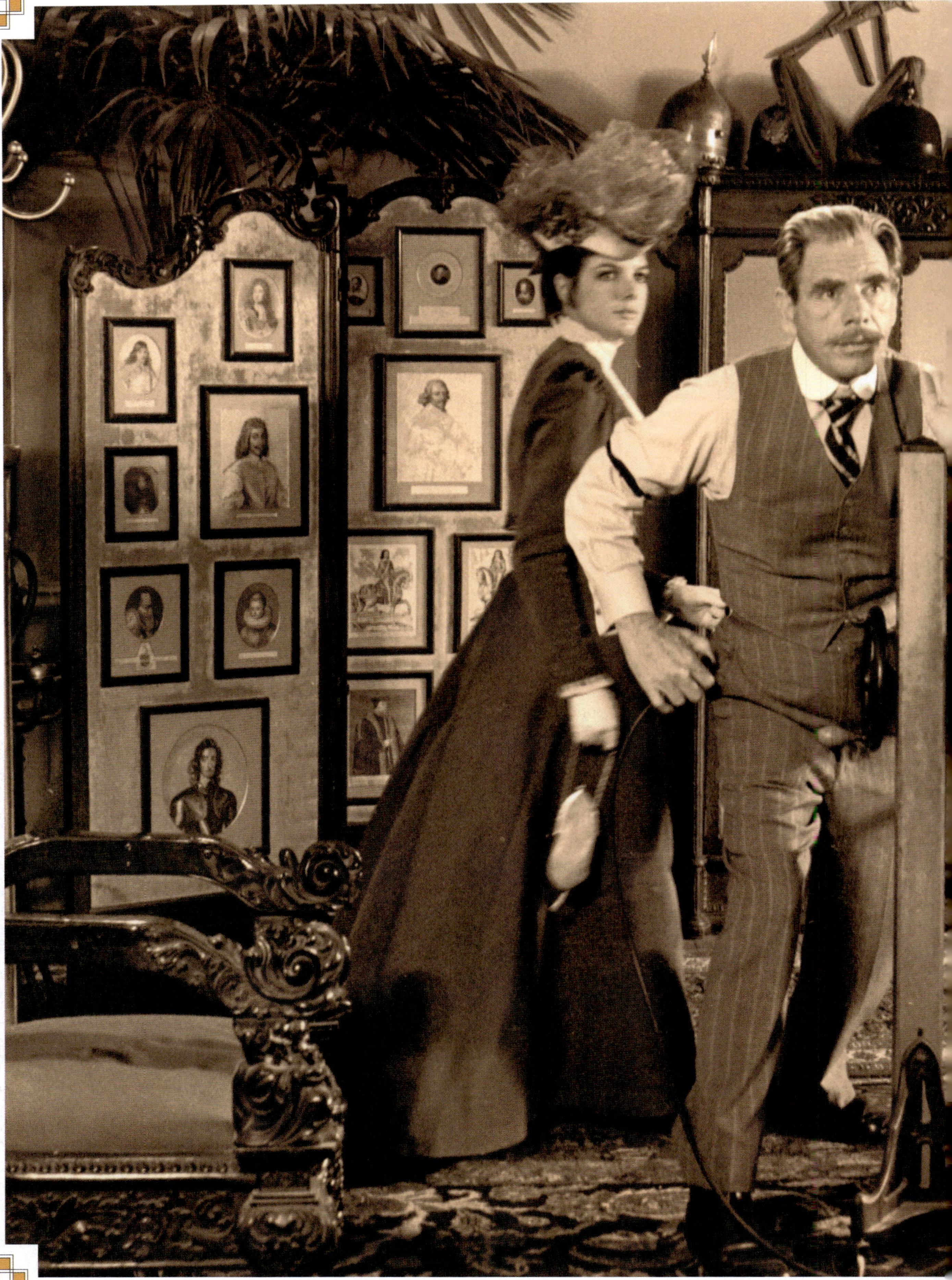

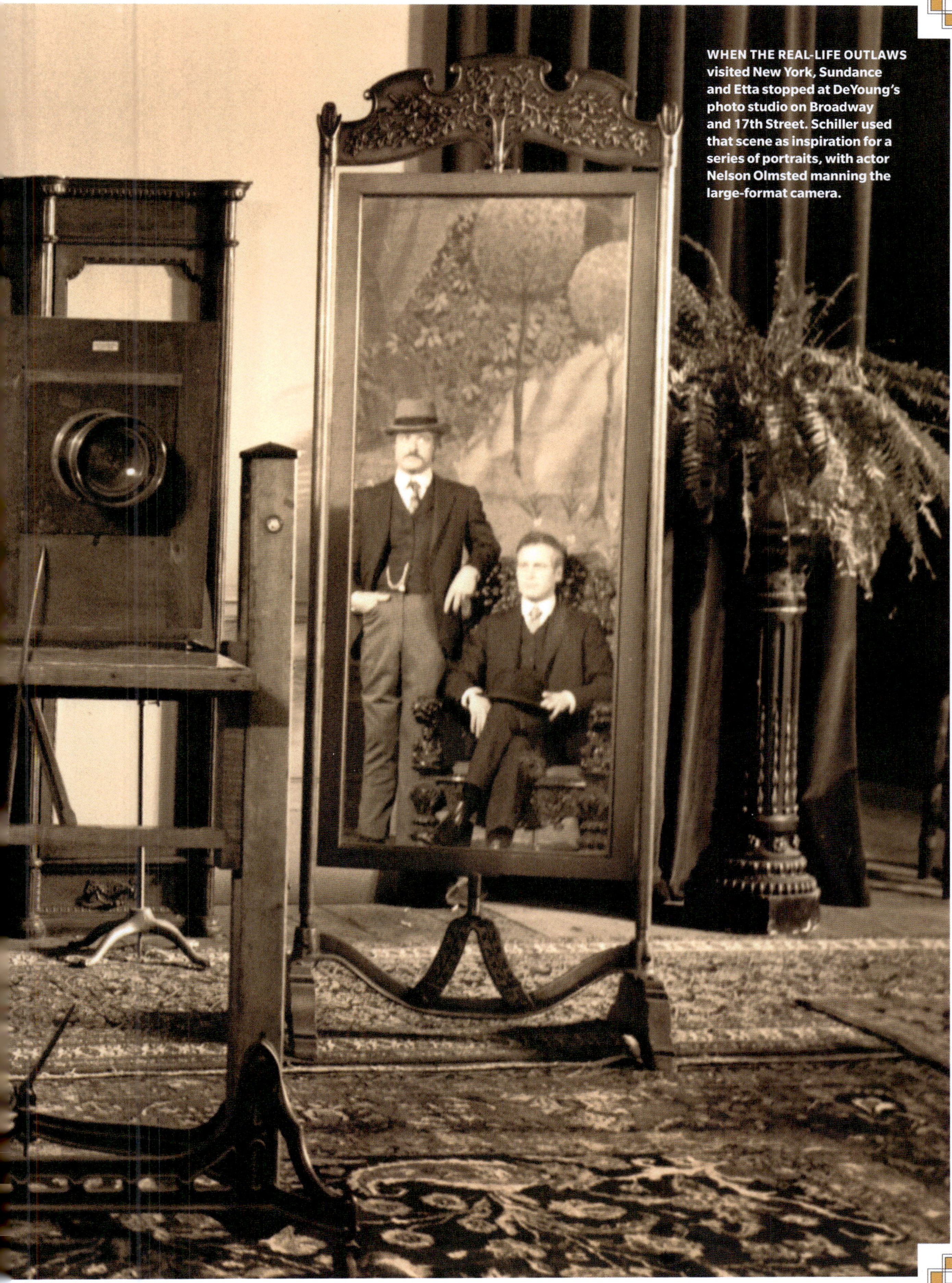

WHEN THE REAL-LIFE OUTLAWS visited New York, Sundance and Etta stopped at DeYoung's photo studio on Broadway and 17th Street. Schiller used that scene as inspiration for a series of portraits, with actor Nelson Olmsted manning the large-format camera.

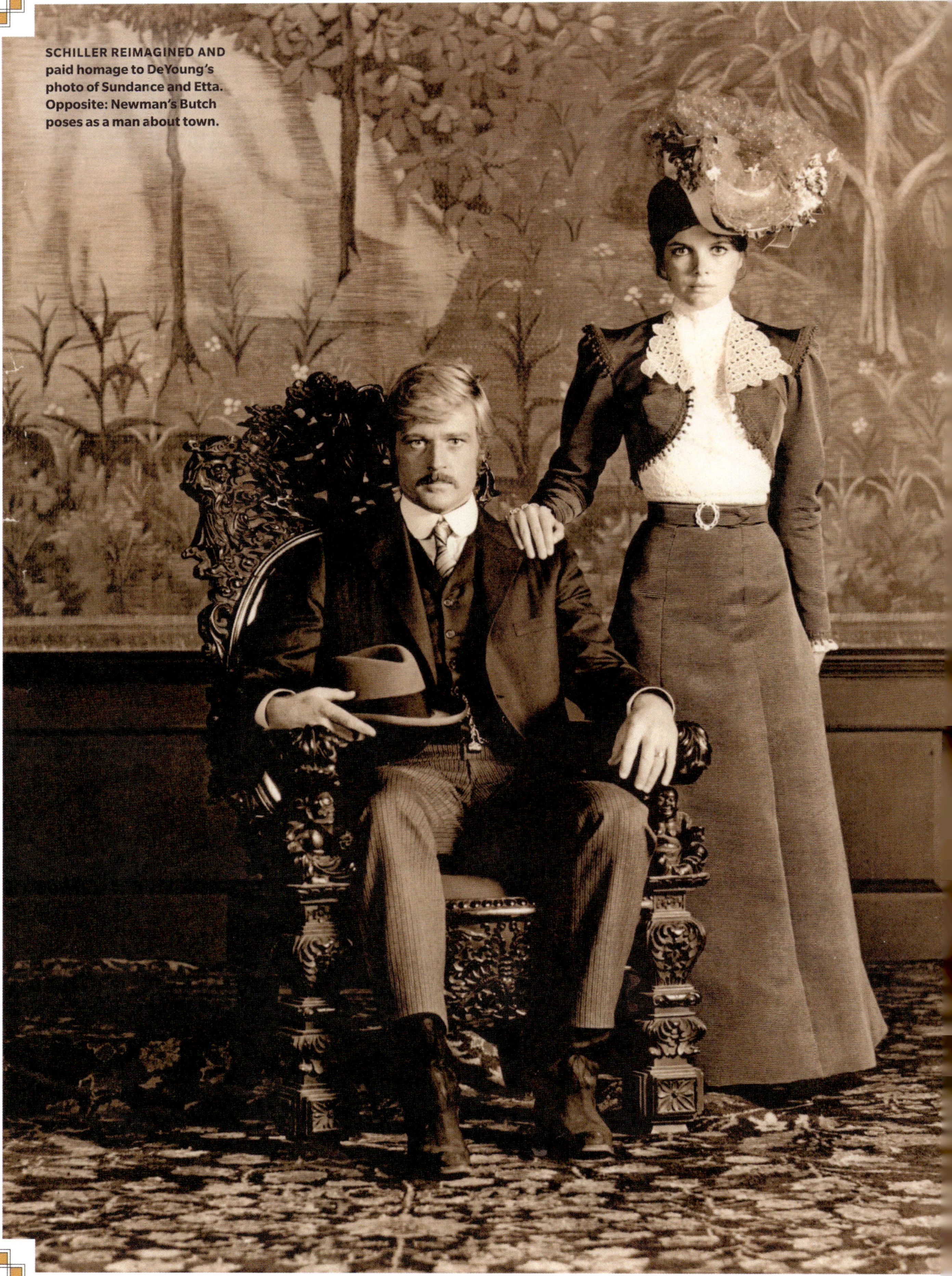

SCHILLER REIMAGINED AND paid homage to DeYoung's photo of Sundance and Etta. Opposite: Newman's Butch poses as a man about town.

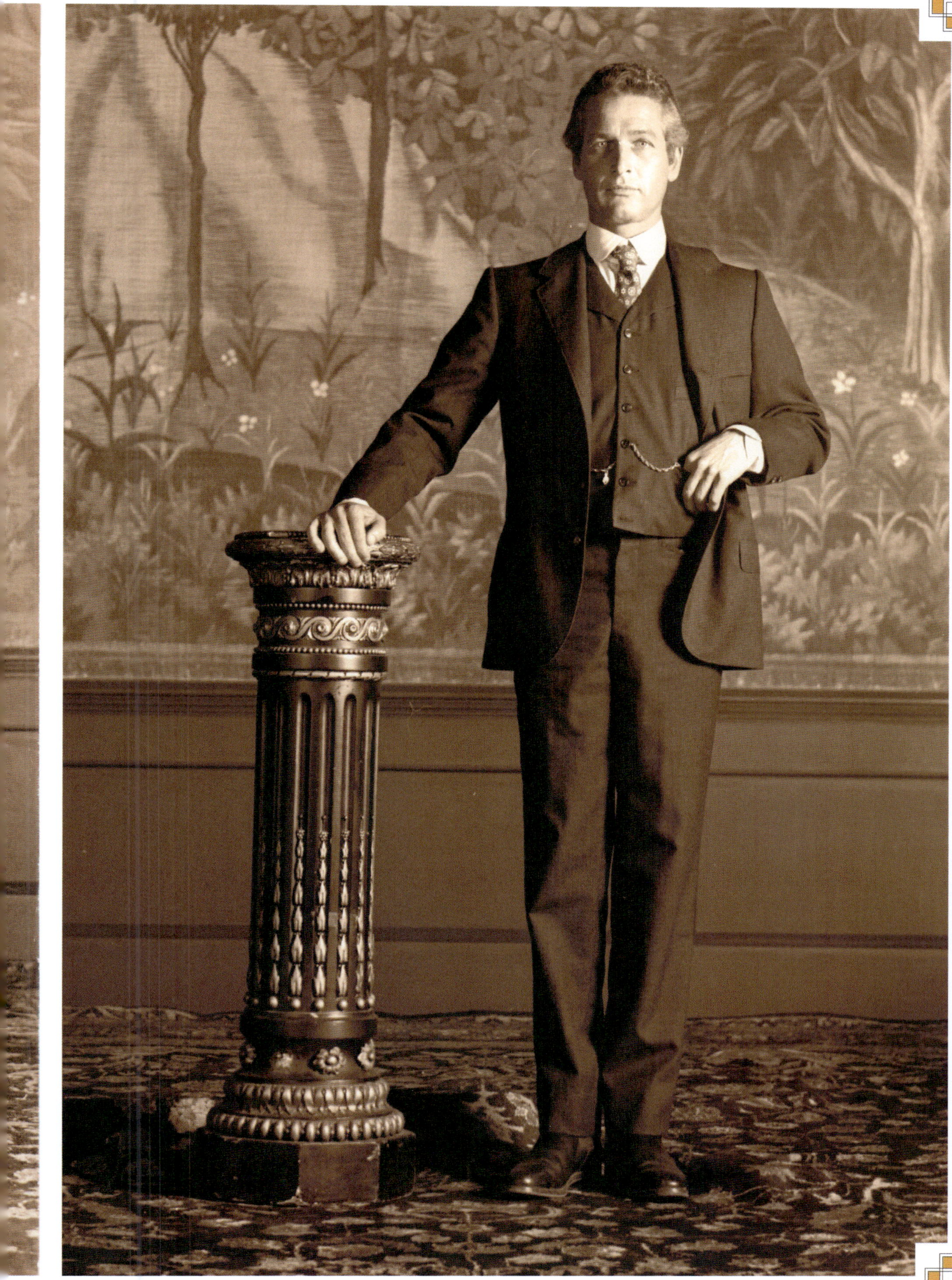

CHAPTER THREE

FROM CINEMA SMASH TO CULTURAL ICON

SOME HIT FILMS ARE QUICKLY FORGOTTEN, BUT *BUTCH CASSIDY* WOULD HAVE A LASTING LEGACY, MAKING A SUPERSTAR OF ROBERT REDFORD AND CREATING A MODEL FOR THE MOVIE BROMANCE

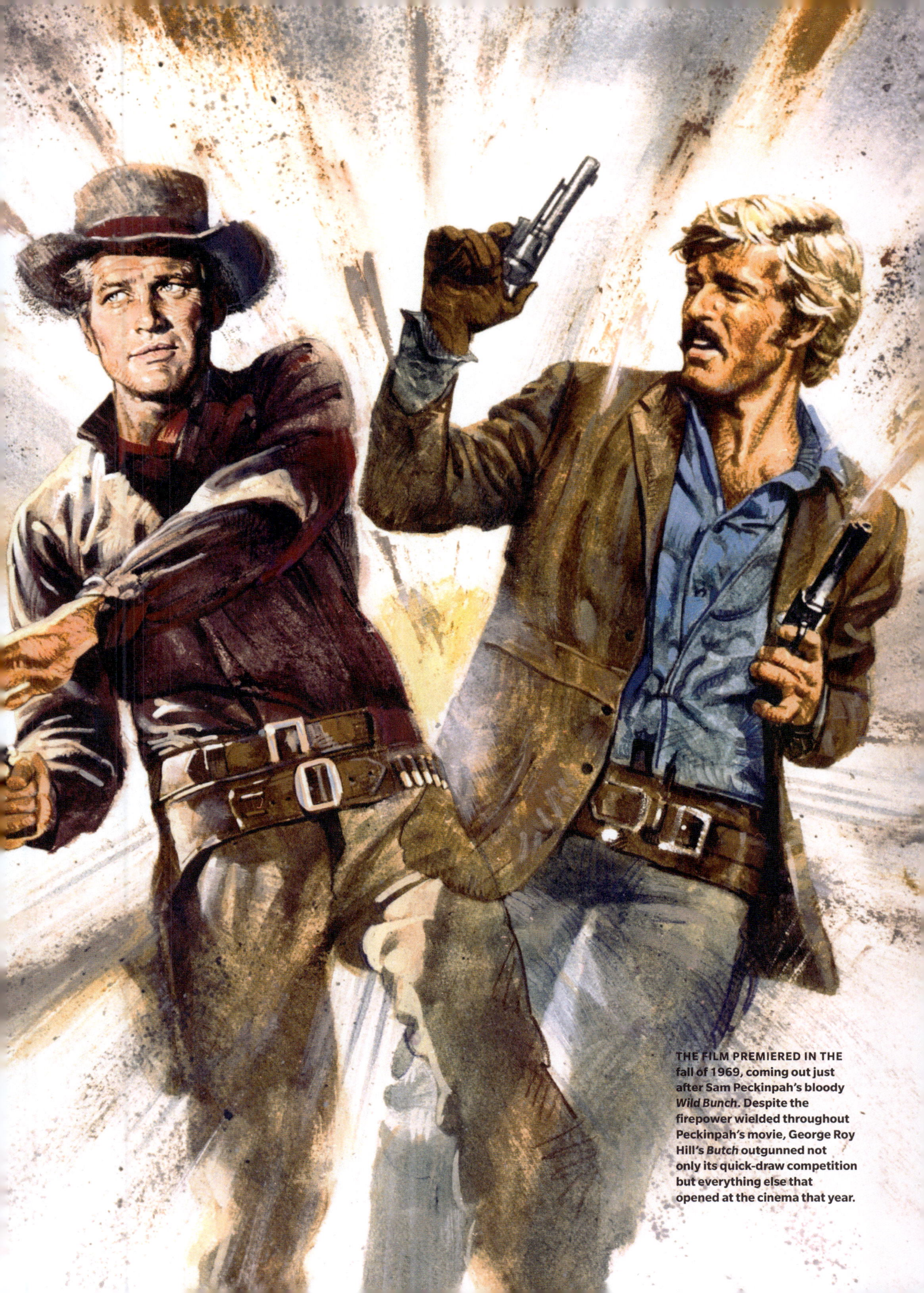

THE FILM PREMIERED IN THE fall of 1969, coming out just after Sam Peckinpah's bloody *Wild Bunch*. Despite the firepower wielded throughout Peckinpah's movie, George Roy Hill's *Butch* outgunned not only its quick-draw competition but everything else that opened at the cinema that year.

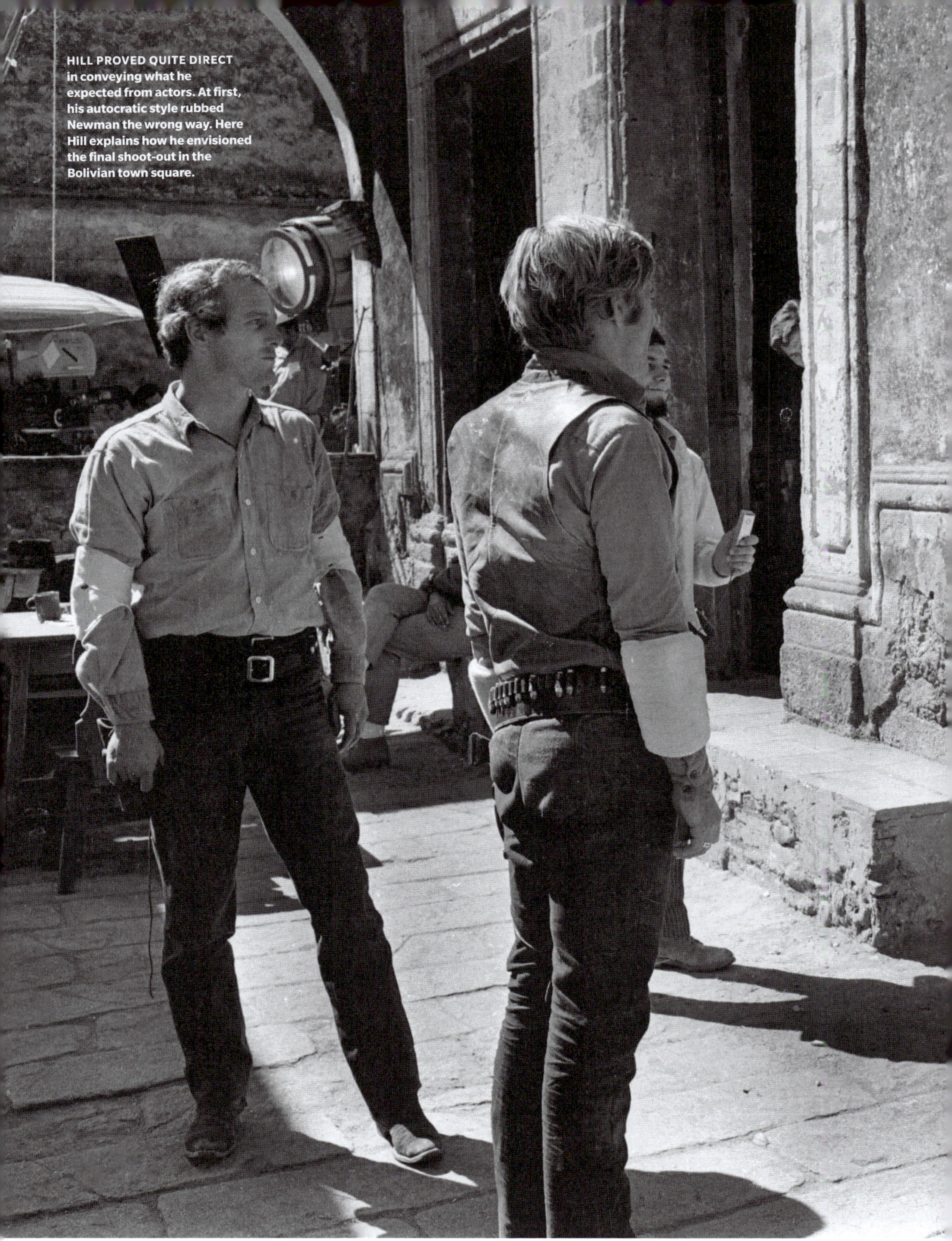

HILL PROVED QUITE DIRECT in conveying what he expected from actors. At first, his autocratic style rubbed Newman the wrong way. Here Hill explains how he envisioned the final shoot-out in the Bolivian town square.

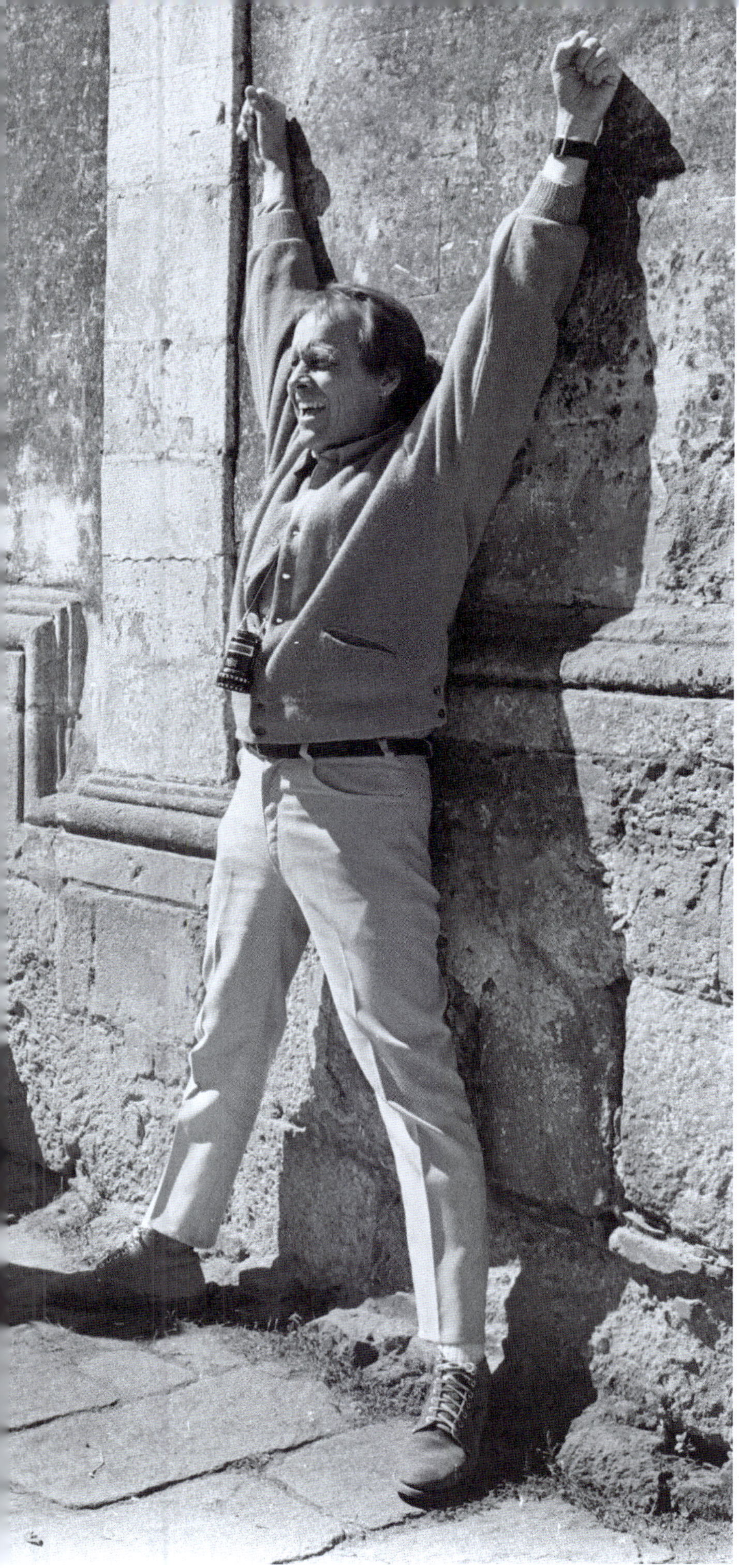

B

BUTCH CASSIDY AND THE SUNDANCE KID is a classic buddy movie in the spirit of Bob Hope and Bing Crosby's comedic *Road* films. While the heroes rob and blow things up, they spend much of their time verbally fencing like an old married couple, giving the film a campy, breezy quality. But during the first previews, audiences found it a little too funny, at least for director George Hill. "They laughed at my tragedy," he lamented—and he took out some of the wisecracks.

Throughout, Hill's film defies conventions. Divided into three parts—the American heists, the posse chase, and the South American sojourn—it's an antiestablishment flick but has no sex to speak of and just one (memorable) curse word. And for a Western, there is limited action and violence, with only two real gunfights. The opening part is shot in sepia. There are three wordless musical montages, and it features a pop tune. Parts of the film also appear to reference François Truffaut's 1962 French New Wave masterpiece *Jules and Jim,* with its love triangle, and the final freeze-frame looks like it came from Truffaut's 1959 *The 400 Blows.*

To be sure, *Butch Cassidy* differs sharply from its obvious competition. As Hill was making the movie, Sam Peckinpah was filming *The Wild Bunch.* Both reference the idea of a vanishing

West. But while *Butch Cassidy* is good natured, *The Wild Bunch* is a bloodbath. To get out ahead of Hill's film, Warner rushed Peckinpah's to theaters by June 1969. Vincent Canby in the *New York Times* praised it as "very beautiful and the first truly interesting American-made Western in years." Yet Canby couldn't help but comment that *The Wild Bunch* is "full of violence—of an intensity that can hardly be supported by the story." Two months later, and a month before *Butch Cassidy* appeared in theaters, Jay Sebring, who styled Newman's hair in the film, was supposed to join Steve McQueen for a dinner at the home of director Roman Polanski and his actress wife, Sharon Tate. As it turned out, McQueen ended up skipping the get-together—fortunately for him, because that evening members of Charles Manson's Family invaded the house and killed Sebring, Tate, and everyone else there (Polanski was out of the country).

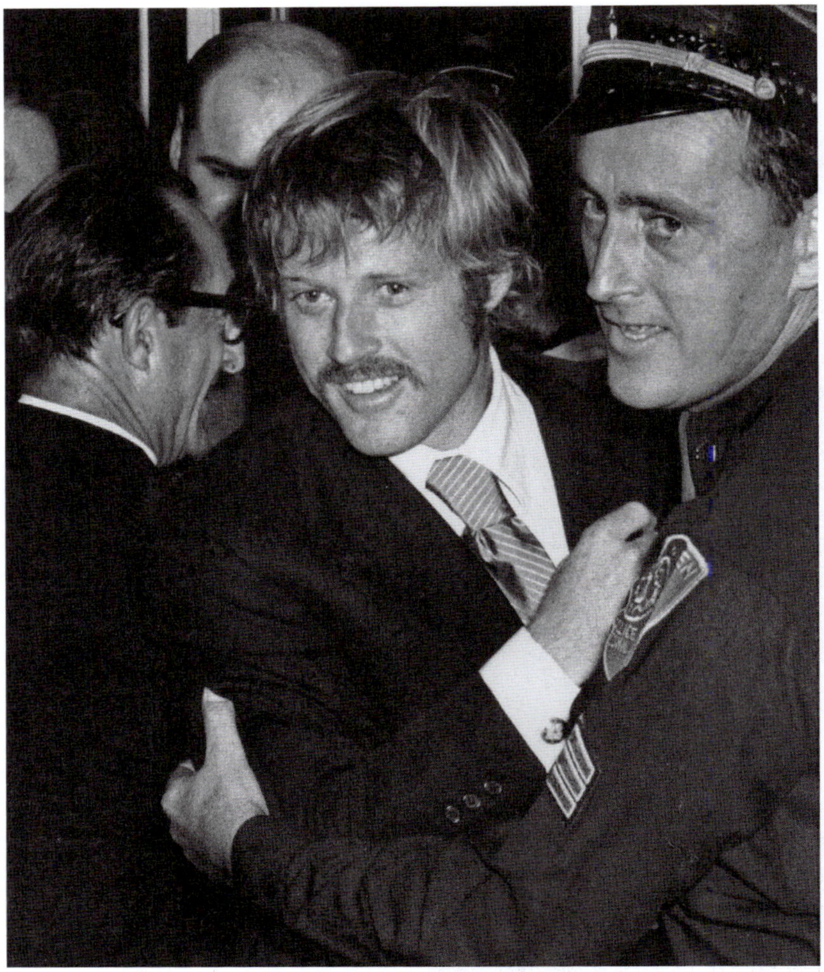

BUTCH CASSIDY AND THE *Sundance Kid* opened in Durango, Colorado, on September 2, 1969, and was then screened three weeks later at Hill's alma mater, Yale University. "We drove up in a limo with George, and there was this milling crowd," recalled Redford of the 6,000 people who turned out. "When we got out, it was terrifying. Pushing, shoving, screaming. The bleachers were overturned." Crowds mobbed Newman and his wife, Joanne Woodward. When they saw Redford, someone yelled out, "Get his hair... get his hair." Barbra Streisand, a close friend of the Newmans', had her dress ripped and needed the help of four policemen to get into the theater.

A calmer postscreening party took place at Mory's, a Yale watering hole, followed the next morning by breakfast in the school's President's Room. Butch's sister Lula Parker Betenson attended as a guest of Newman and Redford's, and when asked what she thought of the film, she replied, "A lot of it is pretty silly." Hill, Goldman, Newman, and Redford then took part in a film seminar. Afterward, Newman, who had spent a year at Yale Drama School, walked around the campus and posed for pictures with the student body, which, he was pleased to note, had gone coed that semester.

THE FILM RECEIVED MIXED REVIEWS. ROGER EBERT OF THE *CHICAGO SUN-TIMES* CALLED IT "SLOW AND DISAPPOINTING."

The film received mixed reviews. "Paul Newman and Robert Redford are afflicted with cinematic schizophrenia," scoffed *Time* magazine. "One moment they are sinewy, battered remnants of a discarded tradition. The next they are low comedians whose chaffing relationship—and dialogue—could have been lifted from a Batman and Robin episode." Canby in the *Times* wrote: "There is thus, at the heart of *Butch Cassidy*, a gnawing emptiness that can't be satisfied by an awareness that Hill and Goldman probably knew exactly what they were doing—making a very slick movie." And Roger Ebert at the *Chicago Sun-Times* noted, "*Butch Cassidy and the Sundance Kid* must have looked like a natural on paper, but, alas, the completed film is slow and disappointing."

By the time Newman and Redford's Butch and Sundance appeared, the Western was declining in America. John Wayne would win his only

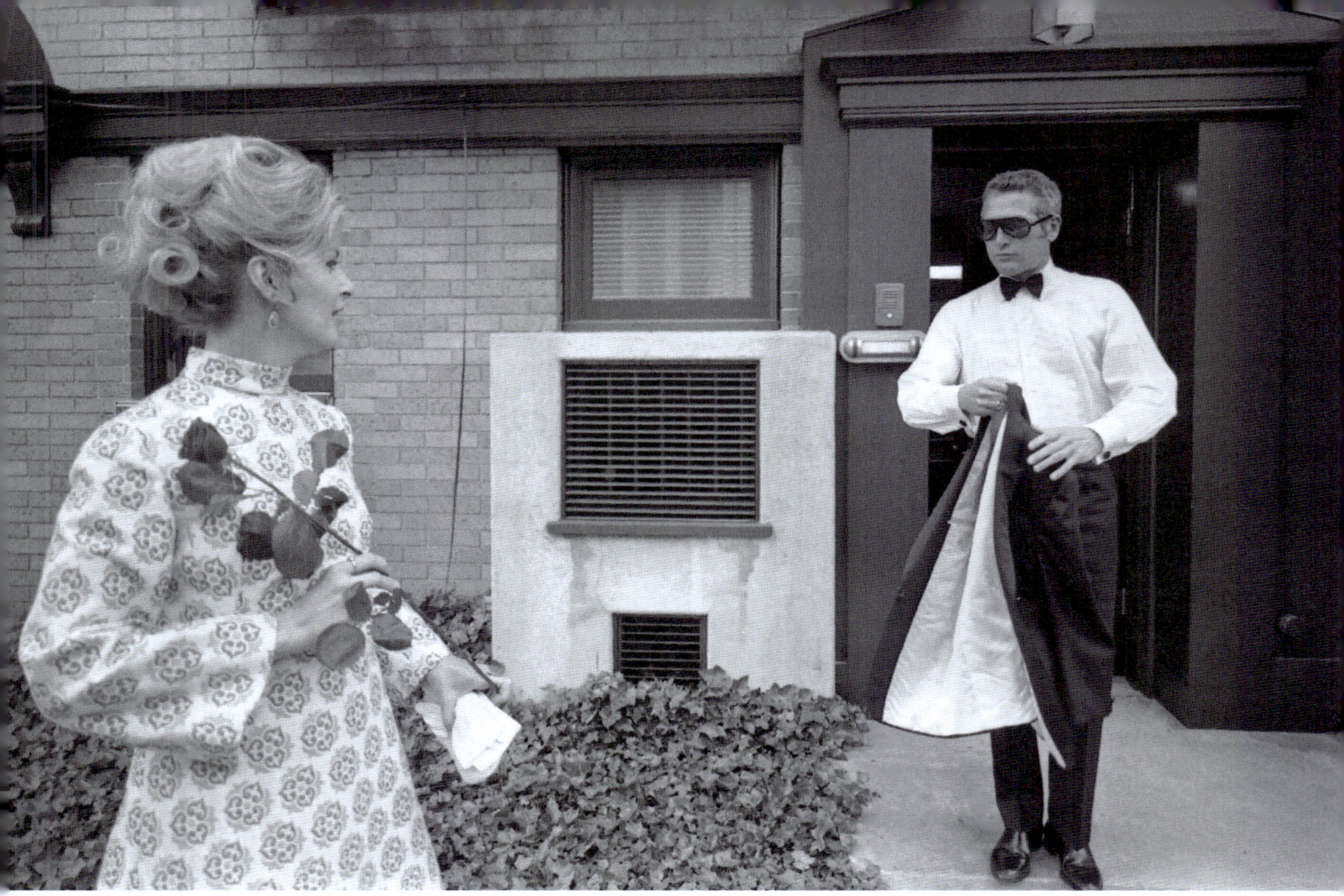

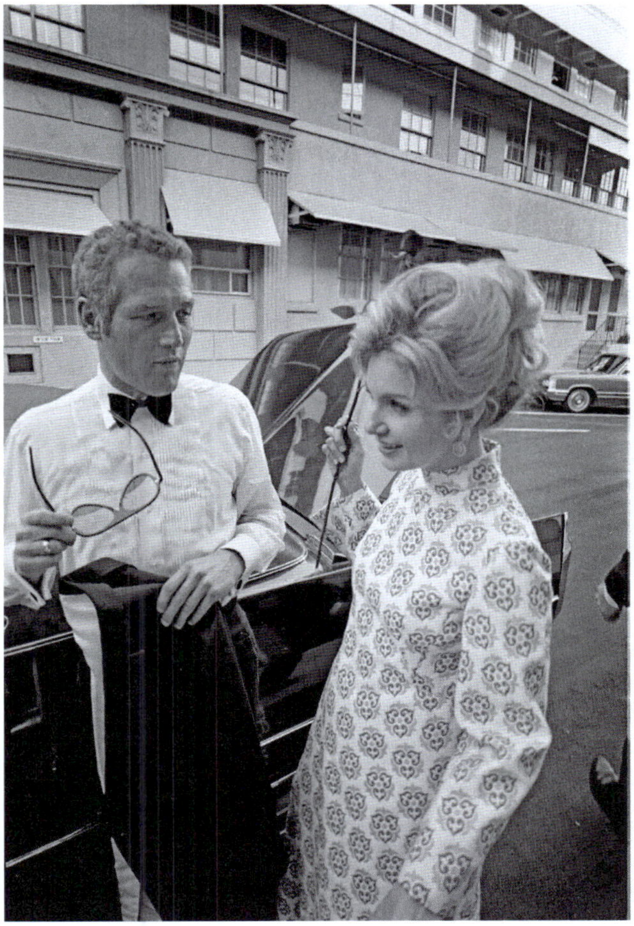

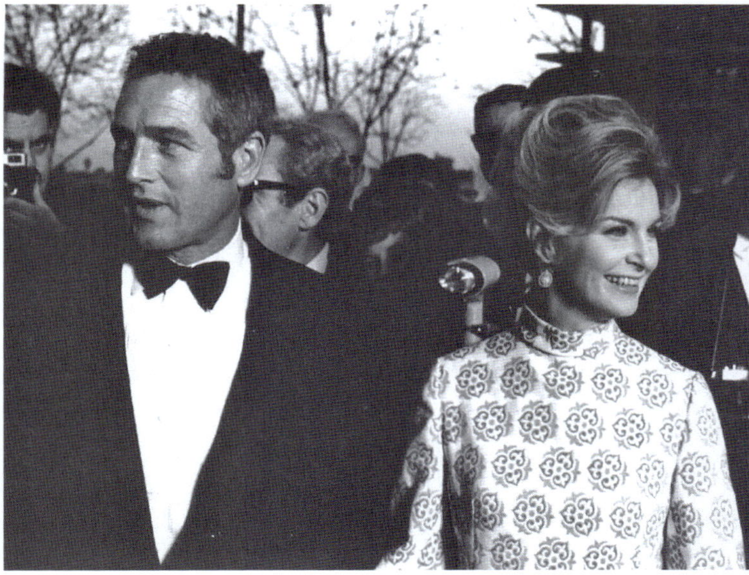

THE PREMIERE IN NEW HAVEN proved to be a madhouse, and required police protection for the stars (opposite). "It was the first time I'd been scared by a crowd. But I also thought it was a good omen," recalled Redford. Newman and his wife, Joanne Woodward (this page), head to the Academy Awards in 1970, where the film won four Oscars, the most statuettes given to any movie that night.

Academy Award that season for his portrayal of Rooster Cogburn in *True Grit*. But while Wayne made a few more such films, including 1972's *The Cowboys,* before his death in 1979, the era saw the rise of the antihero, with audiences embracing such movies as *Easy Rider*.

GLOOM DESCENDED ON ALL those involved with *Butch Cassidy*. "I was walking with the director, George Roy Hill, and we were in despair 'cause we both liked *Butch Cassidy* and it had gotten just crucified in the media," Goldman wrote. "We were talking along the streets of New York at night and George said, 'Let's go into the theatre and talk to the manager.' The manager came up to us and George said, 'Why are you smiling?' and that manager said, 'Because we're selling out every performance and the audience loves us.'"

It wasn't an isolated episode—despite the tepid reviews, people flocked to *Butch Cassidy and the Sundance Kid*. A friend of Goldman's said that when he went to see it, someone from the previous showing came out and yelled, "Hey—it's really worth it." As Redford noted, "It moved by great word of mouth. People saw it and told their friends. It was an instance where the critics meant little. The audiences made up their own minds."

And during a banner year for cinema, which included *Midnight Cowboy, Anne of a Thousand Days, They Shoot Horses, Don't They?, Hello Dolly!, Z, Bob & Carol & Ted & Alice, Take the Money and Run,* and the cult classic *Bambi Meets Godzilla*, Butch and Sundance raided the bank. The film cost $6.5 million to make and bagged $102 million (more than $700 million in 2019), more than double the amount earned by the number two grossing film, *The Love Bug*. It has become one of the most profitable Westerns ever, and one of the 20 top ticket sellers.

Not only was the film a hit, but Burt Bacharach and Hal David's "Raindrops Keep Fallin' on My Head," sung by B.J. Thomas, reached No. 1 on the charts. Redford, who originally had his doubts about the song—"I did not know what it was doing there"—admitted he was dead wrong. "How bad can a guy's judgment be? I hated the song, and suddenly, for the next six months, I had to listen to it everywhere I went. I mean everywhere: cabs, restaurants, stores. There was nowhere to go to get away from it."

The film earned seven Oscar nominations. Goldman received one, but skipped the ceremony because he believed he wouldn't win. He did, however, beating out the writers of *The Wild Bunch*; Katharine Ross, who had just presented another award, had to run back onstage to collect Goldman's statuette. Bacharach earned the Oscar for Best Original Score, likewise besting *The Wild Bunch*—then returned when he and David snagged laurels for Best Song. Conrad Hall, meanwhile, was honored for cinematography, receiving the award from John Wayne. "I would like to thank Katharine," Hall said of Ross, whom he had recently married.

REDFORD'S CAREER TOOK OFF. "This film unquestionably was the film that put me in a new place," he admitted. "This is the one that changed my life where I could no longer live my life the way I had been living normally." He made the cover of LIFE in a piece titled "New Star Robert Redford, a Real Sundance Kid," written by his neighbor and friend, the critic Richard Schickel. "Some people think he stands a fair chance of becoming one of those rare stars who sums up, all by himself, the spirit of his time," Schickel wrote, "as Brando did for the '50s, as no one quite did for the '60s. In any case, Robert Redford is riding very tall in the saddle right now. And, as is his manner, very easy." The actor would soon appear in such hits as 1973's *The Way We Were* with Streisand, 1974's *The Great Gatsby,* and 1976's *All the President's Men;* Redford also directed 1980's *Ordinary People*, for which he won an Oscar, and 1992's *A River Runs Through It*, among other films.

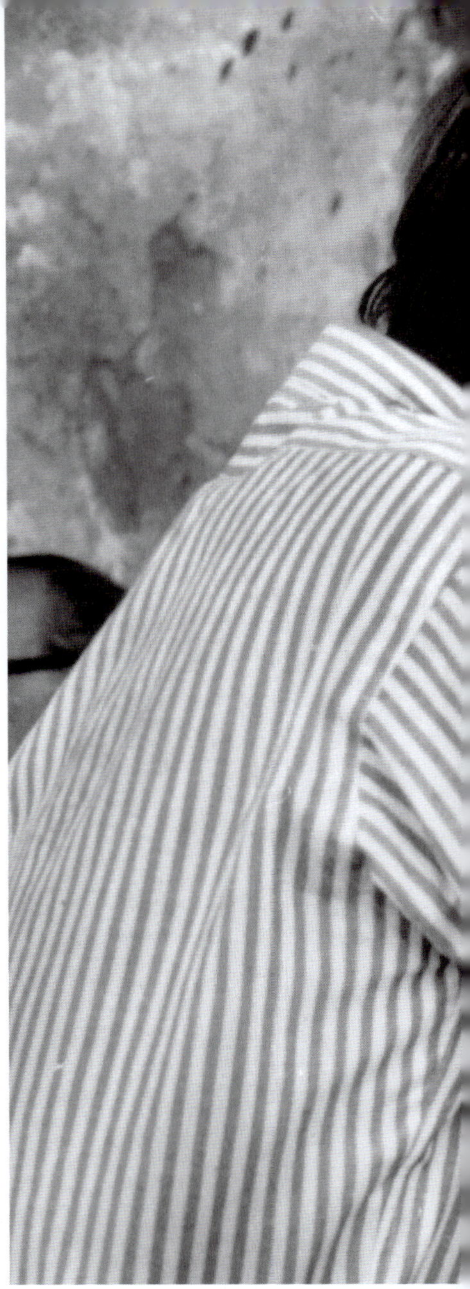

Newman had been a star for years, but *Butch Cassidy* showed his excellent comic chops, which he'd later display in 1977's *Slap Shot*. Meanwhile, Newman and Redford's cowboy chemistry launched the bromance, which has become a Hollywood staple. In 1973 they teamed up again in *The Sting*, also directed by Hill. Newman and Redford discussed doing other films together, and thought of making *A Walk in the Woods*, but Newman's health declined; he retired from film in 2007, dying the following year. (Redford would make *A Walk* in 2015 with Nick Nolte.)

CONTINUED ON PAGE 86

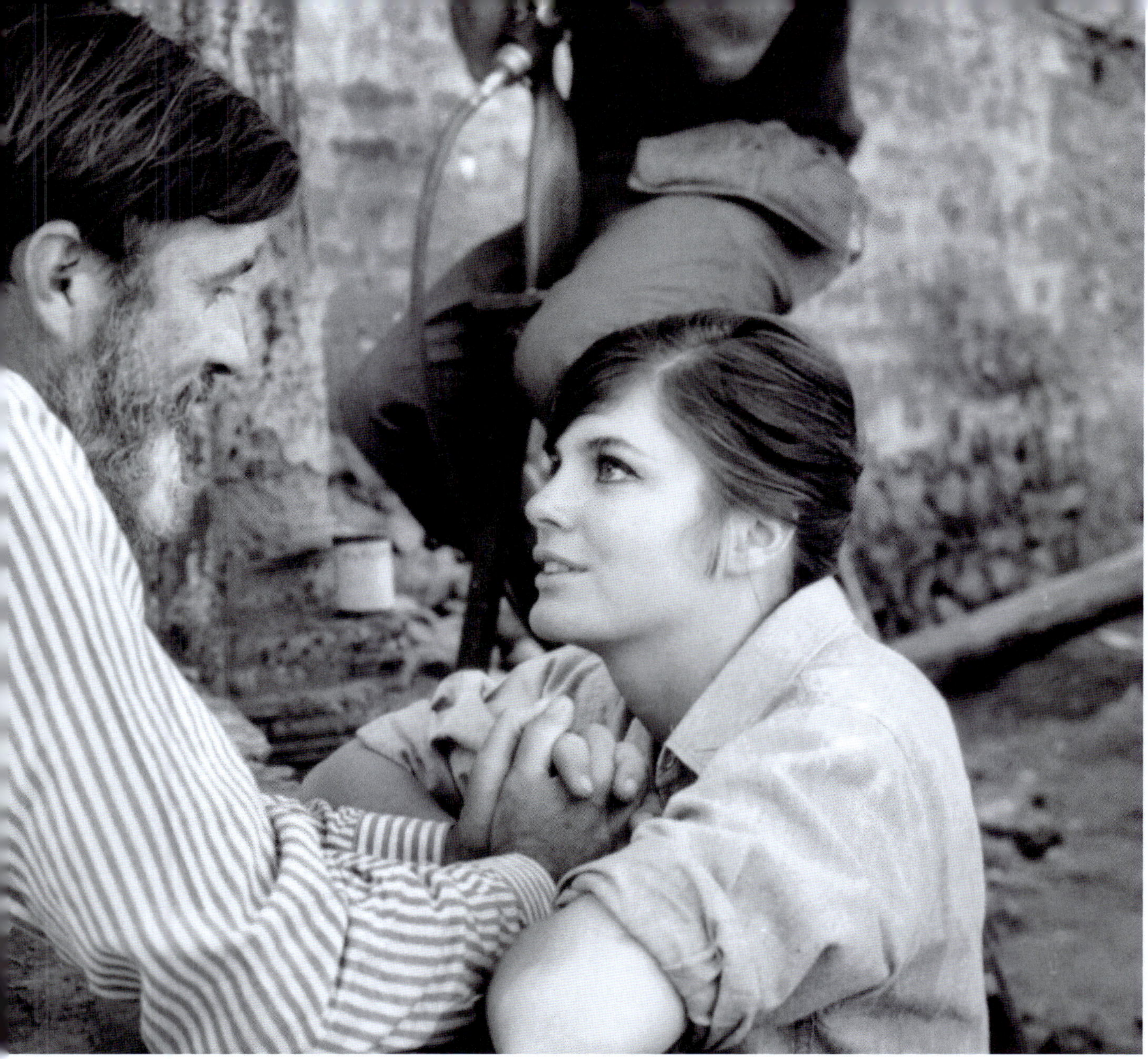

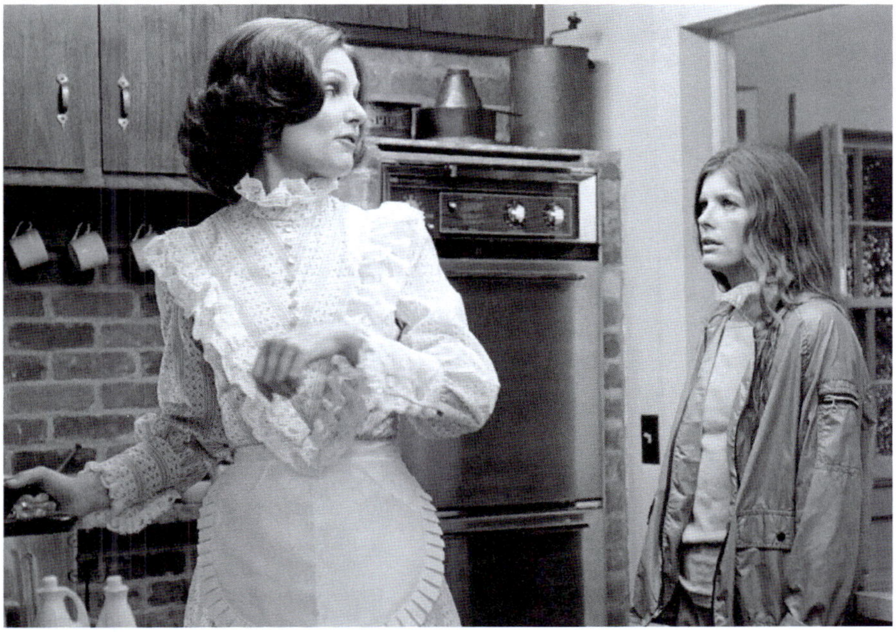

CONRAD HALL AND KATHARINE Ross, above, started dating during the filming of *Butch Cassidy.* "She was with Connie all the time," recalls Lawrence Schiller. They married in 1969. She would go on to make such films as 1975's *The Stepford Wives,* left, with Paula Prentiss. In the film, Ross's character Joanna Eberhart unknowingly moves to a town where the men have replaced their wives with beautiful and submissive robotic mates.

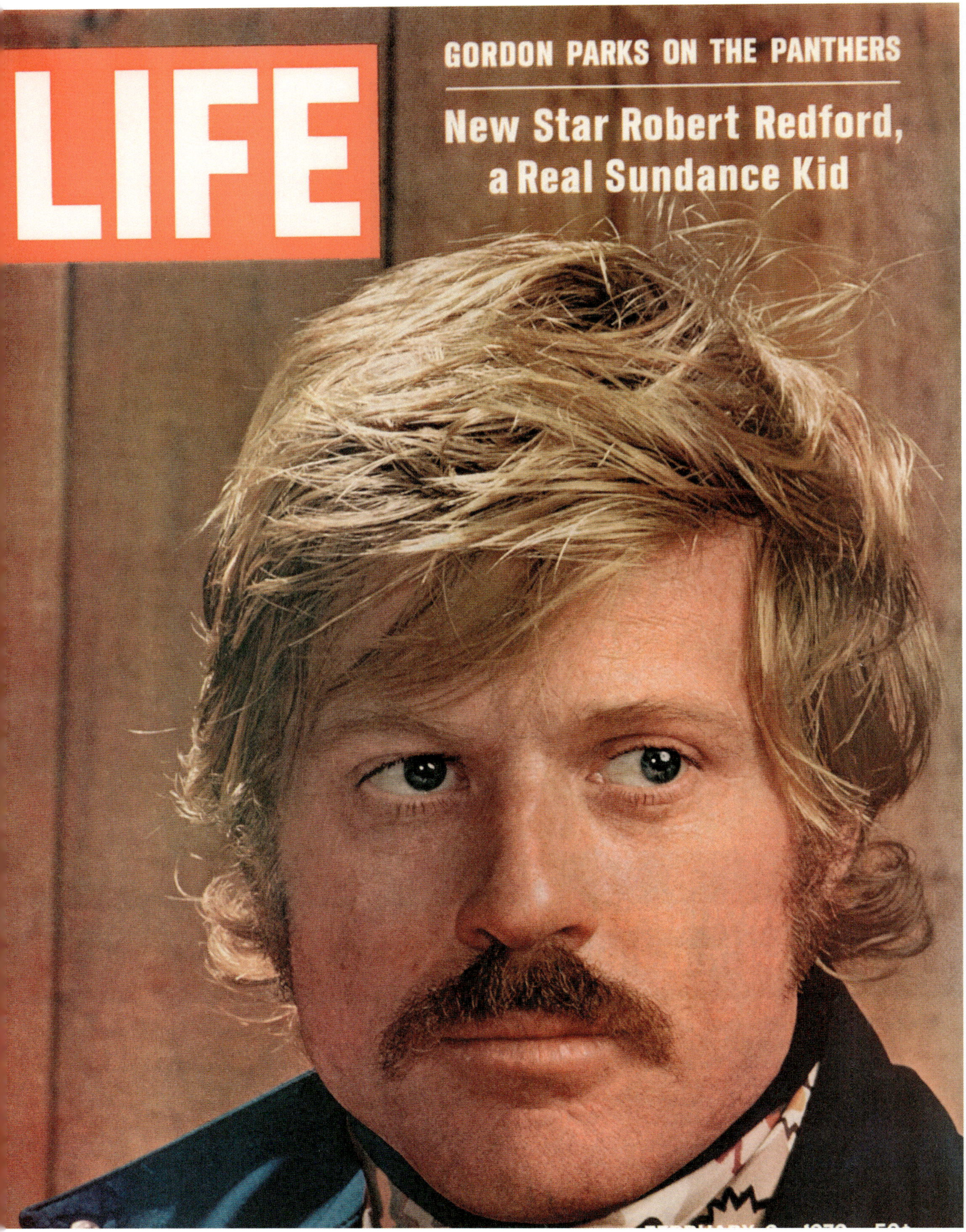
LIFE
GORDON PARKS ON THE PANTHERS
New Star Robert Redford,
a Real Sundance Kid

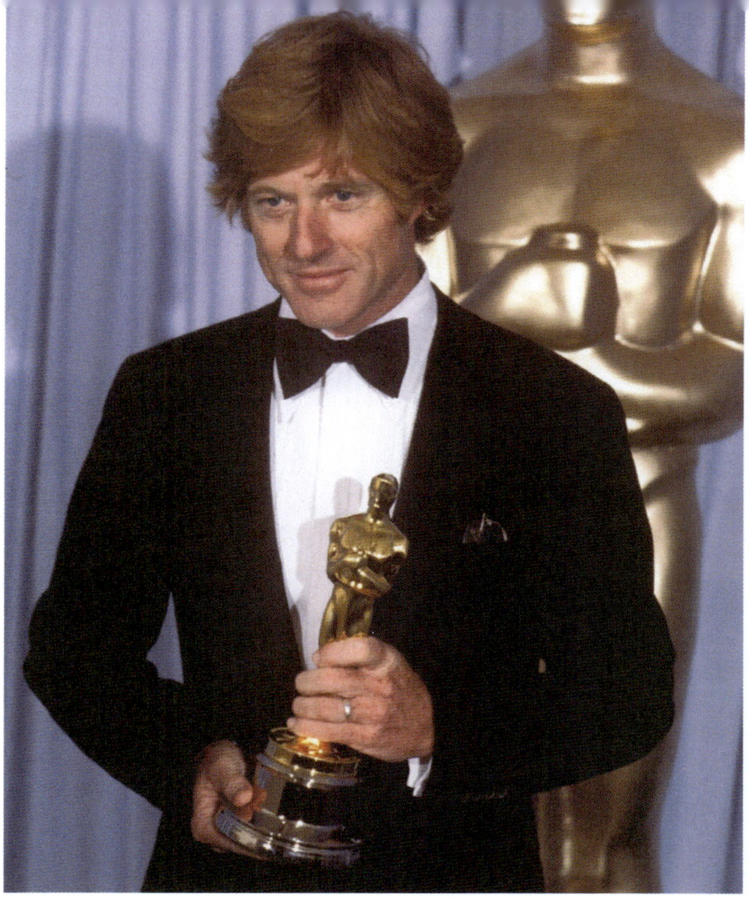

BUTCH CASSIDY AND THE SUNDANCE KID **rocketed Redford to cinematic stardom. He appeared on the cover of LIFE, opposite, and starred in such classics as 1973's *The Way We Were*, 1974's *The Great Gatsby*, and 1976's *All the President's Men*—below, with Jason Robards, Jack Warden, director Alan Pakula, Martin Balsam, and Dustin Hoffman—and won an Academy Award, right, for directing 1980's *Ordinary People*. He has continued directing and acting, appearing in 2019's *Avengers: Endgame*.**

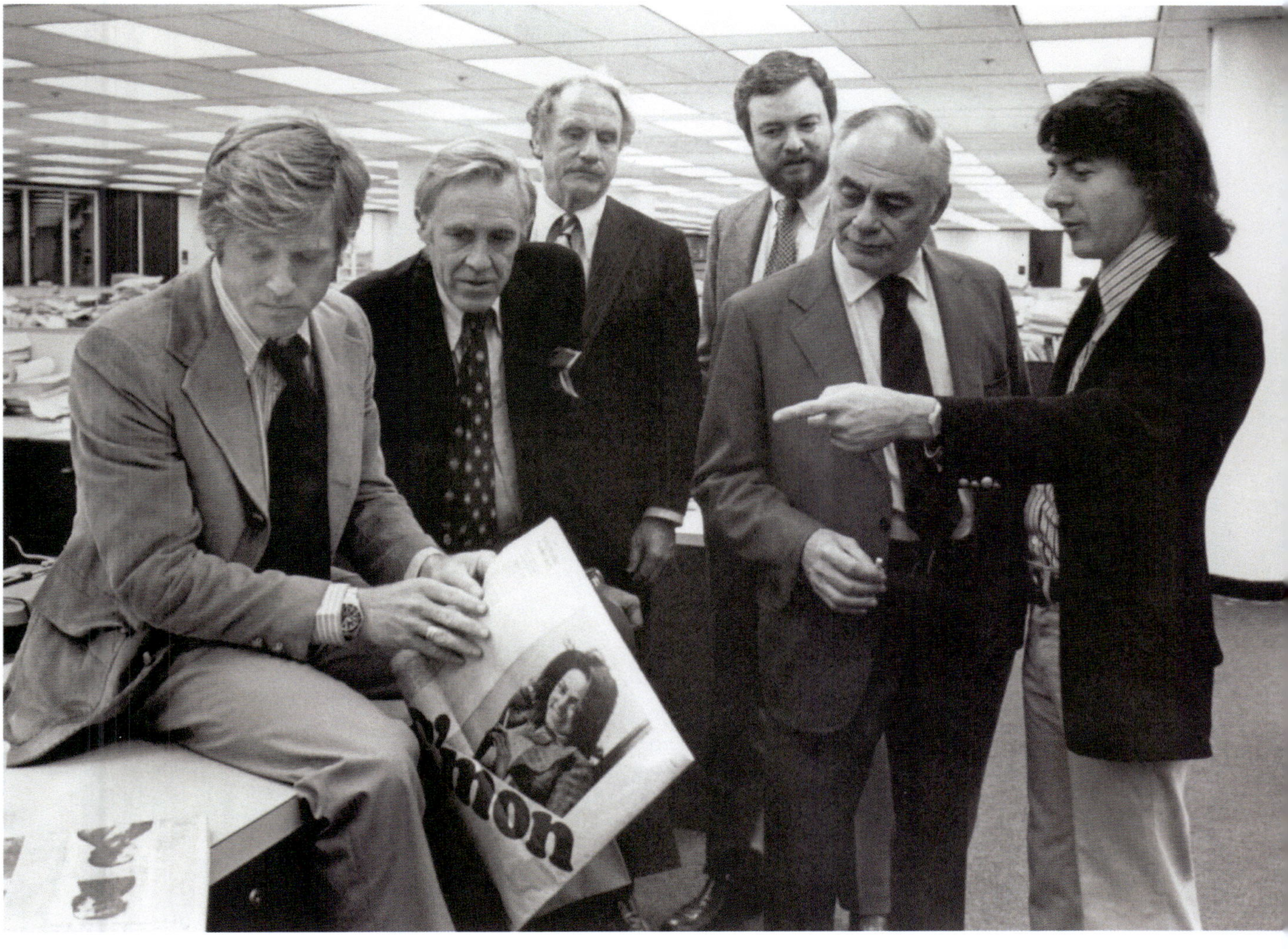

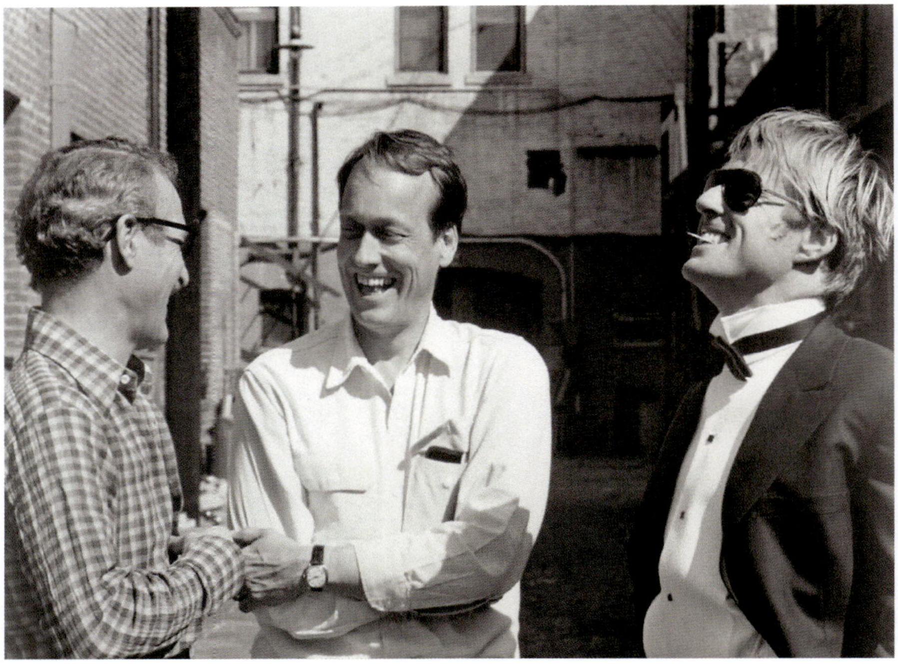

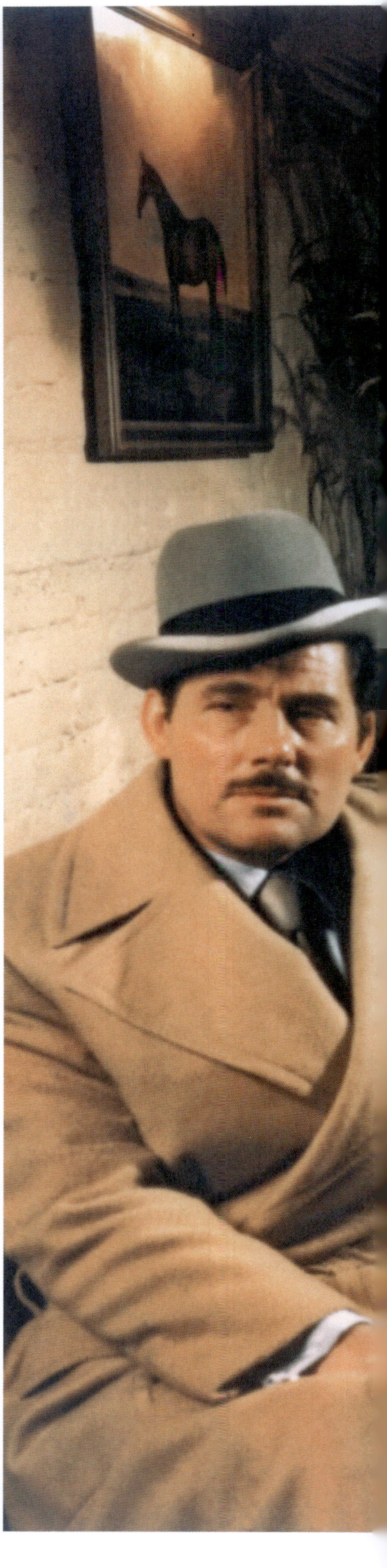

CONTINUED FROM PAGE 82

Over the years, the superstar pals branched out into other areas, with great success. Redford launched the Sundance Institute in Utah in 1981. The institute hosts an annual film festival and has become a major force in promoting independent cinema. Newman and Woodward started the Hole in the Wall Gang Camp, a charity for children and their families dealing with serious medical conditions. And of course there is the Newman's Own Foundation, which started from sales of his home-bottled salad dressing. It would blossom into a philanthropic organization that has so far raised more than $530 million.

As for *Butch Cassidy*'s other major figures, George Roy Hill directed 1972's *Slaughterhouse Five,* which won a Jury Prize at Cannes. Besides reuniting Newman and Redford in *The Sting*, which swept up seven Oscars—Hill won for directing—he did 1975's *The Great Waldo Pepper* with Redford and *Slap Shot* with Newman; Hill died at 81 in 2002.

B*UTCH CASSIDY* WAS WILLIAM Goldman's first original screenplay. The writer turned out scripts for his books *The Princess Bride* and *The Marathon Man*, and did the screenplay for two Redford films, *All the President's Men* and *The Hot Rock* (1972). "I never thought of myself as successful until the *Butch Cassidy* sale," wrote the writer, who died in November 2018 at age 87. "It became the most successful anything I've ever been involved with and that was a huge, huge plus for me."

Katharine Ross and Conrad Hall married in June 1969 and divorced in 1975. Ross would go on to make 1975's *The Stepford Wives* and, the next year, *Voyage of the Damned*. In 1978 she appeared in *The Legacy* with Sam Elliott, one of the poker players at the start of *Butch Cassidy.* Ross and Elliott didn't have any scenes together in *Butch*, and he was too bashful to chat with the Academy Award–nominated actress then. But they started dating while filming *The Legacy*, married in 1984, and have a daughter, Cleo. Hall, who died in 2003 at age 76, would go on to win two more Oscars, one for *American Beauty* (1999) and the other for 2002's *Road to Perdition* with Newman.

In 1971, Robert Crawford's documentary *The Making of "Butch Cassidy and the Sundance Kid"* won an Emmy for Outstanding Achievement in Cultural Documentary Programming. And while Newman and Redford avoided a sequel, *Butch Cassidy* did spawn other films and TV shows. For three

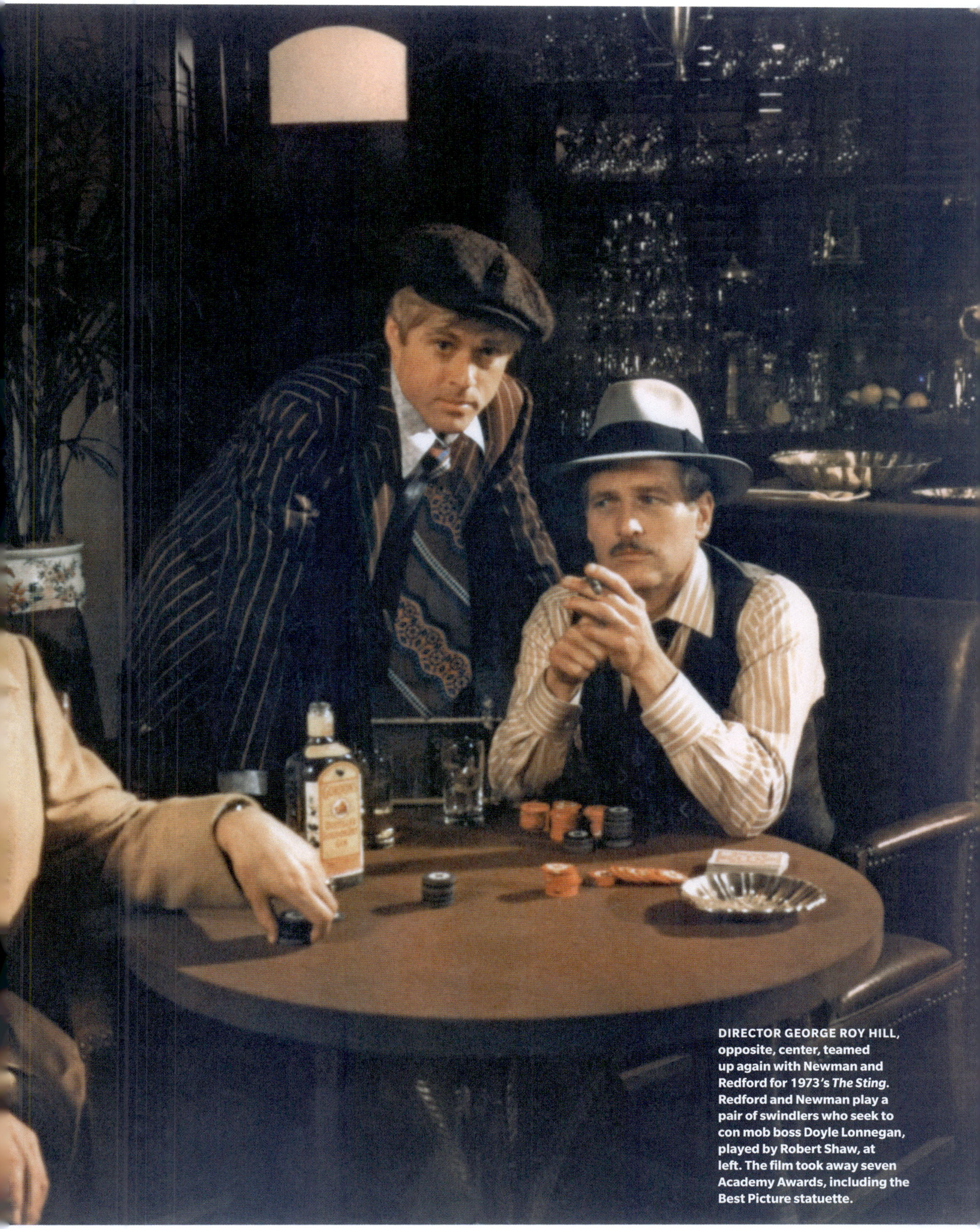

DIRECTOR GEORGE ROY HILL, opposite, center, teamed up again with Newman and Redford for 1973's *The Sting*. Redford and Newman play a pair of swindlers who seek to con mob boss Doyle Lonnegan, played by Robert Shaw, at left. The film took away seven Academy Awards, including the Best Picture statuette.

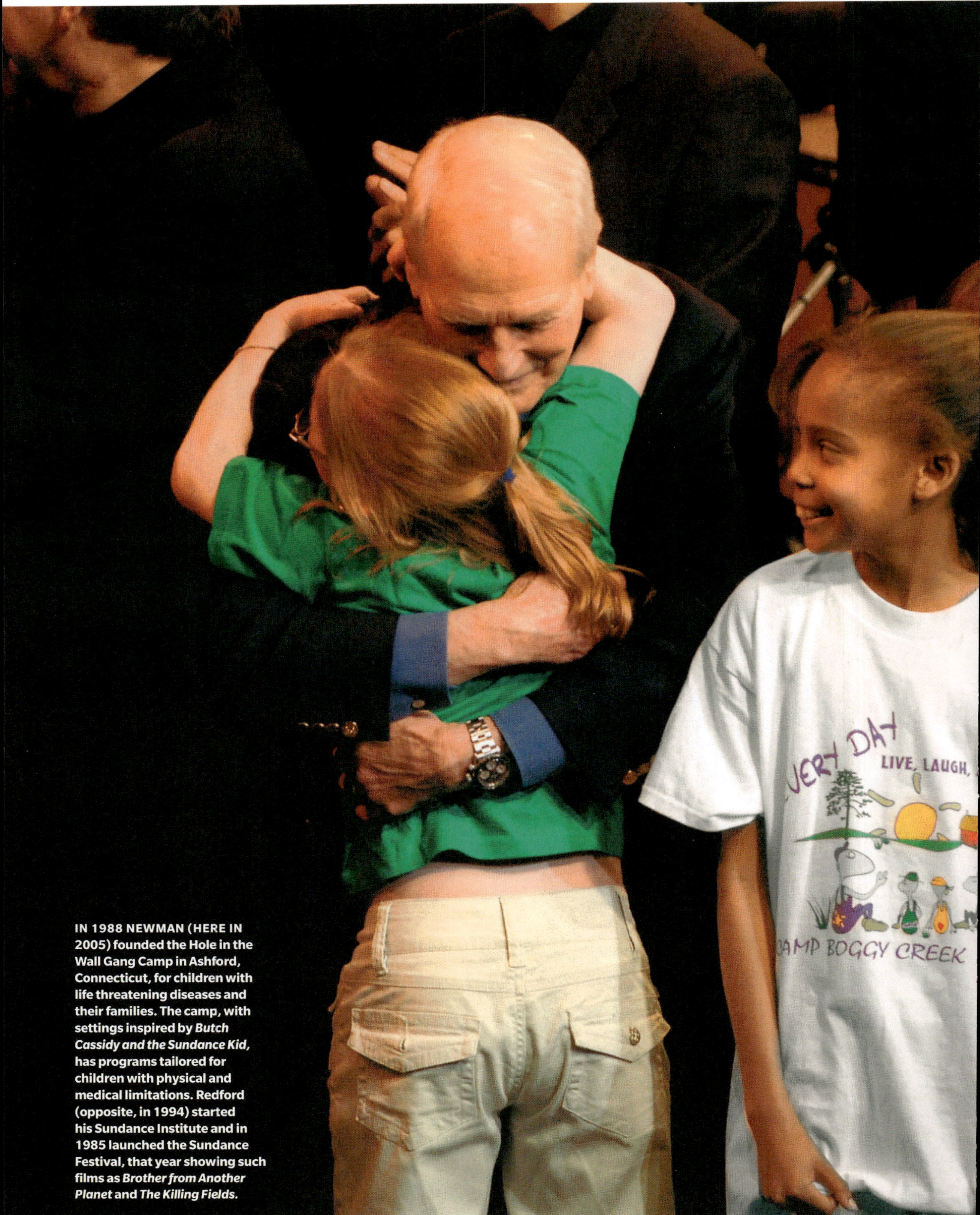

IN 1988 NEWMAN (HERE IN 2005) founded the Hole in the Wall Gang Camp in Ashford, Connecticut, for children with life threatening diseases and their families. The camp, with settings inspired by *Butch Cassidy and the Sundance Kid,* has programs tailored for children with physical and medical limitations. Redford (opposite, in 1994) started his Sundance Institute and in 1985 launched the Sundance Festival, that year showing such films as *Brother from Another Planet* and *The Killing Fields*.

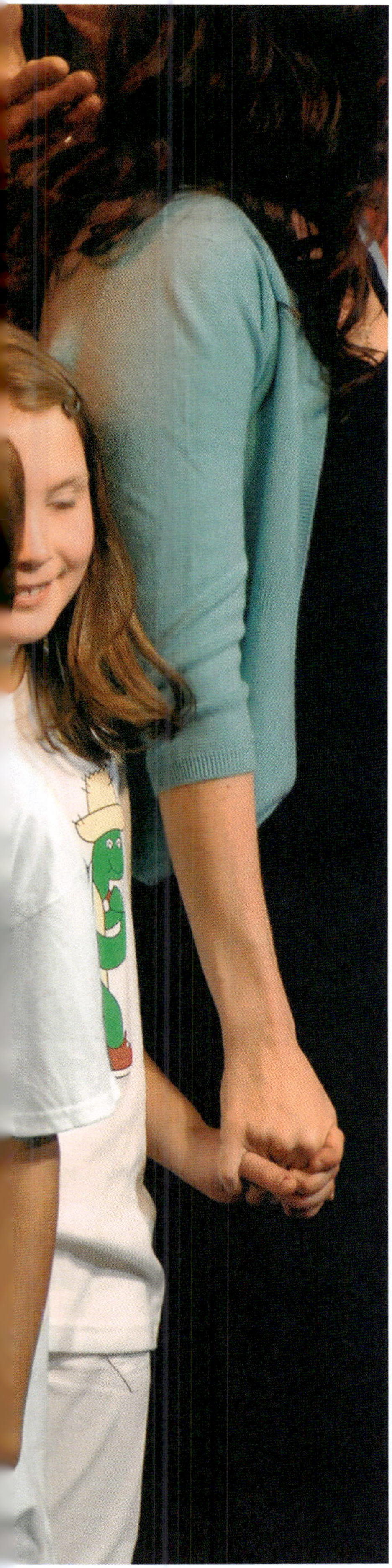

seasons starting in 1971 the Western *Alias Smith and Jones* ran on ABC, the title derived from names Butch and Sundance went by in South America. In 1974, Elizabeth Montgomery portrayed Etta in *Mrs. Sundance*, a TV movie in which her character hears that the Kid is still alive, and sets off to find him.

KATHARINE ROSS WED *BUTCH CASSIDY* CINEMATOGRAPHER CONRAD HALL AND, LATER, SAM ELLIOTT, WHO APPEARED IN THE FILM.

Ross reprised her role as Etta in another TV film, *Wanted: The Sundance Woman,* which takes place following Butch and Sundance's death when she seeks help from Mexican revolutionary Pancho Villa. *Butch & Sundance: The Early Days* appeared in 1979, with Tom Berenger as Butch and William Katt as Sundance; Jeff Corey again played Ray Bledsoe, and Goldman served as a producer. In 2000's *The Way of the Gun,* Ryan Phillippe and Benicio Del Toro are named Parker and Longabaugh, the duo's original surnames. A 2004 TV movie, *The Legend of Butch & Sundance,* starred David Clayton Rogers, Ryan Browning, and Rachelle Lefevre as Butch, Sundance, and Etta. And in 2011, Sam Shepard played a grizzled Butch in *Blackthorn*, depicting the outlaw eager at the end of his life to return to the United States.

And just as *Butch Cassidy* referenced Truffaut's work, other films now nod to Hill's movie. *Thelma & Louise* writer Callie Khouri said that her screenplay for the female buddy film was "winking to *Butch Cassidy and the Sundance Kid,*" with the main characters as female versions of the duo. Hill's film even earned a 1993 homage in *The Simpsons*—at one point Marge and Homer mimic Etta and Butch by sharing a bicycle ride along the streets of Springfield. The couple are singing "Raindrops" as they go pedaling off into a glorious western sunset. ✦

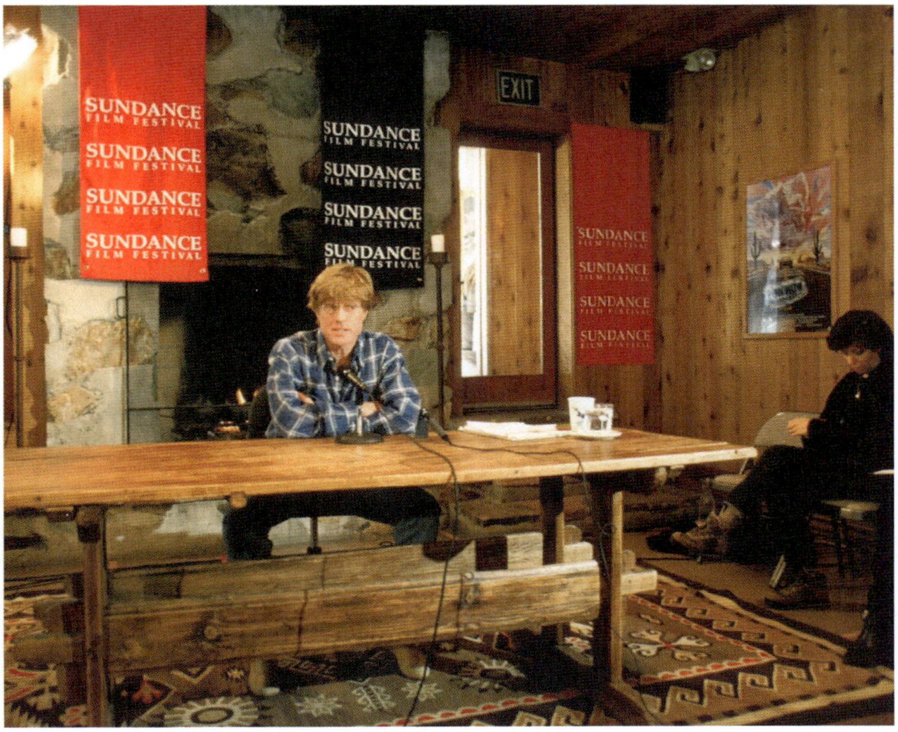

THE AFTERMATH

Into the Sunset

BUTCH AND SUNDANCE SAW THE END OF THE OUTLAW ERA, BUT THE MYTH OF THE OLD WEST ENDURES

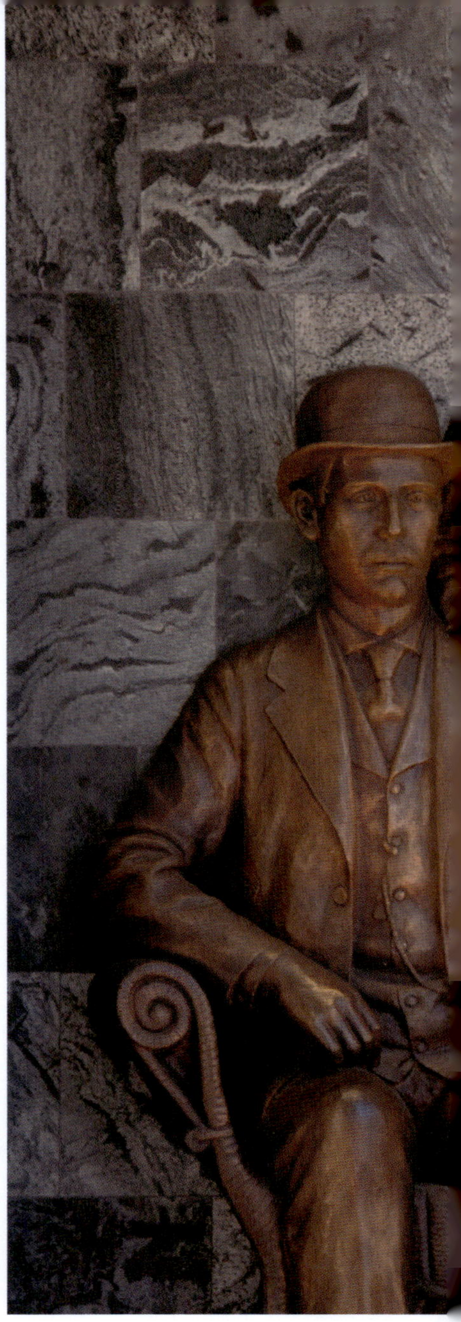

BUTCH CASSIDY AND THE SUNDANCE KID died in a hail of bullets in Bolivia.

Or maybe they didn't.

Rumors swirled for years that the outlaws survived the 1908 shoot-out in San Vicente. Their deaths, or non-deaths, seem in character with George Roy Hill's film *Butch Cassidy and the Sundance Kid,* which begins with the disclaimer "Most of what follows is true." And just as people could not accept the idea that these antiheros perished, Americans refuse to perform a campfire elegy for the Wild West, that figurative geographic region that never quite existed in the way we think of it.

The concept of the West arose long before Butch and Sundance donned dusters and strapped on their six-guns. In 1804, President Thomas Jefferson dispatched Captain Meriwether Lewis and Lieutenant William Clark to explore the newly acquired Louisiana Purchase. Their two-year trek to the Pacific and back was an encounter with the vastness and the possibility of what would become a wide swath of the United States. At Monticello, his home in Virginia, Jefferson touted the glories of the land beyond the Mississippi by displaying Native American buffalo robes, utensils, and beaded leggings in what he christened his "Indian Hall."

By 1860 the United States had 1.4 billion acres of land, up from 512 million in 1783 when the Revolutionary War ended. Congress had been haphazardly distributing the public land, but people clamored for more. Many saw land settlement as a way to free Americans from the industrial servitude that had become a growing part of everyday life. Then in 1862, Congress passed the Homestead Act, which on its 100th anniversary President John F. Kennedy called "the single greatest stimulus to national development ever enacted."

The act helped populate the West by allowing citizens and would-be citizens to claim a quarter section of land, 160 acres. Within 10 years of its passage, settlers claimed homesteads in Ohio, Indiana, Illinois, Missouri, Iowa, Michigan, Wisconsin, Minnesota, Kansas, and Nebraska. The completion of the railroads and the linking of the two coasts in May 1869 dramatically opened up the country. Towns sprang up along the rail lines and farmers laid out their fields, cattlemen founded ranches, and miners sank shafts.

Because of the appeal of owning land, pioneers endured backbreaking labor as they dug wells, hauled water, broke the sod, built homes, raised children and livestock, fought off hostile neighbors and natives, and suffered through droughts, floods, heat waves, and locusts, not to mention the unrelenting loneliness that crushed both seasoned farmers and starry-eyed city folk. And while God-fearing pioneers populated the West, it also had its share of dastardly villains who gravitated to the towns' drinking establishments and houses of ill repute, with lawmen like Wild Bill Hickok, Bat Masterson, and Wyatt Earp seeking to foil the likes of "Killer" Jim Miller, John Wesley Hardin, Belle Starr, Billy the Kid, and Jesse and Frank James.

As the land across the West was plotted and plowed, settlers slaughtered the bison, and the military herded Native Americans from their ancestral lands. The United States took 1.5 billion acres from indigenous people between 1776 and 1887, and corralled them into reservations where poverty, alcoholism, starvation, and disease ravaged their communities.

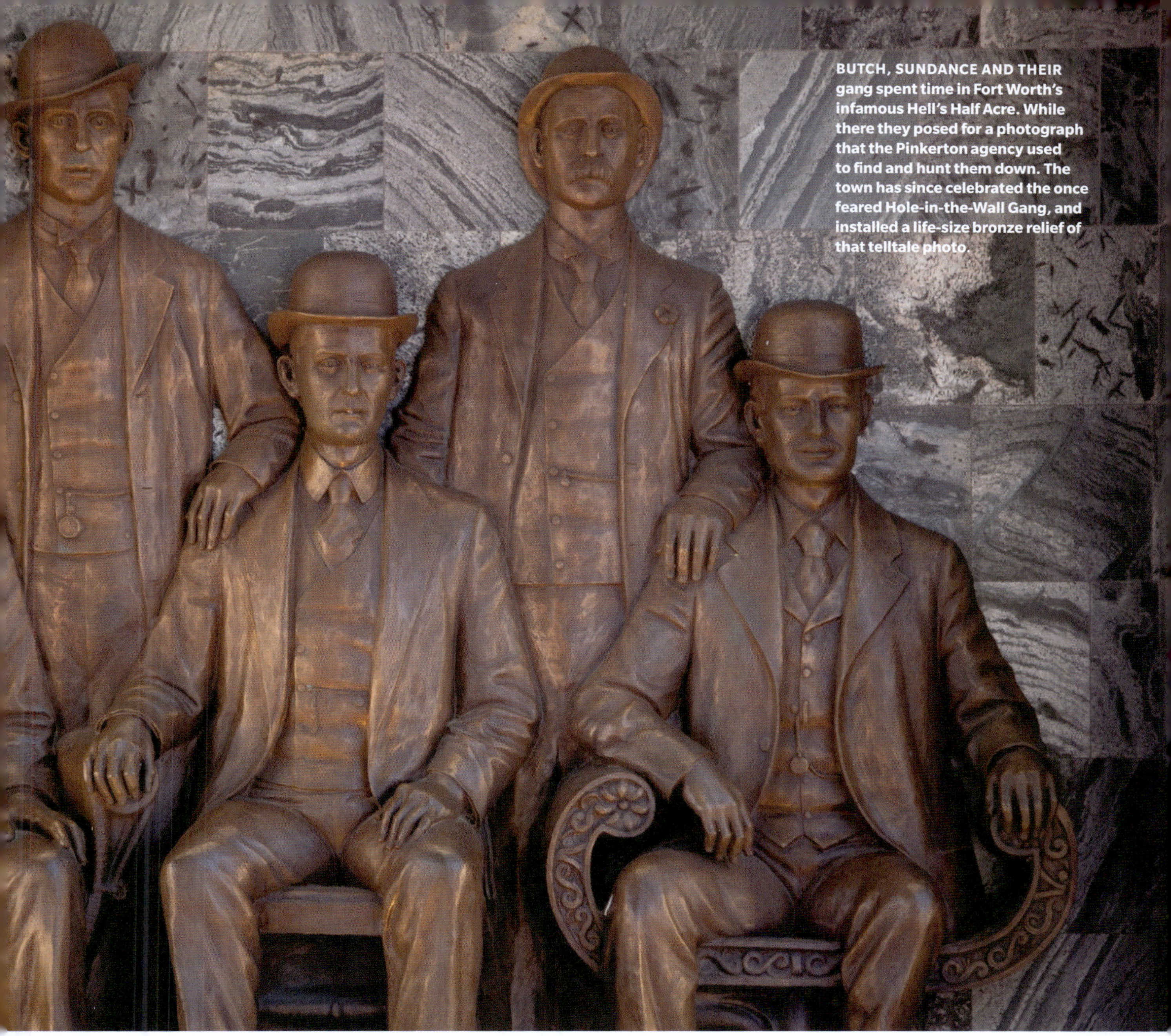

BUTCH, SUNDANCE AND THEIR gang spent time in Fort Worth's infamous Hell's Half Acre. While there they posed for a photograph that the Pinkerton agency used to find and hunt them down. The town has since celebrated the once feared Hole-in-the-Wall Gang, and installed a life-size bronze relief of that telltale photo.

Fearing that the opening of the frontier was wiping out God's pristine creation, photographers headed west to document its wonders. In 1862, Carleton Watkins's photographs of Yosemite drew praise from poet Oliver Wendell Holmes for achieving "a perfection of art which compares with the finest European work." Three years later, Charles L. Weed visited the Yosemite Valley and took luminous images, such as "Mirror Lake and Reflections." And after the Civil War, battlefield photographers like Alexander Gardner captured invaluable images of the land and the Plains Indians. By then collectors and museums started gathering moccasins, pottery, and arrowheads. The artists George Catlin, Frederic Remington, Charles Russell, and Will James captured the nobility and the brutality of both settlers and Native Americans in paintings, illustrations, and sculptures, while others, such as Albert Bierstadt, created grand canvases that glorified the area's Edenesque lushness.

Dime novels featuring western stories first appeared in 1860. Though the tales were often formulaic, they featured such American archetypes as the cowboy and the trapper and brimmed with fast-paced adventure. Readers marveled at the excitement of the West, the nobility of heroes, and the orneriness of outlaws. The pamphlet books, with their colorful covers, captured the imaginations of readers aching for adventure, like the Pennsylvanian Harry Longabaugh, who would soon become known as the Sundance Kid. The characters in these tales seemed to embody the freedom of the land, and confirmed for readers the belief in the American as a proto-superman who could accomplish anything as long as he had a trusty steed and a loaded six-shooter.

As the good, the bad, and the ugly labored and sought to survive, they gathered around campfires and fireplaces and sang songs of the joys, travails, and deadliness of the West. There were tunes like "Home on the Range" extolling the land:

Where the air is so pure and the zephyrs so free,
And the breezes so balmy and light,
That I would not exchange my home on the range,
For all of the cities so bright.

There were likewise songs about the gold rush such as "Oh My Darling, Clementine," as well as others about errors learned too late, most notably "The Streets of Laredo," otherwise known as the "Cowboy's Lament," which told of "a poor cowboy wrapped in white linen / Wrapped in white linen as cold as the clay."

The land continued to attract many hoping for a new start. Bereft after the deaths of both his wife and mother in 1884, the New York–born Theodore Roosevelt moved west, where he ranched, stopped stampedes, and even punched out a gunslinger in Mingusville, Montana. "I struck quick and hard with my right just to one side of the point of his jaw, hitting with my left as I straightened out, and then again with my right," Roosevelt wrote in his autobiography. "He fired the guns, but I do not know whether this was merely a convulsive action of his hands, or whether he was trying to shoot at me. When he went down he struck the corner of the bar with his head . . . he was senseless. I took away his guns, and the other people in the room . . . hustled him out and put him in the shed."

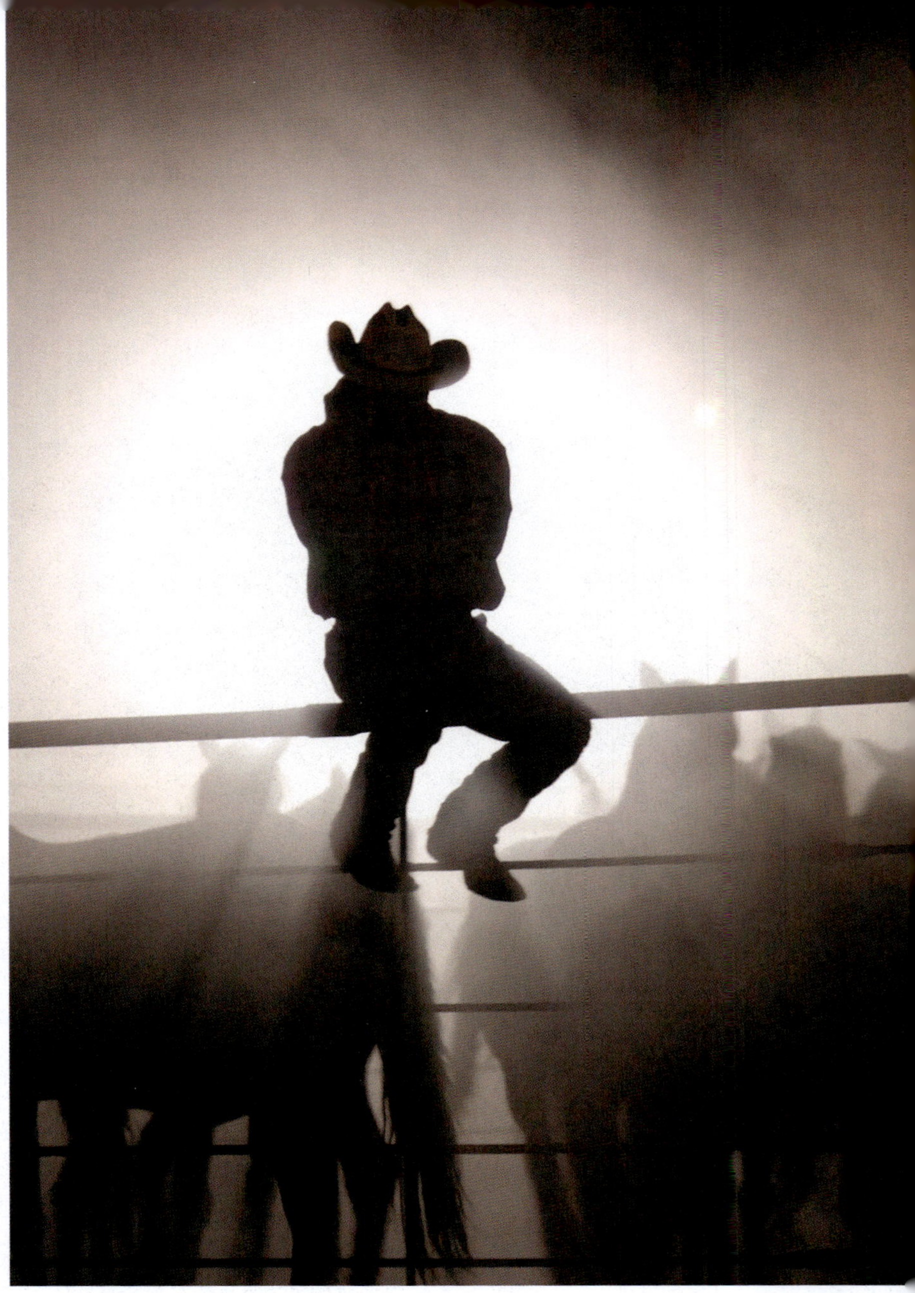

Roosevelt wrote of day-to-day existence out west in his *Ranch Life and the Hunting Trail.* His time there made him America's only true cowboy President, one who held dear the land and the way of life. During the 1898 Spanish American War, Colonel Roosevelt and his band of Rough Riders brought a Wild West charge to Cuba when they captured Kettle Hill. And while in the White House, Roosevelt not only used his "Speak softly and carry a big stick" policy and "cowboy diplomacy" to help make America truly great—a global power—but as the Conservation President, he preserved the land. Appalled by the slaughter of bison and the decline of elk, bighorn sheep, and deer and the destruction of the country's natural beauty, he created the United States Forest Service, established hundreds of national forests, national parks, and federal bird and game reserves, and he saved forever such places as Devils Tower in Wyoming, Arizona's Grand Canyon, and Muir Woods in northern California.

Others wrote of the West and their experiences. Laura Ingalls Wilder's family settled in De Smet, South Dakota, in 1880 on a 160-acre claim, and she would eventually chronicle her life there in her *Little House* book series. The following decade the historian Frederick Jackson Turner proclaimed that the frontier served as "the meeting point between civilization and savagery." And by the turn of the century, novelists started to pen great western books, like Owen Wister's *The Virginian* and Zane Grey's *Riders of the Purple Sage.*

It didn't matter that many authors never actually set foot west of the Mississippi or rode in a prairie schooner. For as the great cattle drives faded at the end of the century, the music, the stories, the legends, and the allure of the cowboy sporting his 10-gallon hat

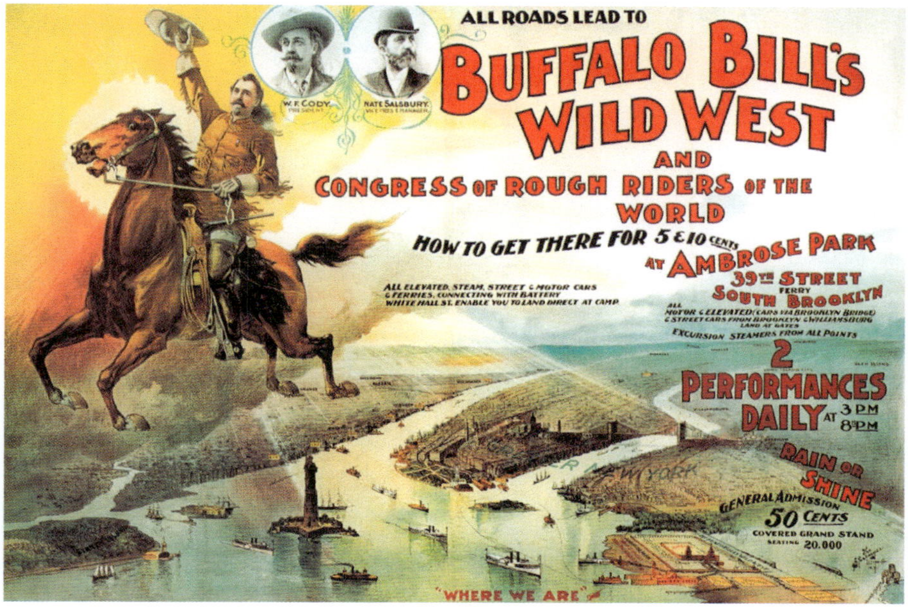

THE WAYS OF THE OLD WEST ARE alive and well, with cowboys still riding the range, herding cattle, and celebrating that long forgotten time. Shows like Buffalo Bill's Wild West, which played in Brooklyn in the 1890s, right, helped popularize images of the West as a land of upright cowboys and strong women, a place where people lived by their wits—and their Colts and Remingtons.

and twirling his Remington revolver only grew larger in the American imagination. Traveling extravaganzas such as William F. Cody's grand Buffalo Bill's Wild West brought trick riding cowpokes, whooping Indians, and charging cavalries to small towns and city slickers.

Cody staged a Wild Bunch Train Robbery based on Butch and Sundance's 1899 Union Pacific heist. The showman likewise appeared in an 1894 Edison Kinetoscope Western along with some of his Native American Oglala and Brule actors. Then, around the time Butch, Sundance, and Etta slipped off for South America, Edwin Porter's 1903 *The Great Train Robbery* flickered on movie house screens. The film also recreated the Union Pacific robbery, and is one of the first motion pictures to tell a complete story.

Westerns quickly became a staple of American cinema. The movies glamorized the West, transformed out-of-work buckaroos into actors, and turned some, like the silent-film leading man Tom Mix, into stars. With the advent of talkies, singing cowboys like Gene Autry became matinee idols, crooning hits such as "Back in the Saddle Again." Then in 1939, John Wayne shot to Hollywood stardom with his role in the John Ford classic *Stagecoach*. Audiences thrilled watching Henry Fonda in 1942's *The Ox-Bow Incident*, Gary Cooper and Grace Kelly a decade later in *High Noon*, and countless more in between. Children played cowboys and Indians, and when Disney aired its *Davy Crockett* miniseries in 1954, raccoon caps became a fashion staple for the under-18 set. By then, many of those young readers whose families had settled in postwar suburbia cherished their dog-eared copies of Wilder's *Little House* books, and their parents eagerly awaited Louis L'Amour's newest "Frontier Stories."

Though John Wayne's *True Grit* appeared in cinemas the same year as *Butch Cassidy and the Sundance Kid*, by the late 1960s the western had declined as a mainstay of cinema. Even so, it survives and has become in many ways darker and possibly more authentic, closely portraying the brutal lives many endured. Clint Eastwood, who had epitomized the lone Man with No Name in such Sergio Leone movies as 1964's *A Fistful of Dollars*, made the haunting 1992 film *Unforgiven*. In this, one of the greatest westerns ever—it won four Academy Awards, including Best Picture—Eastwood plays Bill Munny, a notorious villain out of Missouri. "I've killed women and children," he mutters as he aims his shotgun at the man responsible for the death of his best friend. "I killed just about everything that walks or crawls at one time or another. And I am here to kill you, Little Bill, for what you did

THE MOVIE WESTERN SURVIVES, AND HAS BECOME IN MANY WAYS DARKER AND POSSIBLY MORE AUTHENTIC.

to Ned." And as Munny guns down Little Bill (Gene Hackman) and half a dozen others in a saloon, his latest slaughter transforms him into the bloody defender of the discarded, those often glossed over and ignored in the mythic West.

As the image of the West evolved, one positive change has been the portrayal of Native Americans. Compare the bloodthirsty Geronimo in *Stagecoach* to 1962's *Geronimo!* where the native chief is a defender of his people's ancestral land. A wistful, elegiac vision of the first Americans is on display in films like 1990's *Dances with Wolves,* 1992's *The Last of the Mohicans,* and 2017's *Hostiles.* While the character of Tonto in the mid-century TV show *The Lone Ranger* is demeaning to Native Americans, starting in 1990 the series *Northern Exposure* gave a nuanced, sensitive, albeit humorous view of Alaskan natives—who on Thanksgiving get some payback by flinging tomatoes at local whites.

RESEARCHERS DUG UP BUTCH AND SUNDANCE'S SUPPOSED GRAVES IN 1991, BUT FOUND ONLY THE BODY OF A GERMAN MINER.

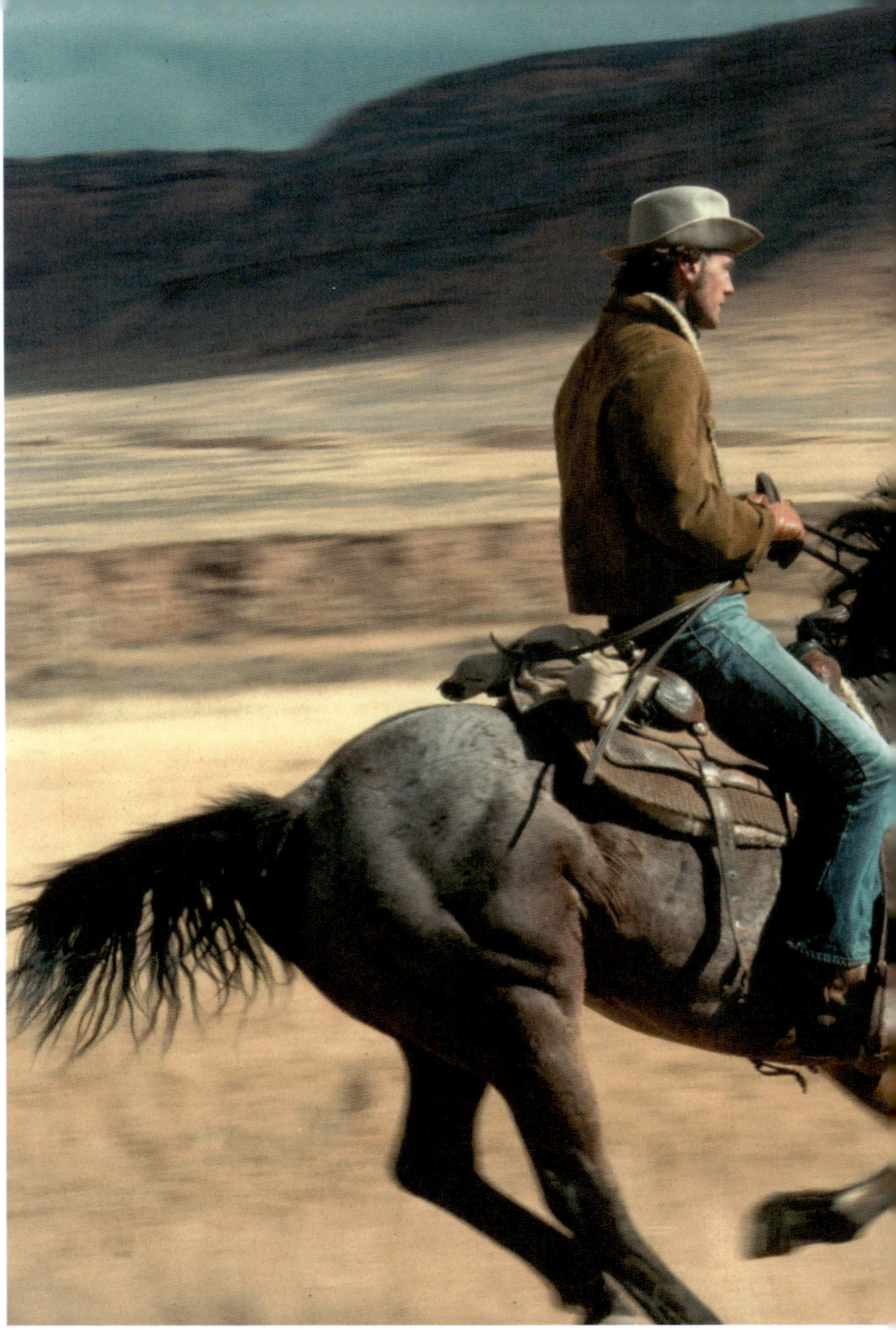

Rodeos are now the closest most people can come to the Old West. Once venues to show off skills at riding and roping, many now hand out big money prizes, at places like Denver's National Western Stock Show & Rodeo, with its parades and horse and agricultural shows. And city slickers hoping for a taste of the West can luxuriate at a dude ranch that offers massages and spas.

Meanwhile the legend of Butch and Sundance and their Hole-in-the-Wall Gang has endured and grown. Following the 1908 shoot-out in San Vicente, where Butch and Sundance were said to have died, there were claims that Sundance continued to live in South America. Others have said Cassidy headed back to the United States. His sister Lula Parker Betenson penned *Butch Cassidy, My Brother*—Redford wrote the foreword—with the claim that he visited the family in Circleville, Utah, in 1925. He then reportedly died of pneumonia in Washington State in 1937.

Researchers seeking answers to what happened to Butch and Sundance dug up their supposed graves in 1991, but found only the body of a German miner. It didn't help that the poorly laid out cemetery had bodies buried together in unmarked plots. Further raising the possibility of their survival was the appearance in 2011 of a 1934 manuscript, *Bandit Invincible: The Story of Butch Cassidy*, which some claim Cassidy penned. And the Pinkerton agency has never officially declared them dead.

The two men continue to haunt the spots they passed through. The town of Circleville restored Butch's childhood home. Telluride, Colorado, where Butch started his downward descent by stealing $20,000, is now a resort town where Butch Cassidy Drive boasts lavish ski

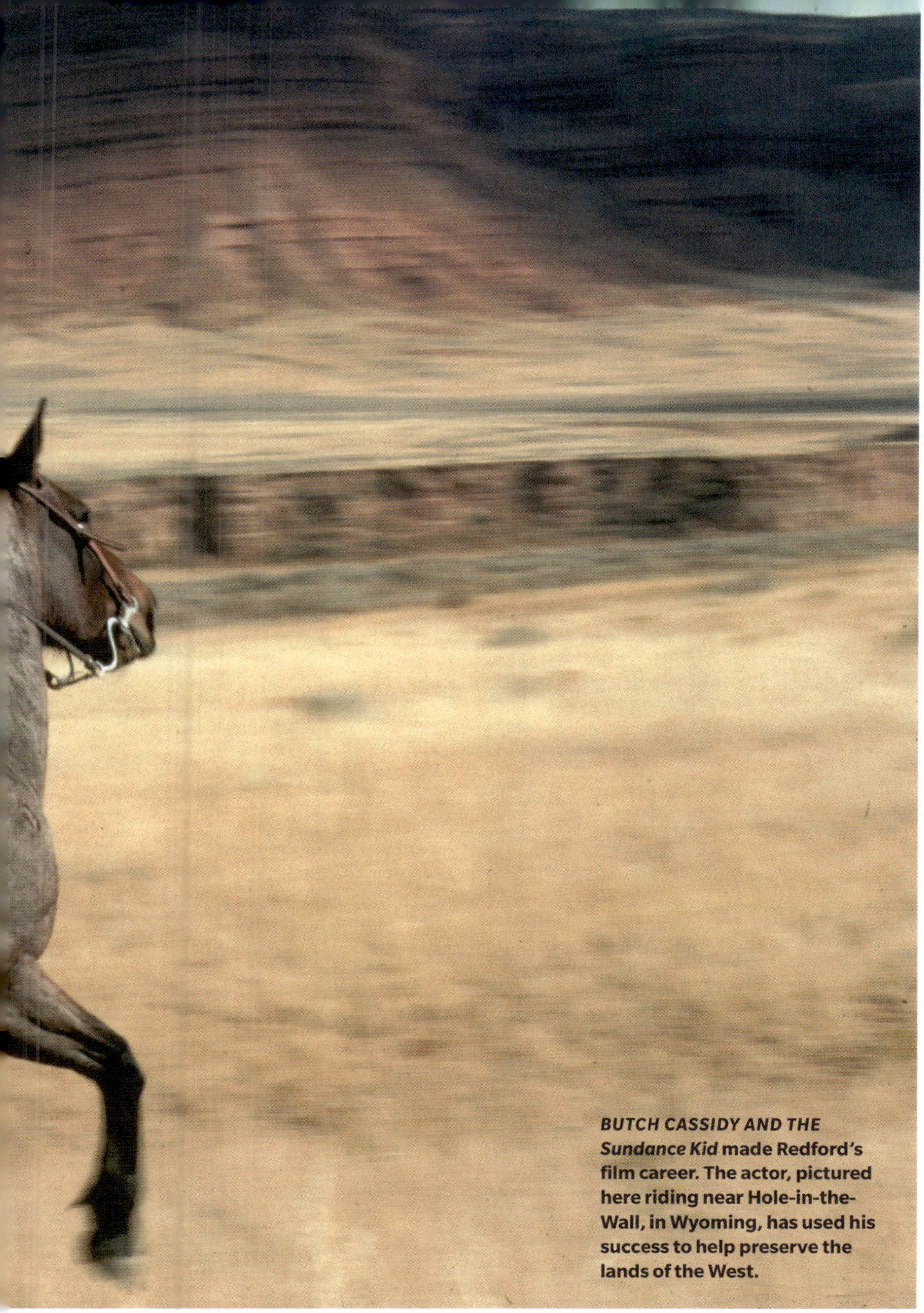

BUTCH CASSIDY AND THE Sundance Kid **made Redford's film career. The actor, pictured here riding near Hole-in-the-Wall, in Wyoming, has used his success to help preserve the lands of the West.**

homes. And Montpelier, Idaho, cherishes its Butch Cassidy Museum, set in the bank he robbed in 1896. Each August, around the time of the heist, locals reenact the holdup.

At the site of the Sundance, Wyoming, jail where the Sundance Kid once cooled his spurs, sits a statue of the fabled inmate. And Fort Worth's former Hell's Half Acre now has a stylish Sundance Square. There tourists can see a life-size bronze relief based on the photo John Swartz took of Butch, Sundance, and friends in 1900. They can also stay at Etta's Place Bed & Breakfast, with such rooms as Butch's Hideout and Sundance's Suite.

And down in Bolivia looms a billboard, "Welcome to San Vicente: Here lie the remains of Butch Cassidy and the Sundance Kid." The community is proud of its Butch Cassidy and Sundance Kid Memorial Museum, a one-room adobe building with a collection of period photos and old guns. They have fenced off the outlaws' putative graves, and in 2008, on the centennial of the shoot-out, townspeople reenacted their famed battle.

Butch, Sundance, and the Wild West live on, their legends only burnished with the passage of time. ✦

Photo Credits

Front Cover: Photograph © Lawrence Schiller, All Rights Reserved/Getty Images **Back Cover** (clockwise from top left): © 20th Century Fox/Courtesy Everett (2); Movie Poster Image Art/Moviepix/Getty **Inside Covers:** ShutterWorx/E+/Getty **Page 1:** Photograph © Lawrence Schiller, All Rights Reserved/Getty Images **Pages 2–3:** Bettmann/Getty

INTRODUCTION
Page 5: Douglas Kirkland/Corbis/Getty

THE LIVES BEHIND THE LEGEND
Page 6 (background): Grafissimo/E+/Getty **Page 7:** Print Collector/Hulton/Getty **Pages 8–9:** Archive/Getty **Pages 10–11:** American Heritage Center, University of Wyoming **Pages 12–13:** John Swartz/American Stock/Archive/Getty **Page 13:** American Heritage Center, University of Wyoming **Pages 14–15:** Johnson County Jim Gatchell Memorial **Page 16** (clockwise from top): Library of Congress (2); Johnson County Jim Gatchell Memorial; Universal History Archive/UIG/Getty **Pages 17–18:** American Heritage Center, University of Wyoming (2) **Page 19:** The San Francisco Call/Library of Congress **Pages 20–21:** Underwood Archives/Archive/Getty **Pages 22–23** (clockwise from left): Granger; Bain Collection/Epics/Hulton/Getty; Florentina Georgescu/Moment RF/Getty

THE MAKING OF A MOVIE CLASSIC
Page 24 (background): Grafissimo/E+/Getty **Page 25:** Photograph © Lawrence Schiller, All Rights Reserved/Getty Images **Page 26:** Bettmann/Getty **Page 27:** LMPC/Getty (3) **Page 28:** Lou Jacobs/Pix Inc./The LIFE Images Collection/Getty **Page 29:** Keystone/Hulton/Getty **Page 30:** Mark Kauffman/LIFE/The Picture Collection **Page 31:** Warner Brothers-Seven Arts/Archive/Moviepix/Getty **Pages 32–33** (clockwise from top left): Charles Bonnay/The LIFE Images Collection/Getty; John Dominis/LIFE/The Picture Collection; Bob Willoughby/MPTVImages **Page 34:** Stanley Bielecki Movie Collection/Moviepix/Getty **Pages 34–35:** Silver Screen Collection/Moviepix/Getty **Pages 36–37:** Stanley Bielecki Movie Collection/Moviepix/Getty **Pages 38–39** (clockwise from top left): Ullstein Bild/Getty; Photograph © Lawrence Schiller, All Rights Reserved/Getty Images; Bridgeman Images **Page 40:** 20th Century Fox/Archive/Moviepix/Getty **Pages 40–41:** © 20th Century Fox/Diltz/Bridgeman Images **Pages 42–43:** Moviestore/REX/Shutterstock **Pages 44–47:** Photographs © Lawrence Schiller, All Rights Reserved/Getty Images (3) **Page 48:** 20th Century Fox/Archive/Moviepix/Getty **Page 49:** Stanley Bielecki Movie Collection/Moviepix/Getty **Pages 50–51:** Photograph © Lawrence Schiller, All Rights Reserved/Getty Images **Page 52:** Bettmann/Getty **Page 53:** Photograph © Lawrence Schiller, All Rights Reserved/Getty Images **Pages 54–55** (clockwise from left): 20th Century Fox/Archive/Moviepix/Getty; Photographs © Lawrence Schiller, All Rights Reserved/Getty Images (2) **Pages 56–57:** Photograph © Lawrence Schiller, All Rights Reserved/Getty Images **Page 58:** 20th Century Fox/Campanile Productions/Newman-Foreman Company/Kobal/REX/Shutterstock **Page 59:** Silver Screen Collection/Moviepix/Getty **Pages 60–61:** Photograph © Lawrence Schiller, All Rights Reserved/Getty Images

URBAN COWBOYS
Pages 62–75: Photographs © Lawrence Schiller, All Rights Reserved/Getty Images (10)

FROM CINEMA SMASH TO CULTURAL ICON
Page 76 (background): Grafissimo/E+/Getty **Page 77:** Silver Screen Collection/Moviepix/Getty **Pages 78–79:** Photograph © Lawrence Schiller, All Rights Reserved/Getty Images **Page 80:** Ron Galella/WireImage/Getty **Page 81** (counterclockwise from left): Photographs © Lawrence Schiller, All Rights Reserved/Getty Images (2); Ron Galella/WireImage/Getty **Pages 82–83:** Photograph © Lawrence Schiller, All Rights Reserved/Getty Images **Page 83** (bottom): Silver Screen Collection/Moviepix/Getty **Page 85** (top to bottom): ABC Photo Archives/Walt Disney Television/Getty; Warner Brothers/Archive/Moviepix/Getty **Page 86:** Silver Screen Collection/Moviepix/Getty **Pages 86–87:** Sunset Boulevard/Corbis/Getty **Pages 88–89:** Kmazur/WireImage/Getty **Page 89:** Tom Smart/Liaison/Hulton/Getty

INTO THE SUNSET
Pages 90–91: Joyce Marshall **Pages 92–93:** Glasshouse Images/Aurora/Cavan Images **Page 93:** Buyenlarge/Archive/Getty **Pages 94–95:** Jonathan Blair/Corbis/Getty **Page 96:** Jonathan Blair/National Geographic/Getty

HOME ON THE RANGE

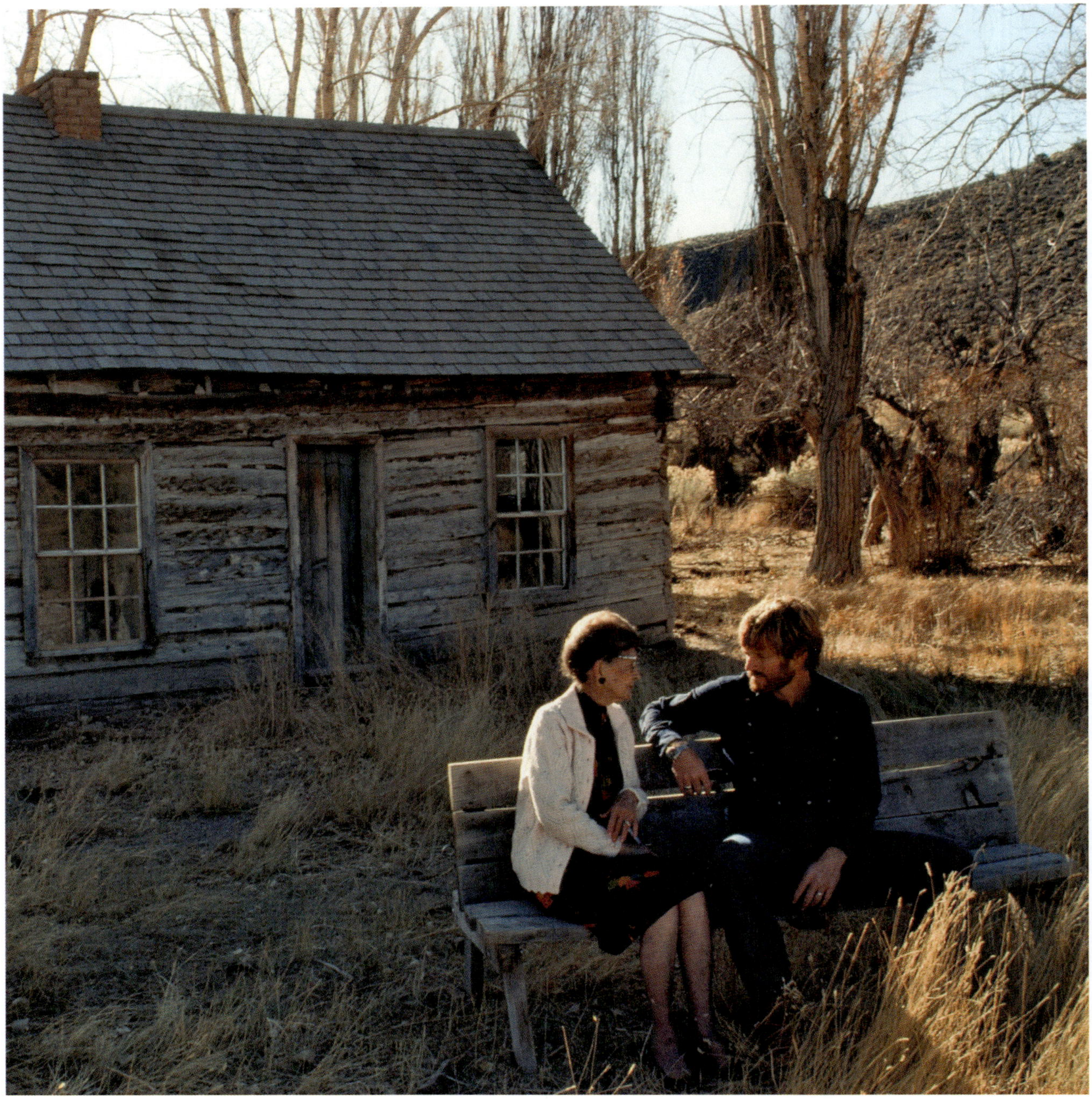

Redford met Butch Cassidy's sister Lula Parker Betenson during the filming of the 1969 movie. The two became friends, and Redford wrote the introduction to her book, *Butch Cassidy, My Brother,* in which she claims that Butch returned to see the family in 1925. Here the two are visiting the childhood home of her once infamous and now celebrated brother near Circleville, Utah.

Printed in Great Britain
by Amazon

37580888R00057